DREAMWEAVER® 4
MAGIC

By Al Sparber, Craig Foster, Gerry Jacobsen,
Linda Rathgeber, and Murray Summers

New Riders

201 West 103rd Street, Indianapolis, Indiana 46290

Dreamweaver® 4 Magic

International Standard Book Number: 0-7357-1046-5

Library of Congress Catalog Card Number: 00-105592

Printed in the United States of America

First Printing: May 2001

05 04 03 02 01   7 6 5 4 3 2 1

Interpretation of the printing code: The rightmost double-digit number is the year of the book's printing; the rightmost single-digit number is the number of the book's printing. For example, the printing code 01-1 shows that the first printing of the book occurred in 2001.

Trademarks

Warning and Disclaimer

Publisher
David Dwyer

Associate Publisher
Al Valvano

Executive Editor
Steve Weiss

Product Marketing Manager
Kathy Malmloff

Managing Editor
Sarah Kearns

Acquisitions Editor
Linda Anne Bump

Development Editor
Barb Terry

Project Editor
Michael Thurston

Copy Editors
Geneil Breeze
Audra McFarland

Technical Editors
Francois Richardson
Vernon E. Viehe

Cover Designer and Project Opener Images
Aren Howell

Interior Designer
Steve Gifford

Compositor
Kim Scott
kim@bumpy.com

Proofreader
Marcia Deboy

Indexer
Joy Dean Lee

Software Development Specialist
Jay Payne

CONTENTS AT A GLANCE

TABLE OF CONTENTS

ABOUT THE AUTHORS

Al Sparber is a founding partner of Project VII, a leading Web development resource site that attracts thousands of visitors daily. Al and the PVII team are reputed for being one step ahead of the leading edge and have authored some of the most exciting Dreamweaver Extensions to be found. PVII's latest claim to fame, the Dreamweaver Design Pack, is the brainchild of Al and partner Gerry Jacobsen. Design Packs are powerful site development tools that have acquired a cult-like following.

Al grew up in the New York City area, lived for baseball, and frequented every disco within a 50-mile radius of the "Apple". He served oxymoronically (his own word) in the U.S. Army Intelligence Corps, and even achieved a Sociology degree, which has served as a dust magnet for nearly a score. Before he found the Web, he was the CEO of a food distribution company in Ohio.

Al lives with his lovely wife Carol, whom he loves madly (his word), and together they have issued several outstanding offspring. Al and Carol love to play tennis and enjoy gourmet foods, art, music, and other highly cultural things.

You can contact Al via e-mail: **asparber@projectseven.com** or on the pviiwebdev newsgroup: **news://forums.projectseven.com/pviiwebdev**

Craig Foster is currently employed as a Web applications designer, desktop publisher, graphics artist, and contractor for the U.S. Navy on the Eastern Shore of Virginia. A Macromedia tech support Evangelist for over two years, Craig has been helping Web design colleagues learn to use Macromedia Dreamweaver by creating a FAQ of questions posted on the Macromedia Dreamweaver newsgroup at **http://cauzway.net/dreamweaver**. Craig also created the Dreamweaver News and Information site, which you can reach at **http://dwnews.owlnet.net**.

Craig says that thousands of Web designers are looking for employment, and only a fraction of them will find Web design employment opportunities. Because of that, he has developed a Cauzway (**http://cauzway.net**), which brings together Web designers and employers.

Craig also uses his knowledge of the Web on a personal level. His middle child, a thirteen-year-old, is deaf, and Craig, along with other local parents of deaf children, formed the DELMARVA Society for Deaf Children nonprofit organization of which he is the secretary and Webmaster. The Web site for that organization is **http://cauzway.net/dsdc**.

Gerry Jacobsen started his career with a BS in finance from Mercy College, NY, and gradually migrated to specializing in developing operational and management software for the Food Industry. In the mid '80s, Gerry developed Unix-based warehouse management systems employing fully integrated online bar code scanning technology. After spending 15 years as a Vice President and MIS Director for a major meat-processing company, Gerry, together with Al Sparber, formed Project VII Development.

Gerry is the programming genius behind Project VII and is a perfect complement to Al's design-side talents. Their Design Packs reveal their talents, enhanced even more by many years of experience in providing first-class support and user documentation. Together, they make a formidable Webdev team with an uncanny sense for what the market needs…and wants!

When he's not developing new code or surfing the Web, Gerry enjoys spending time at home with his wife Diane, and their two children, Chris and Mat. For recreation, Gerry spends a lot of his time playing guitar and tennis and tinkering with his stereo. You can contact Gerry at **www.projectseven.com**.

Linda S. Rathgeber is a former editor and layout and graphic artist for the *Holistic Resource Magazine*, and a contributor to such diverse publications as *Woman's World* and *Dream Quarterly International*. Since turning freelance, her work has been featured by independent film company King Pictures, in book ads for author Bill Stott, on the Fireworks 4 CD-ROM, and on the companion CD-ROM of Joseph W. Lowery's *Fireworks 3 Bible*. Linda is also the creative director of OzTex Alliance.

When not telecommuting with her Australian partner, David C. Nicholls, she can be found in the role of Macromedia Evangelist, coaching newcomers to Macromedia's Fireworks program. She lives in Austin, Texas (Yeeehaw!) with a pet monitor named Missy and a couple of Dell PCs. She can be reached at **www.playingwithfire.com**.

Murray Summers is a Biochemist by training but has spent the last 20 years working in the computer industry. He has served in both a sales and marketing role in this area, and is a long-time user of computers in science and business. Murray's first real exposure to the Internet came in 1987 when the world of email and telecommunications came into sharp business focus for him. Since then, he has participated in the development of the Internet as a commercial vehicle with gusto.

In 1998, Murray started his own Web site production company, Great Web Sights, and has become proficient with the use of Dreamweaver and UltraDev as a development environment in that endeavor. He also participates frequently in the sponsored Usenet forum for Dreamweaver and other products as a Macromedia Evangelist.

Murray and his wife Suzanne share a house in rural Philadelphia with their 11-year-old daughter Carly, a Golden Retriever (Sugar), an Eski-poo (Cookie), a goldfish (Smoochie), and lots of birds outside. Suzanne and Carly can frequently be seen on nearby ski slopes during the winter months, mostly looking down at Murray, buried in large mounds of snow. Murray's Web site can be found at **www.great-web-sights.com**.

ABOUT THE TECHNICAL EDITORS

François Richardson is currently employed with Macromedia as Lead for Dreameaver Technical Support. His experience in real world Web design, writing, and technical research have allowed him to bring a unique combination of skills to the Dreamweaver Magic project. Currently working on the possibilities that Dreamweaver's open-ended architecture offer, François looks forward to pushing the envelope of what can be done with an already amazing program.

Vernon Viehe started his career in the computer industry in 1989 in Birmingham, Alabama, by contracting desktop publishing, consulting, and support. He was the technical director of an Electronic Art Center for many years. For the last several years, Vernon has worked in Technical Support at Macromedia in San Francisco. After serving as Dreamweaver tech support team lead, he moved into support systems management. He has continued his involvement in the Dreamweaver community by serving as consultant and tech editor for books and course materials featuring Dreamweaver.

Vernon lives in San Francisco with his orange tabby manx (Toonces), and shares his desk at Macromedia with a goldfish (Miss Fish).

DEDICATION

We'd like to dedicate this book to the Macromedia Dreamweaver Team. Without you, this book would have been neither possible nor so much fun to write. Thanks, guys!

ACKNOWLEDGMENTS

Al Sparber

I have to thank my beautiful Carol. Without her support and encouragement, there's no way this book could have been done. You kept my spirits up (and the kids busy). Thanks, honey!

Many thanks to my two sweethearts at New Riders, Barb Terry and Linda Bump. I told them to nag me, and they did. But it was so much fun! I couldn't imagine this book getting done without their help, kind words, and enormous talents.

And a special thanks to my partner at projectseven.com, Gerry Jacobsen, for letting me take time away from our business to write. I am truly blessed.

I could never have conceived of writing a book about any software program other than Macromedia Dreamweaver. Dreamweaver is so much more than just software. It's a community of the most wonderful and helpful souls I've ever met. Thank you Lori Hylan and Heidi Bauer for putting up with my incessant JavaScript questions. Thank you, Vern Viehe, for your precision technical editing. Thank you, John Dowdell, Matt Brown, Eric Lerner, Rob Dekoach, Mark Haynes, et al, for helping to maintain and nourish the best online forums in the known universe. Thank you, Craig Foster, Murray Summers, and Linda Rathgeber, for contributing to both this book and to the Dreamweaver community.

Thank you, Sherry London, for showing me the ropes of the book business and for having the confidence in me to undertake this project.

And a very special thank you to everyone on the Project VII Design Pack Newsgroup for your votes of confidence and encouragement.

Thank you one and all.

Murray Summers

Without the tireless and expert efforts of Dreamweaver masters and extensionologists, I wouldn't even be able to spell "Dreamweaver!" They have instructed and nourished me, and shown me what a wonderful development tool Dreamweaver can be with a little inspiration and effort. Included in this amazing fraternity of people are Al Sparber, Massimo Foti, Eddie Traversa, Jaro von Flocken, Joe Milesevic, Drew McClellan, Jag Sidhu, Tom Muck, Ray West, Julian Roberts, Hal Pawluk, Linda Rathgeber, Kleanthis Economou, David Miles, Robert Sherman, Joseph Lowery, and many, many others. Thanks for the ride, guys.

A MESSAGE FROM NEW RIDERS

As the reader of this book, you are our most important critic and commentator. We value your opinion and want to know what we're doing right, what we could do better, in what areas you'd like to see us publish, and any other words of wisdom you're willing to pass our way.

As Executive Editor at New Riders, I welcome your comments. You can fax, email, or write me directly to let me know what you did or didn't like about this book—as well as what we can do to make our books better. When you write, please be sure to include this book's title, ISBN, and author, as well as your name and phone or fax number. I will carefully review your comments and share them with the authors and editors who worked on the book.

Please note that I cannot help you with technical problems related to the topic of this book, and that due to the high volume of email I receive, I might not be able to reply to every message. Thanks.

Email: steve.weiss@newriders.com

Mail: Steve Weiss
         Executive Editor
         New Riders Publishing
         201 West 103rd Street
         Indianapolis, IN 46290 USA

Visit Our Web Site: www.newriders.com

On our Web site, you'll find information about our other books, the authors we partner with, book updates and file downloads, promotions, discussion boards for online interaction with other users and with technology experts, and a calendar of trade shows and other professional events with which we'll be involved. We hope to see you around.

Email Us from Our Web Site

Go to **www.newriders.com** and click on the Contact link if you

- Have comments or questions about this book.

- Want to report errors that you have found in this book.

- Have a book proposal or are interested in writing for New Riders.

- Would like us to send you one of our author kits.

- Are an expert in a computer topic or technology and are interested in being a reviewer or technical editor.

- Want to find a distributor for our titles in your area.

- Are an educator/instructor who wants to preview New Riders books for classroom use. In the body/comments area, include your name, school, department, address, phone number, office days/hours, text currently in use, and enrollment in your department, along with your request for either desk/examination copies or additional information.

Call Us or Fax Us

You can reach us toll-free at (800) 571-5840 + 9 + 3567 (ask for New Riders). If outside the U.S., please call 1-317-581-3500 and ask for New Riders. If you prefer, you can fax us at 1-317-581-4663, Attention: New Riders.

Technical Support for this Book

Although we encourage entry-level users to get as much as they can out of our books, keep in mind that our books are written assuming a non-beginner level of user-knowledge of the technology. This assumption is reflected in the brevity and shorthand nature of some of the tutorials.

New Riders will continually work to create clearly written, thoroughly tested and reviewed technology books of the highest educational caliber and creative design. We value our customers more than anything—that's why we're in this business—but we cannot guarantee to each of the thousands of you who buy and use our books that we will be able to work individually with you through tutorials or content with which you may have questions. We urge readers who need help in working through exercises or other material in our books—and who need this assistance immediately—to use as many of the resources that our technology and technical communities can provide, especially the many online user groups and list servers available.

INTRODUCTION

Macromedia Dreamweaver has long been considered the leading visual Web design tool for professionals—and rightly so. But Dreamweaver also empowers casual users with the tools necessary to produce professional-looking Web sites quickly and easily, without having to write a single line of source code.

Dreamweaver 4 builds on the industry's most powerful toolset with a host of usability and productivity enhancements that raise the bar to new heights. Travel along with us as we take you to the cutting edge of 21st Century Web design with a little Dreamweaver Magic.

WHO WE ARE

Our writers can truly be called a "dream team." Al Sparber is a founding partner of Project VII Development (**www.projectseven.com**), a leading worldwide resource for Dreamweaver learning tools and home to a delicious assortment of Dreamweaver extensions.

Rounding out the writing team are contributing authors Gerry Jacobsen (Al's partner at PVII); and Macromedia Evangelists Craig Foster, Murray Summers, and Linda Rathgeber.

WHO YOU ARE

You know that Dreamweaver 4 is the ultimate visual Web design tool, and you want to explore the full breadth of its capabilities. We assume that you are familiar with the Dreamweaver 4 interface, that you understand the basics, that you are familiar with Dreamweaver's menus and panels, and that you know how to define a Web site and install an extension. We also assume you are ready to take your *Web weaving* to a new level!

If, however, you are a Dreamweaver newbie, don't despair. *Dreamweaver 4 Magic* is a groundbreaking book that comes with a <drum roll> Technical Support Forum. Whoa! We are quite serious about making *Dreamweaver 4 Magic* an immerse experience built around an unprecedented support community where you can interact with fellow readers, as well as this book's authors, on a daily basis.

WHAT'S IN THIS BOOK

Dreamweaver 4 Magic is a project-based book. Each project is an entity unto itself, so feel free to start in the middle, at the end, or in that least likely of spots—the beginning. Projects were picked using a very scientific method. We call it the "ECYVF Test." Translated that means Extremely Cool Yet Very Functional.

There's a lot of DHTML stuff inside. But it all meets the ECYVF test. No gratuitous fluff for us. All DHTML had to meet another, equally stringent test. It had to work in all version 4 and higher browsers including Netscape 6 and Opera 5. The pressure nearly killed us, but we did it. And you'll love it!

Each project is done with Dreamweaver visual tools. No manual coding is required. If a technique required a special kind of JavaScript, we developed a Dreamweaver extension to automate the process. Project VII has created some very cool new behaviors, commands, and objects to make this book's projects very special.

We have drop-down menus, flyout menus, scrolling layers inside stationary widgets, and sliding presentations. We have framesets that don't look like framesets and form buttons that act like image buttons. We have disjoint rollovers, collapsible menus, tree menus, a tabbed interface, a hierarchical jump menu, and a top-secret CSS too-cool-to-even-mention thing. But there's more…

You'll learn a whole lot about advanced CSS and how to properly use that most powerful of Dreamweaver features: the Dreamweaver Template.

We got so excited in writing the projects that we almost forgot the appendices. Rather than do a last-minute emergency appendectomy, we cooked up some cool stuff for the back of the book. We've included a comprehensive list of Dreamweaver resources, a list of our favorite extensions (with guest commentary from the developers), and a list of really cool and inspirational sites made with Dreamweaver.

THE CD

The CD you get is no ordinary CD. It is structured as a Web server would be. As you begin a project, you simply copy the appropriate project folder to your hard drive and use Dreamweaver's Site Manager to define the folder as a proper Dreamweaver site. All the necessary files you'll need to complete a project are contained therein. As a bonus, we've also included the fully editable Fireworks 4 image source files so you can easily customize a project to your heart's content. Each project folder contains a finshed_project subfolder that holds a finished version of the project.

The CD also contains an Extensions folder with subfolders for actions, commands, and objects—all in Dreamweaver Exchange .MXP format for click-click easy installation. Also included, are links to Macromedia.com where you can download the 30-day trial versions of Dreamweaver 4, Fireworks 4, and Flash 5.

OUR ASSUMPTIONS AS WE WROTE THIS BOOK

The Dreamweaver Community is a special place. Kind of like a small town that spans the globe. It's full of nice, friendly, helpful souls. We've been a part of that community for quite some time, and it's helped us to formulate some educated assumptions about what would make for a successful Dreamweaver book.

You Need More Than Just Another Dreamweaver Reference

These days, some great Dreamweaver reference books are available. The last thing we wanted to do was rehash the basics. And Dreamweaver does come with a good printed manual and a fabulous online help system, so every Dreamweaver user has the material at his or her disposal to learn the basics. You already paid for them, so we assume you've taken advantage of them!

You Want Exciting, Cutting-Edge Stuff That Can Actually Be Used in a Real Web Site

We've seen all the cutesy stuff in how-to books from A to Z. You don't want to burden your Web sites with one single line of code unless it is a functional enhancement. You don't want to learn how to fly text across your screen with timelines that waste hundreds of lines of precious bandwidth. If you do want those things, you won't find it in this book!

You want fully functioning and logically structured navigation systems that can manage a working Web site you'll be proud of. You want usable DHTML that works in Microsoft Internet Explorer 4 and higher, Netscape Navigator 4 and higher, and Opera 5. You want cool stuff that works to make a visit to your site that much more enjoyable.

You Want a Book That Contains Visually Striking Design

We were absolutely fanatical about the quality of the images used in our projects. Text and background contrast had to be just so. GIFs had to be perfectly blended into our pages. Clean and crisp was the order of the day every day we worked on *Dreamweaver 4 Magic*.

So we assume, after all is said and done, that you really want a book like *Dreamweaver 4 Magic*!

CONVENTIONS USED IN THIS BOOK

Every computer book has its own style of presenting information. As you flip through the book, you'll notice we have an interesting layout going on here. Because we know most of you are really into graphics, the project openers contain way-cool eye candy. Then the real meat of the projects starts on the next page.

In the left column, you'll find step-by-step instructions for completing the project, as well as succinct but extremely valuable explanations. The text next to the number contains the action you must perform. In many cases, the action text is followed by a paragraph that contains contextual information. Note that if you want to perform the steps quickly and without any background info, you need to read only the text next to the step numbers.

In the corresponding columns to the right, you'll find screen captures (and/or code) and captions, illustrating the steps. You'll also find Notes and Tips, which will provide you with additional contextual information or customization techniques.

At the end of each project, you'll find unique customization information. Each *Magic* project is designed to be highly customizable; therefore, we provide many tips and examples of what you can do with the techniques you've learned so that you can apply them to your own work quickly and easily.

THE DREAMWEAVER MAGIC COMMUNITY: A VERY SPECIAL PLACE

The real value of Dreamweaver lies in its wonderful and supportive community, evident in Macromedia's Dreamweaver Newsgroup, Project VII's Dreamweaver-Design Pack Newsgroup, various mailing lists, and now…

The Dreamweaver Magic Forum. You can set up a new News account from within your newsreader (Outlook Express, for example), using the following server name:

forums.projectseven.com

In response, you will get a list of all the forums on the news server. Simply pick pviiwebdev and subscribe to it. You will be able to communicate with other *Dreamweaver 4 Magic* readers and with this book's authors.

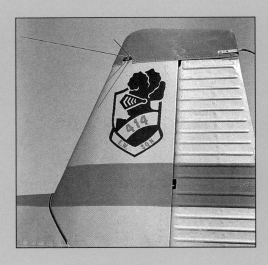

USING CASCADING STYLE SHEETS TO MAKE SELECTABLE THEMES

"While browsing through the Web one day, it occurred to me that I was not alone. Then it all made perfect sense."

—ANCIENT PVII PROVERB

THE INCREDIBLE CSS COOKIE MONSTER

Wouldn't it be cool if you could offer your site's visitors a choice of design themes? What if you could make it so that whatever theme a visitor chose would stick with him throughout his session? And maybe it would be totally cool if a visitor's chosen theme could be remembered so that if he returned, say, a week later, the same theme would be selected.

All in all, what we have here is a technique with an off-the-scale wow factor. Imagine that

- You have a persnickety client who can't decide whether he wants blue text or green text (yuck).
- Your boss wants dark text on a white background, but her boss wants light text on a dark background.
- Your husband wants your family business Web site to look like the Cleveland Browns team uniform, but you prefer something a bit more subtle.

Well, you could use this technique to make everyone happy. Just give them all a link to their own preferred style (they can draw straws over whose style is the default). Or you could use it as the ultimate prototyping tool to quickly show your clients different versions of the same page with just a click of a link.

The Incredible CSS Cookie Monster is a peacemaker of grand proportions. We rank it up there with Roosevelt, Churchill, and Ghandi. Of course, they never had this technique available to them or history might well have taken a completely different course.

Using Cascading Style Sheets to Make Selectable Themes

by Al Sparber and Gerry Jacobsen

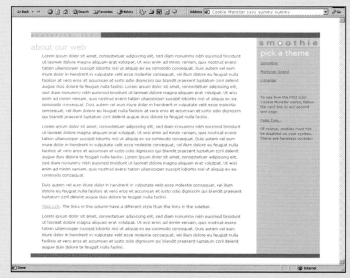

Our page is rendered with its default style sheet.

IT WORKS LIKE THIS

A visitor is presented with a heading that says something like "Choose a Theme." Under the heading is a set of links. Each link describes a theme. For example, Soft Blue, Lemon Yellow, Happy Holidays, and Large Text.

Upon clicking one of the links, a small JavaScript in the page writes a little cookie to the visitor's system. The cookie simply states the name of a style sheet to use and how long the cookie will remain on the visitor's system. It takes a millisecond to write the cookie, after which the script reads back the cookie, tells the page which style sheet to use, and reloads the page to make the changes take effect.

The magic begins when the visitor goes to another page. Our little script reads the cookie as it's loading the new page and voilá! The new page loads with the selected theme. But the magic doesn't stop here.

The same page after selecting the Mortimer Snerd theme.

The cookie contains not only the style sheet name, but also an expiration date (that you set). So long as the cookie has not expired, your visitor's selected theme will be chosen every time he visits your site. This is one smart cookie.

What happens if a visitor has cookies disabled? That's simple, we are going to place a default style sheet link in our page. If cookies are not allowed, the default theme (based on the default style sheet) will work perfectly.

A Class Act: CSS is the straw that stirs it all.

Our JavaScript works by reading a cookie that tells the browser which style sheet to use. The style sheet used determines the theme. Here's a little example:

Theme1.css

```
.examplestyle {  font-family: Verdana, Arial, Helvetica, sans-serif; font-size:
12px; color: #000000}
```

Theme2.css

```
.examplestyle {  font-family: Verdana, Arial, Helvetica, sans-serif; font-size:
16px; color: #FFFFFF}
```

The secret is to make sure that each CSS file contains the same classes. If, for example, a paragraph on your page is assigned the .examplestyle class, it will reflect the rules contained in the CSS file relating to the chosen theme. If a visitor has chosen Theme1, the text in the paragraph will be 12px black. If Theme2 is chosen, the same paragraph will be 16px white. Why? Because both style sheets contain the same class (.examplestyle) with different rules. Obviously, then, Cascading Style Sheets are vital components of this project!

The three CSS files necessary for this project are included in the assets/style_sheets folder. We're going to set up our home page now, but don't worry, we will have a full style sheet discussion later.

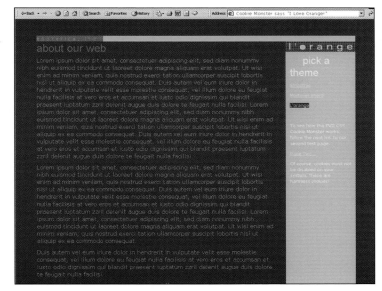

The same page after selecting the L'Orange theme.

DRIVEN BY STYLES

The CSS classes assigned to your page elements are contained in multiple style sheets. Each style sheet contains the same named classes; we just change the style rules in each sheet. This causes our page to transform.

Note: You may notice that the code in this book sometimes wraps to the next line. That wrapping is caused by the narrowness of the column within this book. Dreamweaver does not restrict the length of the line; the code appears on one line.

PREPARING TO WORK

Let's go through the routine. You need to install some extensions, copy the project folder from the CD to your hard drive, and then fire up Dreamweaver and define a new site using the copied project folder as the local root folder.

1   Install the P7 CSS Styles Cookie Monster Suite:

   • Browse to the Extensions folder on the CD.

   • Open the Extensions\Commands subfolder.

   • Double-click p7setCSS.mxp to install the suite. The suite contains both a command and a behavior.

2   Install the NN4 Return False Fix and the Scrubber commands:

   The NN4 Return False Fix command eliminates Netscape showing the hourglass cursor when clicking a null link to fire a JavaScript. This command must be applied for our project to function correctly in Netscape. The Scrubber can be used to eliminate the focus lines around clicked links in MS Internet Explorer.

   • Browse to the Extensions folder on the CD.

   • Open the Commands subfolder.

   • Double-click the file called N4 Return False Fix.mxp to install the command.

   • Repeat to install scrubber.mxp.

3   Copy the projects folder:

   • Browse to the projects folder on the CD.

   • Copy the project_one folder to a convenient location on your hard drive.

4   Define a new Dreamweaver site using the project_one copy as your local root folder.

BROWSER COMPATIBILITY

We have tested this interface and found that it is fully functional in the following browsers:

MSIE 4 (Windows and Mac)

MSIE 5 (Windows and Mac)

MSIE 5.5 (Windows)

NN4.08–4.76 (Windows)

NN4.5 (Mac)

Opera 5.01 (Windows)

Netscape 6 (Windows and Mac)

Note: If you want to see how the completed site looks in either Dreamweaver or your browser, you can find all the files in the test_site folder.

Tip: At Project Seven we use the PC platform to develop extensions. Macintosh systems will sometimes not recognize the MXP file format. However, double-clicking the file will still execute a proper installation of the extension.

SPECIAL NOTES

This project presents a very powerful tool. To implement it correctly, you need to remember these points concerning both the design and the underlying code. The points raised here are covered in detail during the course of the project. This section serves only to emphasize their importance.

Previewing

The site you build will only function on a remote server (to ensure Netscape 4 compatibility). If, at any time, you wish to preview a locally working version of the site, use the index page inside the test_site folder. The test files have been specially prepared for local previewing in MS Internet Explorer and Netscape 6. The test files are linked to your real working style sheets, so this is a good place to do your editing, too.

Absolute Paths

Netscape 4 requires you to use absolute paths to your CSS files because of the way the script works. There is no other way. An absolute path looks just like a normal hyperlink. In a normal page, a linked style sheet would have a document relative path and might look like:

../assets/styles/mystyles.css

If your Web domain is www.boris-natasha.com, then the absolute path to the above style sheet would be:

http://www.boris-natasha.com/assets/styles/mystyles.css

However, you do use a document relative style sheet link in the head of your working page. It's there so that you see a styled page as you work in Dreamweaver. Once the page is up on the Web, your JavaScripts take over and actually write the CSS links on the fly.

Style Sheet Position

The position of the style sheet in your page is important, too. Even though you are using absolutely pathed CSS files written on the fly by our scripts, you still have a presentational style sheet relatively pathed in your page (so you see something pretty as you work!). If you attempt to have Dreamweaver link a style sheet to a page that contains any JavaScript, Dreamweaver will write the link below the closing **</script>** tag. Under normal circumstances this wouldn't matter. But this technique requires that the style sheet link be in the proper position—above the opening **<script>** tag. If you follow the project step-by-step, this won't be an issue. It will only be a problem if you use Dreamweaver's CSS panel to change the CSS link after you've inserted the JavaScripts. Why is this a problem? Our scripts write the style sheet link to the proper position above the opening **<script>** tag and below where a normally linked style sheet would be declared. If there is a style sheet linked to below the closing **</script>** tag, then it will be given precedence to any style sheets listed above it. We have included instructions in the project that explain how to manually change the position in your source code.

The NN4 Return False Fix

This command places return false; after the onClick events that fire the CSS Cookie Monster scripts. The command must be applied to your page or the script will not work correctly in Netscape browsers. The NN4 Return False Fix can be applied as many times as you please. It will only fix those events that need fixing! So it's a good idea to apply it after an editing session just in case!

Now, on with the show!

CREATING THE HOME PAGE

In this section, we add three tables to form the structure of our design. If at any time you want to see the finished pages, you will find them in the test_site folder. The reason we've used test_site rather than the project folder will become apparent as we proceed.

1 Open the file named index.htm in the root of your project_one site.

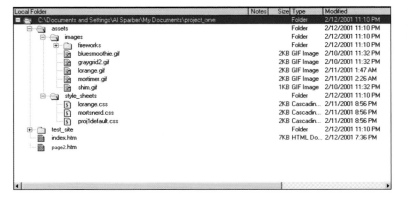

Open the file named index.htm in the root of your project_one site in the Dreamweaver Site window.

2 Insert a new table:

- In the Insert Table dialog, enter these settings:

  Rows: **1**
  Columns: **1**
  Width: **90%**
  Border: **0**
  Cell Padding: **0**
  Cell Spacing: **0**

- Use the property inspector to set Align to Center.

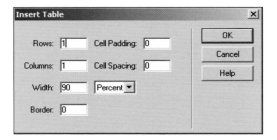

In the Insert Table dialog, enter the settings for the new table.

3 Insert a second table:

- In the Insert Table dialog, enter these settings:

  Rows: **1**
  Columns: **2**
  Width: **90%**
  Border: **0**
  Cell Padding: **0**
  Cell Spacing: **0**

- Use the property inspector to set Align to Center.

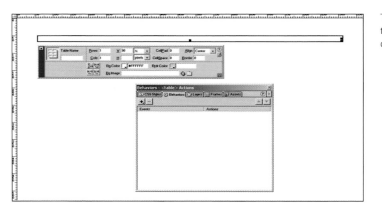

The first table should look like this after you've inserted and centered it.

4   Insert a third table identical to the first:

- In the Insert Table dialog, enter these settings:

  Rows: **1**

  Columns: **1**

  Width: **90%**

  Border: **0**

  Cell Padding: **0**

  Cell Spacing: **0**

- Use the property inspector to set Align to Center.

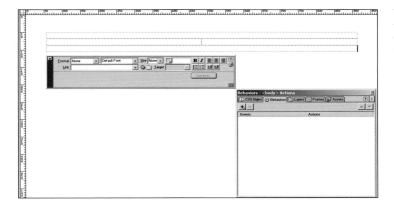

Your page should look like this when you have all three tables inserted and ready to be styled and populated.

POPULATING THE TABLES ON THE HOME PAGE

We've included all the style sheets you'll need and all are preformatted for you. Before we can apply styles to the tables, we need to link the default CSS to the home page.

1   Link the default style sheet:

- Click the Pencil icon at the bottom of the CSS Styles panel to open the Edit Style Sheet dialog.

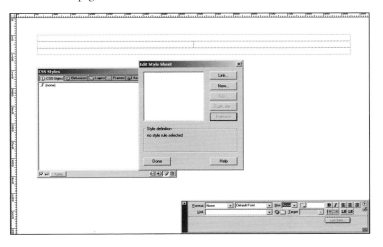

Click the Pencil icon at the bottom of the CSS Styles panel to begin linking a CSS file.

- Click the Link button on the Edit Style Sheet dialog, and the Link External Style Sheet dialog opens.
- Browse to proj1default.css in the style_sheets sub-folder of the assets directory, off the root of your project_one defined site.

Click the Link button on the Edit Style Sheet dialog and then click the Browse button on the Link External Style Sheet dialog.

- Click the Select button to execute the link and then click the Done button on the Edit Style Sheet dialog.

  The CSS file is now linked to the home page.

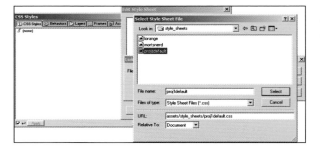

Browse to the style_sheets folder in the assets directory, choose proj1default.css, and click the Select button.

2 Enter the header text in the top table:
- Click inside the top table and type **esoterica, ltd.**

3 Enter the middle table header and placeholder text:
- Click inside the left column of the middle table and type **about our Web**.
- Press Enter and type a few paragraphs of placeholder text.

4 Enter the copyright in the bottom table:
- Click inside the bottom table and type © **2001 ESOTERICA LTD- ALL RIGHTS RESERVED**.

5 Size the right column of the middle table:
- Click inside the right column of the middle table and set its width to **200** on the property inspector.

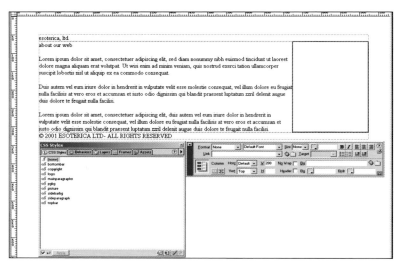

After typing in the headings, copyright, and placeholder text, set the right column of the middle table to a width of 200 on the property inspector.

Tip: Sometimes tables will collapse when you enter text inside one cell. To get to the next cell to the right, press your Tab key while in the left cell. To move to the next cell left, press Shift+Tab.

6 Enter the sidebar heading, links, and text:

- Click inside the right column and type the following:

   pick a theme

   Smoothie

   Mortimer snerd

   L'Orange

   To see how the CSS Cookie Monster works, follow the next link to our second test page: Page 2

7 Insert a nested table inside the right column:

- Place your cursor just to the left of the "p" in pick a theme and insert a table inside with these settings:

   Rows: **1**

   Columns: **1**

   Width: **200 pixels**

   Border: **0**

   Cell Padding: **0**

   Cell Spacing: **0**

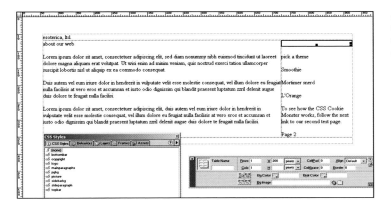

After typing in the sidebar content, insert a 200-pixel wide table inside the right column of the middle table.

ASSIGNING CSS CLASSES TO THE HOME PAGE ELEMENTS

By assigning classes to headers, text, and table cells, we'll see the home page begin to take shape.

1 Assign a class to the header in the top table:

- Select the text esoteric, ltd.

- Right-click (Ctrl+click) and choose Wrap Tag.

- Click inside the little box that pops up with an empty tag <>and type **span** so that it looks like **<span>**.

- Press Enter to close the box.

- Insert your cursor somewhere inside the text esoterica, ltd.

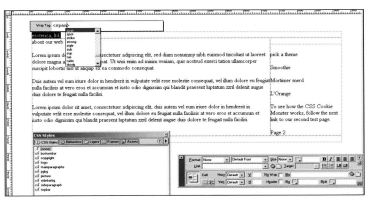

Use Dreamweaver's powerful Wrap Tag feature to insert a **<span>** tag pair.

11

- Select the **<span>** tag on the Dreamweaver status bar (lower-left window border) and right-click (Ctrl+click).
- Choose Set Class/logo.

  The text is now dark gray on a light gray background.

Note: We are using several methods of applying CSS classes because Dreamweaver behaves differently under certain situations, and we have chosen the methods that work most accurately in each situation.

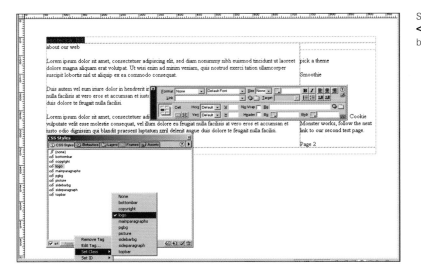

Set the CSS class of the **<span>** tag via the status bar context menu.

2 Assign a class to the top table's row:

- Insert your cursor in the top table row (next to esoterica, ltd.) and right-click (Ctrl+click) the **<td>** tag on the status bar.
- Choose Set Class/topbar.

  The table row is now colored blue.

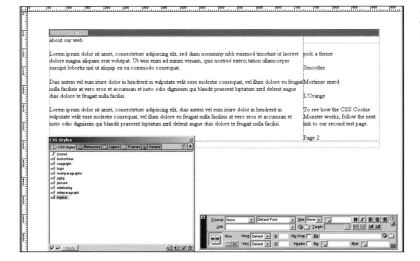

Apply the topbar class to its **<td>** tag to make the top table row turn blue.

3 Assign a class to the heading in the left column–middle table:

- Place your cursor on the same line as the heading "about our Web."
- Drop down the format menu on the property inspector and choose Heading1.

Apply the H1 format to the headings.

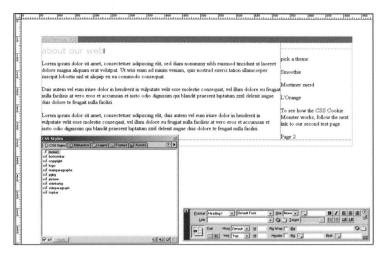

When the H1 format is selected, the heading becomes instantly styled.

4 Assign a class to the paragraphs in the left column–middle table:

- Place your cursor inside the first paragraph below the "about our Web" heading.
- Right-click (Ctrl+click) the **<p>** tag on the status bar.
- Choose Set Class/mainparagraphs.
- Repeat this class for the remaining paragraphs in the column.

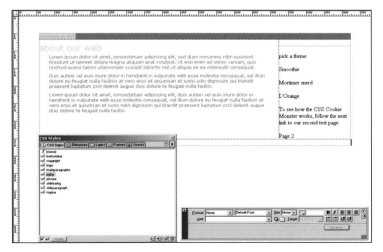

Apply the mainparagraphs class to each **<p>** tag in the first column.

5 Assign classes to the sidebar and its content:

- Place your cursor on the same line as the heading "pick a theme" in the right column of the middle table.

- Drop down the format menu on the property inspector and choose Heading2.

  The text will seem to disappear. We'll fix that in a moment.

- Place your cursor inside the first paragraph below the "pick a theme" heading.

- Right-click (Ctrl+click) the **<p>** tag on the status bar.

- Choose Set Class/sideparagraphs.

- Repeat this class for the remaining paragraphs in the column.

- Click inside any of the sidebar paragraphs we just styled.

- Right-click (Ctrl+click) the **<td>** tag on the status bar.

- Choose Set Class/sidebarbg.

6 Assign classes to the lower table:

- Select the text © 2001 ESOTERICA LTD- ALL RIGHTS RESERVED.

- Right-click (Ctrl+click) and choose Wrap Tag.

- Click inside the tag markers and type **span** so that it looks like **<span>**. Press Enter to close the box.

- Insert your cursor somewhere inside the text © 2001 ESOTERICA LTD- ALL RIGHTS RESERVED.

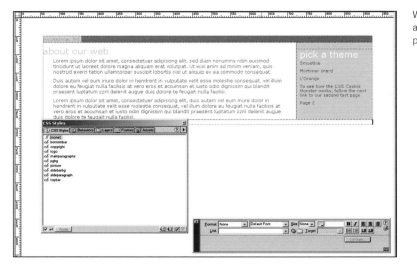

With paragraphs, headings, and the sidebar styled, our page is really taking shape.

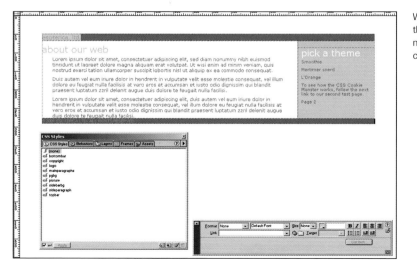

Wrap a **<span>** tag around the text to style the copyright notice and then set the copyright.

- Select the **<span>** tag on the status bar and right-click (Ctrl+click).
- Choose Set Class/copyright.

7 Assign a class to the lower table's row:

- Insert your cursor in the bottom table row and right-click (Ctrl+click) the **<td>** tag on the status bar.
- Choose Set Class/bottombar.

  The table row is now colored blue.

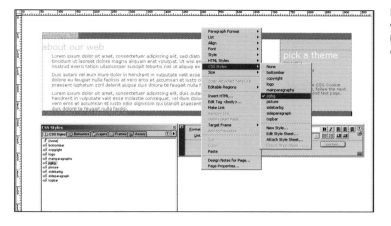

Right-click (Ctrl+click) anywhere on the page below the bottom table to set the body class.

SETTING UP A SWAP IMAGE WITH CSS

Now the real magic starts! Remember the little nested table we placed at the top of the sidebar? We have a special CSS class for that baby.

1 Assign a class to the nested table's row:

- Click inside the nested table that is inside the sidebar.
- Right-click (Ctrl+click) the **<td>** tag on the status bar.
- Choose Set Class/picture.

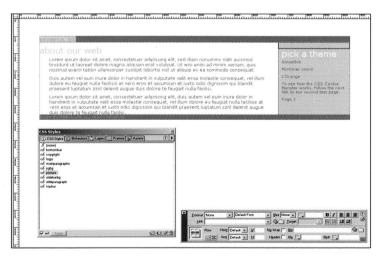

Set the **<td>** of the nested table to the picture class.

2 Insert a transparent GIF inside the nested sidebar table:

- Click inside the nested table.
- Open the Assets panel and scroll down to the image called shim.gif.
- Click the Insert button on the Assets panel to insert the image inside the table.

  The image we've provided is already properly sized at 200 pixels wide by 32 pixels high.

> **Note:** The transparent GIF serves to hold the table open to allow a background image to show through. The CSS class .picture assigns the background image to the table cell. Each of our three CSS files sets a different image, so when a user chooses a theme, the image changes along with the style sheet. However, if you preview the page at this stage, you will not see the image. Don't worry; this is perfectly normal. We'll fix that in a moment.

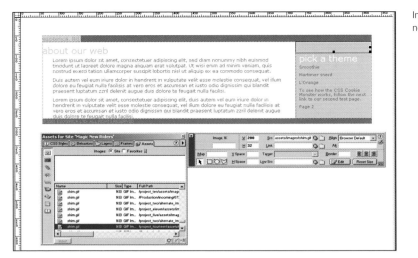

Insert shim.gif inside the nested table.

SETTING THE BACKGROUND IMAGE URL IN STYLE SHEETS

We'd love for this part to be just a little easier, but we are committed to supporting Netscape 4, and that browser needs a little workaround to render images declared in externally linked style sheets.

1 Enter an absolute path for our CSS background images:

- Click the Pencil icon at the bottom of the CSS Styles panel to open the Edit Style Sheet dialog.
- Double-click proj1default.css to edit the CSS file.
- Double-click the .picture class.
- Choose the Background category.
- In the Background Image field, type the fully qualified path to the default background image relative to your actual Web server, using this format as an example:

  http://www.yourdomain.com/assets/images/ bluesmoothie.gif

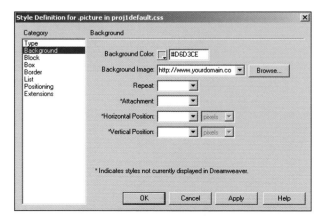

Enter the absolute URL to the background image of our table cell.

2 Enter an absolute path for the Mortimer Snerd background image:

- Open the site window and double-click mortsnerd.css

- Double-click **.picture** and repeat the preceding steps to enter the absolute URL for mortsnerd.css, using this path:

  http://www.yourdomain.com/assets/images/ mortimer.gif

3 Open the l'orange.css file and enter an absolute path for the L'Orange background image:

  http://www.yourdomain.com/assets/images/ lorange.gif

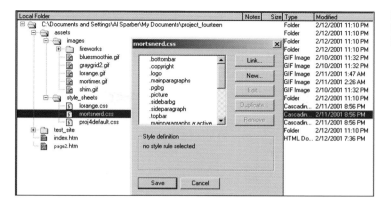

Double-click mortsnerd.css in the site window to open the CSS Editor.

Tip: If you are unsure of your actual domain, ask your network administrator, ISP, or hosting company to give you the proper path.

Note: By default, Dreamweaver opens the CSS dialog unless you have customized your settings in the Preferences window.

APPLYING THE COOKIE SCRIPT COMMAND AND BEHAVIORS

We're now ready to insert the script that writes the CSS cookie. Once again, you'll be setting the absolute URL to the CSS files. This is vitally important for Netscape 4 compatibility (and also to enable you to use a Dreamweaver template to manage a multiple-folder site).

1 Apply the P7 CSS style cookie:

- From the Commands menu, choose Studio VII/P7 CSS Style Cookie.

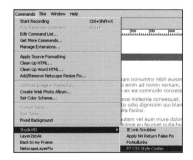

Choose Commands/Studio VII/P7 CSS Style Cookie.

- Click the Insert button.

  The cookie script is now in the document.

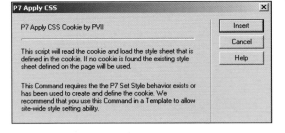

Click the Insert button to apply the P7 CSS Cookie script.

2 Prepare the text links to accept the P7 Apply CSS behaviors:

- Select Smoothie from the sidebar. Type **javascript:;** into the Link field on the property inspector.
- Repeat the preceding steps to apply JavaScript links to Mortimer Snerd and L'Orange.

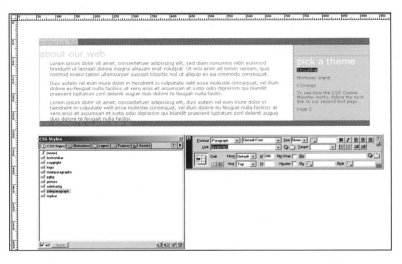

Select the word "Smoothie" in the sidebar and type **javascript:;** into the Link field on the PI.

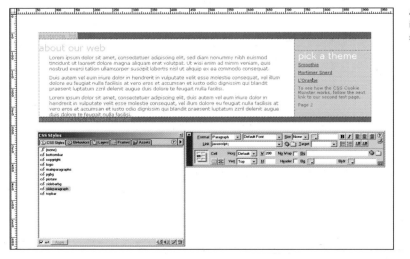

Add null links to the remaining two theme names in the sidebar.

3 Apply the P7 CSS behaviors:

- Select the Smoothie link.
- Open the Behaviors panel menu, click the + sign to open the Behaviors menu, choose Studio VII, and then choose P7 setCSS.

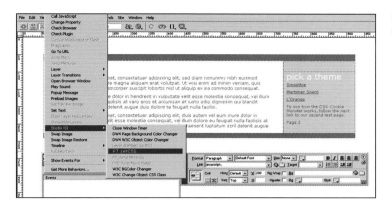

Select the Smoothie link and apply the P7 setCSS behavior.

- Enter an expiration date into the Days to Expire field or keep the default setting of 30 (days).
- Type the fully qualified absolute URL to the proj1default.css style sheet in the Set To Style Sheet field. For example:

  http://www.yourdomain.com/assets/ style_sheets/proj1default.css

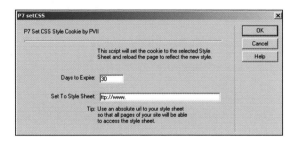

Enter an expiration date for your cookie and the absolute URL to the default style sheet.

- Make sure that the event is set to onClick.
- Repeat the preceding steps to apply the P7 setCSS behavior to the Mortimer Snerd and L'Orange links. Remember to set the absolute URLs:

  http://www.yourdomain.com/assets/ style_sheets/mortsnerd.css

  and

  http://www.yourdomain.com/assets/ style_sheets/lorange.css

Make sure that the event is set to onClick.

APPLYING THE NN4 RETURN FALSE FIX AND THE SCRUBBER COMMANDS

The NN4 Return False Fix must be applied for our project to function correctly in Netscape. The Scrubber can be optionally used to eliminate the focus lines around clicked links in MS Internet Explorer. Apply these commands to both the index.htm and page2.htm pages.

1   Apply the NN4 Return False Fix:

   • Choose Command/Studio VII/Apply N4 Return False Fix.

   • Click the Apply button.

2   Apply the Scrubber:

   • Choose Command/Studio VII/IE Link Scrubber.

   • Click the Scrub Em! button.

USING A SECOND TEST PAGE TO SEE IF THE BROWSER IS READING THE COOKIE

It's a good idea to create a second page to test the scripts on your local system. The page should have the P7 Apply CSS command and it should be styled using the CSS classes from our style sheets. We've taken the liberty of including this page in the root of your project folder. Test the cookie, using the provided second page as described in the next section.

1   Select the text page 2 in the sidebar of the home page.

   • Use the property inspector to create a normal hyperlink to page2.htm.

   • Open page2.htm, select the text back to the index in the sidebar.

   • Use the property inspector to create a hyperlink back to index.htm.

Note: Please read this paragraph. Do not overlook it. It is so important that we set it up as a separate section.

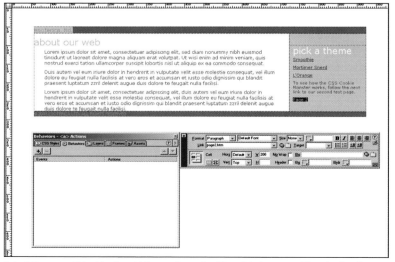

Select the page 2 text in the sidebar and use the PI to link it to page2.htm in the site root.

2 Save your work and close index.htm and page2.htm.

Now you're ready to begin working on the pages in the test site folder.

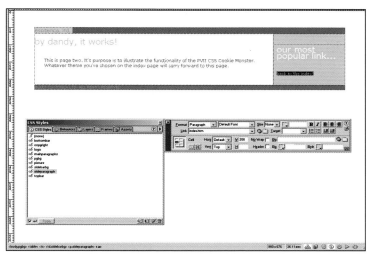

Open page2.htm, select the text "back to the index," and use the PI to link it to index.htm.

USING THE SUPPLIED TEST SITE

Because we need to use absolute URLs to link our style sheets, local previewing and style sheet edits would be difficult without a dedicated test page or two. The test page functions locally to permit previewing through Dreamweaver. We've created two test pages for you and placed them in a folder called test_site.

We've linked the test page to all three style sheets. **Do not link the second and third style sheets to your actual site pages, only to the test pages!**

By linking all three CSS files in the test pages, we made it possible for you to toggle the active style sheet so that you can edit the styles *and* see your changes in Dreamweaver.

The mortsnerd.css is being used as the active sheet because we've placed it below the links to the other style sheets in the document's head. The word "cascading" in Cascading Style Sheets means (among other things) that you can link multiple style sheets in a document and the browser places precedence on the one listed last.

> **Note:** This section is all about managing the finished site by using test pages that remain on your local system and do not get uploaded to your actual Web server.

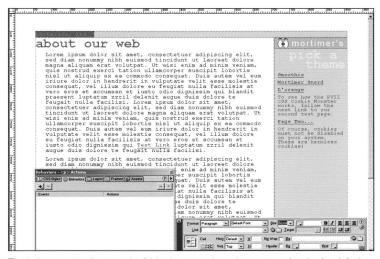

The index page in the test_site folder is set to show the mortsnerd styles by default.

> **Note:** When a page contains JavaScript, Dreamweaver places a newly linked style sheet below the closing **<script>** tag, just above the opening **<body>** tag. This is incorrect and prevents the cookie script from executing properly. This is not a problem if you link a style sheet before adding scripts to the page. If you encounter this problem, simply cut the style sheet link and paste it just above the first **<script>** tag at the top of the document.

We've set the source of the image atop the right sidebar to mortimer.gif by simply changing the source on the property inspector so you can visualize it onscreen. If you wanted to make L'Orange the active style sheet for your test page, you'd change the image source to lorange.gif to get an accurate preview.

```
1  <html>
2  <head>
3  <title>Chapter 14 - Test Site</title>
4  <meta http-equiv="Content-Type" content="text/html; charset=iso-8859-1">
5  <link rel="stylesheet" href="../assets/style_sheets/lorange.css" type="text/css">
6  <link rel="stylesheet" href="../assets/style_sheets/proj14default.css" type="text/css">
7  <link rel="stylesheet" href="../assets/style_sheets/mortsnerd.css" type="text/css">
8  <script language="JavaScript">
9  <!--
10 function P7_getCSS(a) { // v1.6 PVII
11    var i=0,j=0,e=0,theSheet="";
12    a=a+"=",t="<",u="LINK";
13    var alen=a.length,clen=document.cookie.length;
14    while (i < clen) {
15      j=i+alen;
16      if(document.cookie.substring(i,j)==a) {
17        e = document.cookie.indexOf(";",j);
18        if (e==-1) (e=clen)
19        theSheet = unescape(document.cookie.substring(j,e));
20        document.write(t+u+' rel="stylesheet" type="text/css" href="' + theSheet + '">');
21        break;}
22      else (i=document.cookie.indexOf(" ",i)+1;
23        if (i==0) break; ) }
24  }
25  P7_getCSS('p7styler');
26
27  function P7_setCSS(d, theStyle) { // v1.6 PVII
28    var expDays=parseInt(d),path = "/";
29    var expdate = new Date();
30    expdate.setTime(expdate.getTime() + (expDays*24*60*60*1000));
31    document.cookie = "p7styler=" + escape (theStyle) + "; expires=" + expdate.toGMTString() +'; path=' + path;
32    top.location.reload();
33  }
34  //-->
35  </script>
36  </head>
37  <body bgcolor="#FFFFFF" text="#000000" class="pgbg">
38  <p> </p>
```

The style sheet links must be above the opening **<script>** tag in your document's **<head>**.

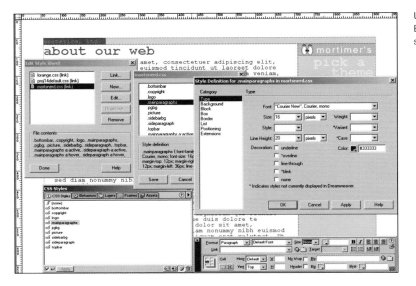

Use Dreamweaver's CSS Editor to customize the style sheets.

If you want to edit a style sheet in the test site, there are some things you need to know. The index.htm page in the test site is linked to the same style sheets used by the real index page. As mentioned earlier, it is actually linked to all three style sheets. This is the most efficient approach to take in a test scenario because if you used Dreamweaver to re-link multiple style sheets, it would place the CSS link under the JavaScript, and the script would not work.

Editing the CSS in the test pages is fine because you are using the same CSS files linked to the real site. The following is the process for editing:

1 Click the Pencil icon on the CSS panel to open the Edit Style Sheet dialog, which lists all three linked sheets.

2 Double-click the sheet you want to edit.

3 Double-click a class to open Dreamweaver's Style Definition window.

The style sheet listed last in the Edit Style Sheet dialog is the active style sheet. Editing that sheet enables you to see your changes immediately.

The style sheet listed last in the Edit Style Sheet dialog is the active style sheet. Changing the order of your linked style sheets sets their precedence.

Tip: To make a style sheet active, go into the source code and move it to the bottom of the list.

AN IN-DEPTH LOOK AT PROJECT ONE'S CSS DEPLOYMENT

We know that our cookie script sets one of three style sheets as the active one. To make this work properly, we assigned classes to our page elements. We also redefined some tags so that any element within a redefined tag is automatically styled. We created and edited the styles in Dreamweaver's CSS Editor. If you want to follow our tracks and then play around with changing our styles, complete the steps in this section.

1   Access the CSS Editor:

- Open index.htm in the test_site folder.

- Open the CSS Styles Panel and click the little Pencil icon along its bottom border to open Edit Style Sheet dialog and see the list of linked CSS files.

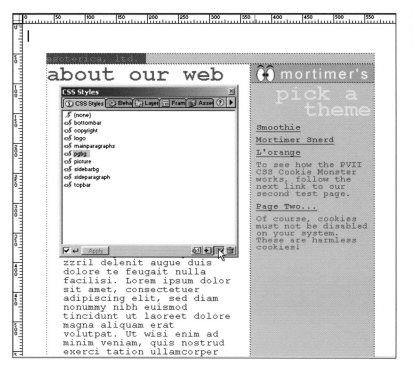

Click the CSS panel's Pencil icon to open the Edit Style Sheet dialog.

- Double-click the active (bottom) style sheet file mortsnerd.css to open a window that lists the styles in the mortsnerd.css file.

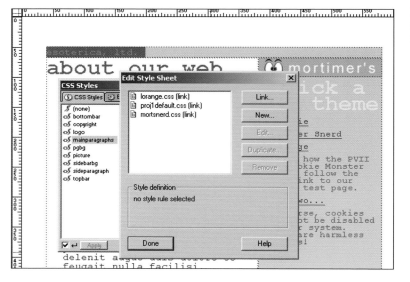

Double-click the active (bottom) style sheet to open the styles list.

- Double-click any style to open the CSS Editor window.

The CSS Editor title bar displays Style Definition for .whateverstyleyouchoose in mortsnerd.css. The Editor window displays these categories: Type, Background, Box, Border, List, Positioning, and Extensions.

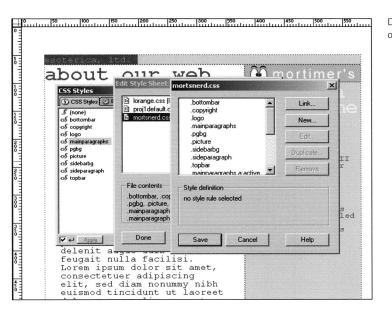

Double-click any style to open the Editor window.

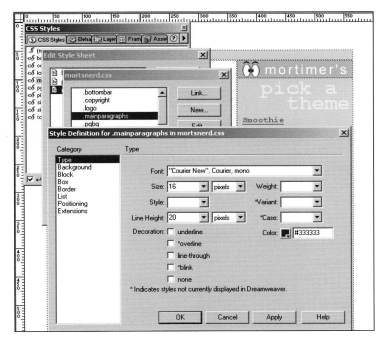

In the Editor window, select the category you want to work with.

2 Look at the styles one-by-one:

- Double-click the style called h1.

   h1 { font-family: "Courier New", Courier, mono; font-size: 36px; font-weight: bold; color: #666666; line-height: 36px; margin-top: 6px; margin-right: 0px; margin-bottom: 12px; margin-left: 0px}

   This is a redefinition of the h1 (Heading 1) tag. Font-family tells the browser to use Courier New. If Courier New is not present on the client system, the choice cascades to Courier. If Courier is not present, the browser looks for Mono (the default mono-spaced font on the system). If Mono isn't found, the browser chooses the client system's default monospaced font. Font size, font weight, color, and line-height are all selected in the Type Category of the Editor window. Margin settings are made in the Box category.

- Double-click .topbar.

   .topbar { background-color: #C6E3C6}

   .topbar is a custom style (denoted by a leading period). Custom styles are always applied manually, via the CSS panel or by right-clicking (Ctrl+clicking) the tag on the status bar. Both the .topbar and .bottombar styles are applied to the **<td>** tags in the top and bottom table rows of our page. We have made two styles to give us the option of making each cell a different color.

- Double-click .bottombar.

   .bottombar { background-color: #C7E2C7}

   Background colors and images are entered in the Editor's Background category.

- Double-click .mainparagraphs.

   .mainparagraphs { font-family: "Courier New", Courier, mono; font-size: 16px; color: #333333; margin-top: 12px; margin-right: 36px; margin-bottom: 12px; margin-left: 36px; line-height: 20px}

The custom style .mainparagraphs is used to style the paragraphs in the main content column of our page.

- Double-click .sideparagraph.

   .sideparagraph { font-family: "Courier New", Courier, mono; font-size: 14px; color: #666666; margin-top: 12px; margin-right: 12px; margin-bottom: 12px; margin-left: 12px; line-height: 16px}

   The custom style .sideparagraph is used to style the paragraphs in the sidebar column of our page.

- Double-click .sidebarbg.

   .sidebarbg { background-color: #C7E2C7}

   The custom style .sidebarbg is applied to the **<td>** tag of the sidebar column.

- Double-click .h2.

   h2 { font-family: "Courier New", Courier, mono; font-size: 36px; font-weight: bold; color: #E2F1E2; line-height: 36px; margin-top: 6px; margin-right: 6px; margin-bottom: 0px; margin-left: 12px; text-align: right; text-indent: 0px}

   The redefined h2 tag has a text-indent, which is applied in the Block category. It is set to 0 because other style sheets do have an indent set. If a particular property is used in any of the three style sheets, it must be present in all three, even if it is 0. Why? Because if not explicitly stated, the browser continues to use the last declared value for that property until we tell it otherwise.

- Double-click .logo.

   .logo { font-family: "Courier New", Courier, mono; font-size: 16px; color: #999999; background-color: #666666; letter-spacing: 2px}

   This custom style is the one we applied to the **<span>** tags surrounding esoterica, ltd. in the top bar of our table.

- Double-click .copyright.

  .copyright { font-family: "Courier New", Courier, mono; font-size: 10px; color: #333333; text-indent: 3pt}

  This custom style is the one we applied to the **<span>** tags surrounding the copyright notice in the bottom bar of our table.

- Double-click .sideparagraph a:link.

  .sideparagraph a:link { color: #0000CE; text-decoration: underline}

  This is a contextual selector. Huh? Any link inside an element that has the .sideparagraph custom style applied to it will automatically render according to this style. In other words, the browser selects and accordingly styles all links (**<a>** tags) in the context of elements that have a class of .sideparagraph.

- Double-click .sideparagraph a:visited.

  .sideparagraph a:visited { color: #993399; text-decoration: underline}

  This is the style selected for all visited links according to the contextual selector.

- Double-click .sideparagraph a:hover.

  .sideparagraph a:hover { color: #0000CE; text-decoration: underline; background-color: #C6E3C6}

  This is the style selected while hovering the mouse over the links styled with the .sideparagraph selector. Hover is a CSS-2 property and is currently supported by MSIE4, 5, and 6 series browsers, Netscape 6, and Opera 5. We don't want the Mortimer theme to have a changed background on hover, but because the other themes have this effect, we need to declare a background color; otherwise, the browser would render the background from the last selected theme. So, in this case, we set the background color to the same color as the table cell background in .sidebarbg.

However, if you compare the two, you'll note that the color numbers are slightly different. This seems to be a bug (at least on our three test systems) in Dreamweaver's color picker tool. The colors are similar and render fine in the browser. Feel free to change them, but we wanted to document the actual results of our page-building process!

- Double-click .sideparagraph a:active.

  .sideparagraph a:active { color: #333333; text-decoration: underline}

  This is the style selected while the mouse is being pressed down on .sideparagraph links.

- Double-click .body.

  body { background-color: #FFFFFF}

  This is the redefined body tag. It simply sets the background color.

- Double-click .mainparagraphs a:link.

  .mainparagraphs a:link { color: #0000CE; text-decoration: underline}

  This is a contextual selector for all links within paragraphs to which the .mainparagraphs custom style is applied. So, we can have more than one style of link on our pages. Cool!

- Double-click .mainparagraphs a:visited.

  .mainparagraphs a:visited { color: #996699; text-decoration: underline}

  This is a contextual selector for all visited links within paragraphs to which the .mainparagraphs custom style is applied.

- Double-click .mainparagraphs a:hover.

  .mainparagraphs a:hover { color: #0000CE; text-decoration: underline; background-color: #FFFFFF}

  This is the style selected while hovering the mouse over the links styled with the .mainparagraphs selector.

- Double-click .mainparagraphs a:active.

   .mainparagraphs a:active { color: #333333; text-decoration: underline}

   This is the style selected while the mouse is being pressed down on .mainparagraph links.

- Double-click .picture.

   .picture { background-color: #99CC99; background-image: url(http://www. yourdomain.com/assets/images/ mortimer.gif)}

   Shssh… keep this one to yourself. It's really a cool trick. This is the custom style that's applied to the **<td>** tag in the nested table atop the sidebar. When a visitor chooses a theme, a different background image is loaded because each of our three style sheets has different images declared.

   Note: The image path must be absolute to accommodate a Netscape 4 bug.

3 Edit a style:

   It's real easy to manage and edit the style sheets using the test_site index page technique. We already linked all three style sheets to the test page, and you've learned how to manipulate the order of a sheet (in the source code) to make it the active sheet. So, you're ready to edit a theme—if you want.

- Make the theme style sheet the active sheet.

- Use Dreamweaver's CSS Editor to make changes.

   As you make a change, Dreamweaver renders the style on the page.

AUTOMATICALLY APPLYING A LINK STYLE TO ALL LINKS ON A PAGE

If you want to have a link style that automatically applies to all links on your page (except those to which a contextual selector applies), then you would define them using the CSS selector in the New Style dialog:

- a:link { blah; blah; blah}

- a:visited { blah; blah; blah}

- a:hover { blah; blah; blah}

- a:active { blah; blah; blah}

Note: Dreamweaver renders most styles in the document window. The styles it is incapable of rendering are marked with asterisks in the CSS Editor. However, those styles are rendered when you preview in your browser (if the browser supports them!).

4 Add a new style:

If you want to add a new style, there are some steps you should take to make sure you get the results you want. Let's say that you want a certain paragraph in the main body to stand out.

- Open the CSS panel.
- Click the Pencil icon.
- Double-click the active (bottom) style sheet. In this case, I've made the active sheet lorange.css because I'm tired of looking at green screen captures!
- Click the New button.

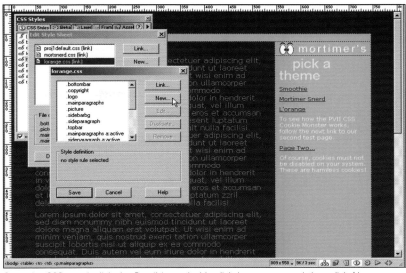

Open the CSS panel, click the Pencil icon, double-click lorange.css, and then click New.

- Make sure that Type is Use CSS Selector and Define In is lorange.css.
- Type **.mainparagraph i** into the Name field.
- Click OK and the Editor window opens with the Type category selected.

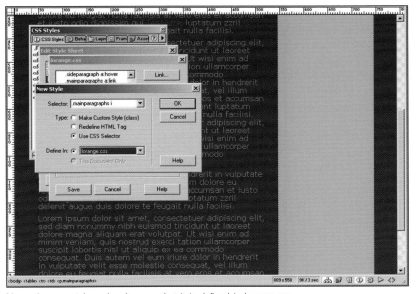

Name the new style and make sure that it is defined in lorange.css.

- Enter **#6699CC** in the Color field and normal in the Style field.
- Leave all other fields blank.

> **Tip:** To create a new style, you can simply click the + icon on the CSS panel's bottom (to the left of the Pencil icon). This opens the New Style dialog. We took a purposefully circuitous route to make sure that you are familiar with all the CSS dialogs.

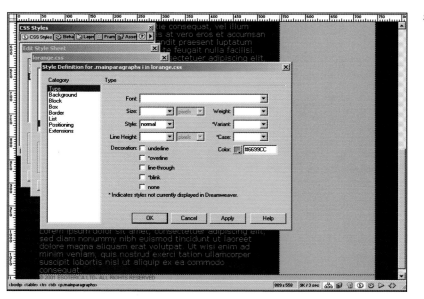

Set the style and color.

5 Apply the new style:

We have a special new style. A Contextual Selector just like our special link styles. But this Selector does not do links. It styles text with an assigned class of .mainparagraph that has also been set to italic (**<i>**).

> **Tip:** I use this technique often because I never use italic text. It tends to look pretty ugly on the Web. So why waste a perfectly good tag!

- Select any block of text within a paragragh that has the .mainparagraph class applied.
- Click the Italic button on the PI.

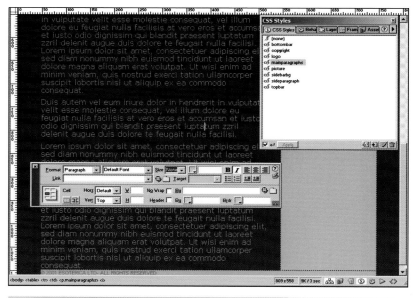

Apply the style by selecting a block of text in the main table column and then clicking the Italic button in the PI.

> **Note:** This style is not included in the supplied style sheets. But do feel free to make your own selectors. If you do, make sure that you make identically named selectors in your other style sheets.

MODIFICATIONS

The nature of this project leaves room for easy and efficient modifications. You can change an existing theme in just a few minutes. You can add additional themes just as easily by adding new style sheets.

The easiest way I've found to add more themes is to open one of the style sheets in my default text editor (Notepad, for example). Use the text editor's File menu to save the .css file with a new name, thereby creating a duplicate.

Link the new style sheet to your test page. Make sure that you go into Code view and move it above the opening script tag (this is explained in greater detail earlier in the project).

Edit the style sheet in the Dreamweaver CSS Editor, from within the test page; and then create a new link beneath the last theme (L'Orange) and apply the P7 setCSS behavior. Set this instance of the behavior to "call" your new style sheet. It's that simple!

Test it and then place the link and behavior on your real index page, using the techniques you've learned in this project!

Don't forget! The CSS links in your test site can be document relative, but the links from your real site must be absolute (http://don't_forget!).

And always use the test page technique to edit and preview your themes locally! If you try to preview your real pages, your browser will attempt to connect with your remote server via the Internet. So it's usually best to use the test page.

BUILDING A DHTML

DROP-DOWN MENU

"If someone has to think about how to

navigate your Web site, they won't."

—AL SPARBER

A DHTML DROP-DOWN MENU

When I was a little boy, I thought I'd grow up to be a famous athlete or scientist. Little did I know that my name would be inextricably tied to DHTML drop-down, flyout, and popup menus. They are all over our Web site. They are even in my home. You can't take three steps without running into one. We are especially careful when opening closet doors. The flyout menus are actually the most painful. But if you are really careful, they can be enormously useful (and intuitive) Web navigation tools—and cool to boot.

Project 2

Building a DHTML Drop-Down Menu

by Al Sparber

IT WORKS LIKE THIS

Clicking the little arrows to the right of each main menu heading pops open a contextual submenu below it. Some submenu items have right-pointing flyout arrows to indicate that there is a contextual menu that flies out beside it. I've set up the menu so that the flyouts are actuated onMouseOver, but this is easily changed to onClick if that suits you better. The idea is to create a visually attractive navigation system that holds many links without dominating the page. The key is to design it so that its purpose is apparent. I'll give you an example:

Many famous sites (Microsoft, Adobe, and Quark come to mind) have drop-down menus. The casual surfer, however, would never know it because they left out one important piece—the downward pointing arrow. Arrows are metaphors. They usually say, "Click me and I will make something appear over there in the direction to which I am pointing." If I encounter a drop-down menu without something obvious to click on or wave my mouse over, then I don't. You see, I can keep a secret as well as the next guy! The moral here is that if it looks like a menu, it probably is. Now back to my point.

So you click or move the mouse over the arrows, and submenus appear in the area the arrow is pointing to. Pretty simple.

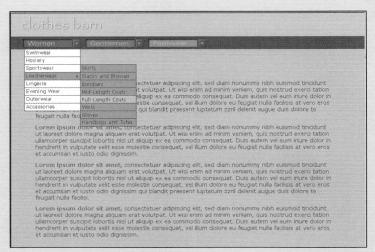

In the finished Menu, clicking the down arrow reveals submenus. Mousing over the right-pointing arrows reveals flyout menus.

The middle menu heading also has a drop-down menu, which has a flyout, too.

34

This particular menu is made with images. Even for the submenu links. Why? Because it looks neater and allows us to weave some magic that would not otherwise be possible. The images are transparent (except, of course, for the text), which allows the underlying table cell background to show through. So I can use CSS and a little JavaScript to change the color of the table cell when you mouseover the transparent image, and thereby create a swap image (rollover) effect with a single image. But I was very economical and made sure that the images were optimized to death in Fireworks. Each menu item image is less than one-third of one kilobyte. So, even if a design required 60 links on a page (an unusually high number), the total image weight would be around 15KB. Of course, the techniques used to create this menu would work just as well if you chose to use plain old text.

BROWSER COMPATIBILITY

We have tested this interface and found that it is fully functional in the following browsers:

MSIE 4 (Windows and Mac)

MSIE 5 (Windows and Mac)

MSIE 5.5 (Windows)

NN4.08–4.76 (Windows)

NN4.5 (Mac)

Opera 5.01 (Windows)

Netscape 6 (Windows and Mac)

Note: The images used in this project were made with Fireworks 4, and the original (editable) source files are included on the accompanying CD. The secret to making the menu item text images (those that appear in the drop-down and flyout menus) is to make them on a transparent canvas, turn off anti-aliasing, and set transparency to Alpha. I used 12pt Tahoma for text and set its color to #666666 (dark gray).

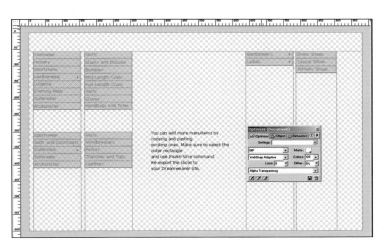

This main image, as seen in Fireworks, has slices turned on.

PREPARING TO WORK

Let's go through the routine. You need to install some extensions, copy the project folder from the CD to your hard drive, and then fire up Dreamweaver and define a new site using your copied project folder as the local root folder.

1 Install the PVII Auto Layers behavior (if you haven't already done so) and the DW4 W3C Object Color Changer behavior:

   • Browse to the Extensions folder on the CD.

   • Open the Behaviors/Actions subfolder.

   • Double-click P7_autoLayers.mxp to install the behavior.

   • Repeat these steps to install DW4w3ccolorchanger.mxp.

2 Install the NN4 Return False Fix and the Scrubber commands:

   NN4 Return False Fix, a Project VII command, eliminates Netscape showing the hourglass cursor when clicking a null link to fire a JavaScript. The Scrubber removes the residual focus lines from around clicked links in MSIE.

   • Browse to the Extensions folder on the CD.

   • Open the Commands subfolder.

   • Double-click the file called N4 Return False Fix.mxp to install the command.

   • Repeat these steps to install scrubber.mxp.

3 Copy the projects folder:

   • Browse to the projects folder on the CD.

   • Copy the project_two folder to a convenient location on your hard drive.

4 Define a new Dreamweaver site using the project_two copy as your local root folder.

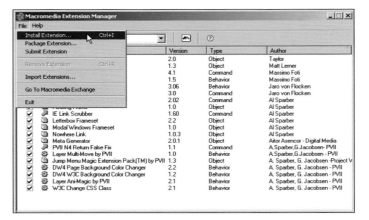

If you have any problems installing an extension via the Manage Extensions command in Dreamweaver, open the Extensions Manager directly using your computer's Programs menu.

Tip: Should you encounter difficulties installing an extension, you can access the Extension directly via the Manage Extensions Manager program by selecting Manage Extensions from the Commands menu inside Dreamweaver.

There have been reports that under certain conditions and in some operating systems, double-clicking an MXP file will not invoke the installation procedure. In that event, you can simply open the Extension Manager itself (as described previously) and use its File/Install Extension command to browse to the appropriate MXP file.

Note: Remember, if you want to see how the completed site looks in either Dreamweaver or your browser, you can find all the files in the finished_project folder.

USING CSS TO STYLE A PAGE

If you have the urge to dive right into the menu-building process, resist it. We need to set the stage by making a nice page to fit it into. I took a little of the work off your hands by creating the style sheet and linking it to your work page. Because the background image is part of the style sheet, it's going to be there when you open the page.

1 Open the working project file and inspect the Cascading Style Sheet:

- Open index.htm from the root of the project_two folder.
- Open the style sheet editor by clicking the Pencil icon on the bottom of the CSS panel.

Notice the linked external CSS file called proj2.css. Beneath that is a style called body. The body style is separate because it is not in the linked sheet—it is contained (embedded) directly in the document. Why? Well, Netscape 4 does not know how to resolve image paths in external style sheets if the page and the CSS file are in different folders. Because the page background image is declared in the CSS body style, we need to ensure that in a working site, pages placed in folders other than the root will render a background image in Netscape 4.

The background image ch2bg.gif is set to repeat along the X-axis of the page. Because the image is 1600 pixels wide by 92 pixels high, the result is a band that spans the top of the page. The area below 92 pixels picks up the background color I've set to #D6D3CE. Notice that the darker strip along the bottom of the background image covers the bottom 32 pixels of the image, which is precisely the height of the three trigger (menu header) images.

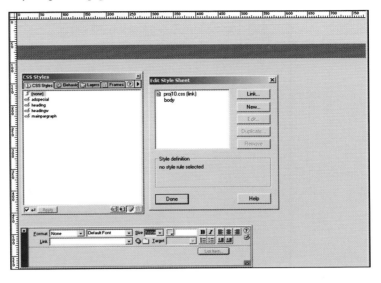

When you open the working project page, the background image is applied, and the CSS is all ready to go.

The background image creates a band effect across the top of the page that will fill up a browser window as wide as 1600 pixels.

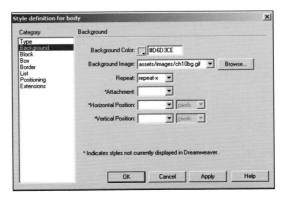

The background image is declared in an embedded body style and set to repeat only along the X-axis. A background color fills the area below the images.

2 Insert the logo layer on the page:

- Insert a new layer onto the page.
- Use the property inspector to set these attributes:

   Name: **logolayer**
   Tag: **DIV**
   L: **0px**
   T: **0px**
   W: **668px**
   H: **59px**

   Leave all other fields in their default states.

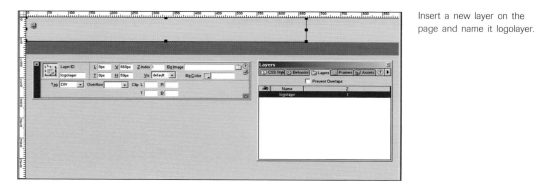

Insert a new layer on the page and name it logolayer.

3 Insert the logo image inside the logo layer:

- Open the Assets panel.
- Select the Images category.
- Scroll down to find logo.gif.
- Click inside logolayer.
- Select logo.gif in the Assets panel and drag it up inside the layer. Release the mouse button to drop the image inside the layer.

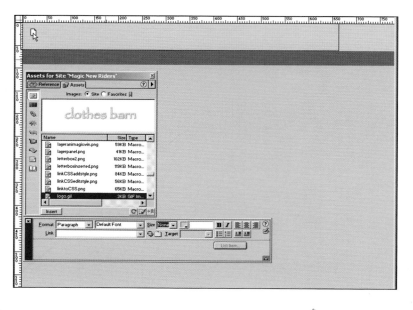

Use the Assets panel to insert logo.gif into logolayer.

Note: You can also use the Insert button at the bottom of the Assets panel to insert the image by clicking inside the layer to establish a flashing insertion point and then clicking the button.

Tip: It's a good idea to save your work after each step!

INSERTING THE TRIGGER AND MENU LAYERS

To ensure that our menus always line up perfectly with their trigger images, both the trigger images and the menus need to be in layers. The trigger images, are the buttons you click to cause the drop-down menus to appear.

1 Insert the trigger image layers:

The trigger images are the menu headings that users click to open the drop-down submenus.

• Insert three new layers onto the page.

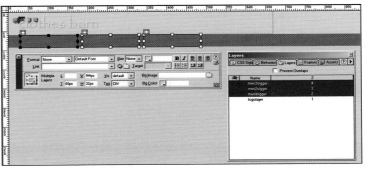

Insert three new layers to accommodate the menu trigger images.

• Use the property inspector to set the attributes shown in the table.

The Top position of 60px places the layers precisely inside the bottom band of the background image, which is color coordinated especially for the trigger images.

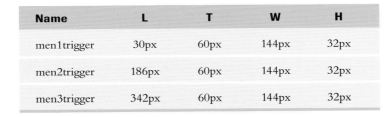

Name	L	T	W	H
men1trigger	30px	60px	144px	32px
men2trigger	186px	60px	144px	32px
men3trigger	342px	60px	144px	32px

Create these new layers and set their attributes in the property inspector.

2 Insert the trigger images:

• Use the Assets panel to insert these trigger images (the menu headers) into their respective layers:

men1trigger	ch2iface4menhead1.gif
men2trigger	ch2iface4menhead2.gif
men3trigger	ch2iface4menhead3.gif

Each image is precisely 144px wide by 32px tall, the exact dimensions of the layers.

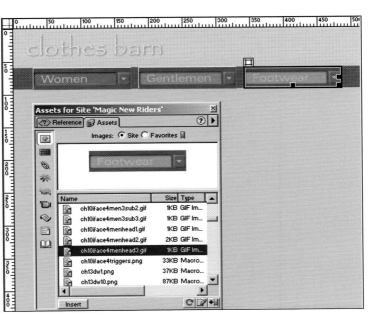

Insert the three trigger images into the new layers using the Assets panel.

3 Insert the submenu layers:

- Insert three new layers onto the page.

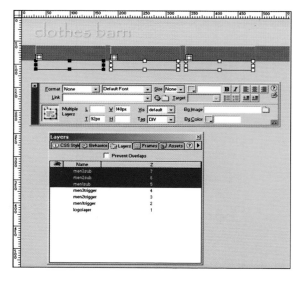

Insert the three submenu layers under the trigger layers.

- Use the property inspector to set the attributes shown in the table.

Name	L	T	W	H
men1sub	30px	92px	140px	blank
men2sub	186px	92px	140px	blank
men3sub	342px	92px	140px	blank

Insert three new layers, applying the appropriate attributes.

4 Insert the submenu tables:

- Insert a table inside each of the three submenu layers that has these attributes:

  Rows: **1**
  Columns: **1**
  Width: **140 pixels**
  Border: **0**
  Cell padding: **0**
  Cell Spacing: **0**

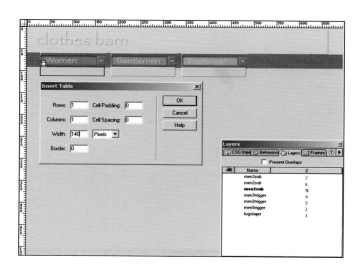

Insert a single cell table inside each submenu.

40

- Use the property inspector to color each cell white (#FFFFFF).

You may be asking why we're using just one cell. The answer is simple. We are going to apply a JavaScript behavior to the first cell of each table and then use the Tab key to create the additional needed cells. In this way, the new cells will pick up the JavaScript behavior from the previous cell. Cool!

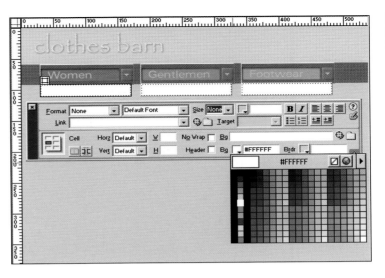

Set the background color of the cell (not the entire table) to white in all three tables.

5 Study the table showing the background colors of the submenu table cells:

The Color Changer inserts a JavaScript that will cause the table cell to change color onMouseOver. Because the text images we will be inserting inside the table cells are transparent, the illusion created will be that of a swap image rollover. However, instead of the two images (up and over), we need only one.

Because we want to have the cells containing the fly-out menu arrows color coordinated with the color of the flyout menus themselves, we did some advance work and charted it out:

Note: When designing a page like this, it's always a good idea to chart out colors and interactions before diving into Dreamweaver. It will save you a lot of time.

men1sub	men2sub	men3sub
Cell 1 is white #FFFFFF	Cell 1 is white #FFFFFF	Cell 1 is white #FFFFFF (flyout)
Cell 2 is white #FFFFFF	Cell 2 is white #FFFFFF	Cell 2 is pink #E2C5C5 (flyout)
Cell 3 is white #FFFFFF	Cell 3 is mint #DEE3D6 (flyout)	
Cell 4 is rose #CC9999	Cell 4 is white #FFFFFF	
Cell 5 is white #FFFFFF	Cell 5 is white #FFFFFF	
Cell 6 is white #FFFFFF		
Cell 7 is white #FFFFFF		
Cell 8 is white #FFFFFF		

Use this table to define the color of each cell. The cell colors depicted represent the default color of each cell in its resting state, and also its color onMouseOut. The onMouseOver color for all cells is #D6D3CE (medium gray).

6 Apply the DW4 W3C Object Color Changer behavior to the submenu table cells:

We're going to apply the Color Changer behavior to the **<td>** tags (the table cells), so we need to set our Behaviors panel to show events for version 5 and higher browsers. Netscape 4 will degrade gracefully and simply ignore the script.

- Open the Behaviors panel and click the + button to open the Behaviors menu.

- Choose Show Events For and select IE5.0. (NN6 also supports these events but does not appear in the menu because it was released after Dreamweaver 4 shipped.)

- Click inside the table cell in layer men1sub.

- Open the Behaviors panel again.

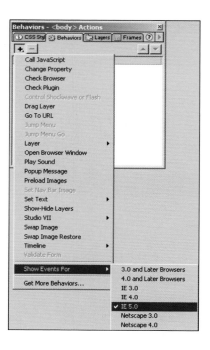

In the Behaviors panel, choose Behaviors/Show Events For, and select IE5.0.

- Click the + button and choose DW4 W3C Object Color Changer from the Studio VII flyout menu.

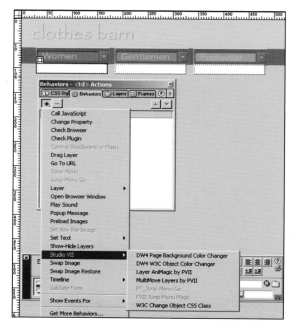

In the Behaviors panel, choose Behaviors/Studio VII, and select DW4 W3C Object Color Changer.

42

- Type **#D6D3CE** into the Select New Color Value field.
- Click OK and make sure that the event set on the Behaviors panel is onMouseOver.
- Leave your cursor in the table cell and apply the DW4 W3C Object Color Changer behavior again.

In the DW4 W3C Object Color Changer dialog, type **#D6D3CE** into the Select New Color Value field.

- Type **#FFFFFF** into the Select New Color Value field.
- Click OK and make sure that the event set on the Behaviors panel is onMouseOut.
- You've created a W3C rollover! Mousing over the table cell changes its color from white to medium gray. Mousing out changes its color back to white.
- Repeat the preceding procedure for the table cells inside layers men2sub and men3sub.

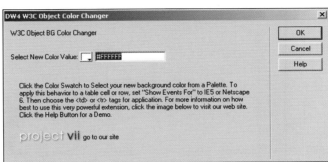

In the DW4 W3C Object Color Changer dialog, type **#FFFFFF** into the Select New Color Value field.

7   Add the remaining necessary table cells to each table in the three submenu layers:

- Click inside the first table (inside layer men1sub) and press your Tab key seven times to add seven new rows.
- Click inside the second table and add four new rows.
- Click inside the third table and add one more row.

Using this method to add rows also duplicates the JavaScript behaviors, so every table cell now carries the identical onMouseOver and onMouseOut events you placed on the original cells in each table!

However, when we charted the background colors, we determined that the fourth cell in the first table, the third cell in the second table, and the second cell in the third table need to be different colors: rose, mint, and pink.

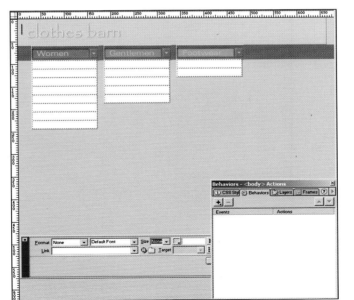

Add the new rows that create the cells you need for the tables.

8 Color the table cells that relate to the flyout menus:

- Click inside row 4 of the first table.
- Use the property inspector to set its background color to rose (#CC9999).
- Click inside row 3 of the second table.
- Use the property inspector to set its background color to mint (#DEE3D6).
- Click inside row 2 of the third table.
- Use the property inspector to set its background color to pink (#E2C5C5).

Note: Throughout this book we use the terms *row* and *cell*. A cell is the box created by the intersection of a row and a column. A single-column table row is considered a cell and is associated with the **<td>** tag, whereas a row can be comprised of two or more contiguous cells and is associated with the **<tr>** tag. Applying a JavaScript action to either a **<tr>** or **<td>** tag in a single-column table will have the same results.

9 Update the W3C Object Color Changer on the newly colored cells:

The new background colors you just set need to become the onMouseOut color in the Object Color Changer behavior.

- Click inside the rose-colored cell in the first table.
- Open the Behaviors panel and double-click the onMouseOut event.
- Click the Select New Color Value color square.
- Use the Eyedropper tool to pick up the rose background from the table cell.
- Click OK.
- Repeat this process to change the onMouseOut events for the mint and pink-colored cells in the second and third tables.

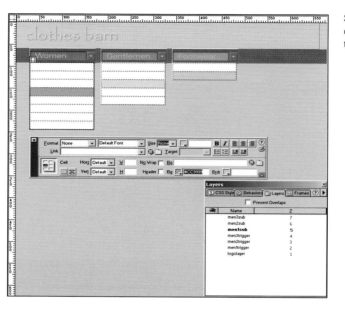

Set the background color of each cell that is related to a flyout menu.

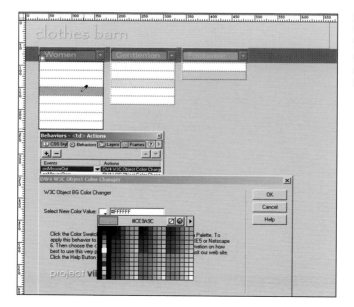

In the W3C Object Color Changer, use the Eyedropper tool to pick up the background color from the table cells that relate to the flyout menus.

INSERTING FLYOUT MENU LAYERS

We're almost done! Let's add the menus that fly out from the submenu layers. But first
let's make it easier to see the new layers we're about to create by temporarily setting
layers men1sub, men2sub, and men3sub to hidden.

1 Temporarily hide the submenu layers:

- Open the Layers panel.

- Select men1sub and click in the left column of the
panel until you see the closed eye icon.

- Repeat for layers men2sub and men3sub.

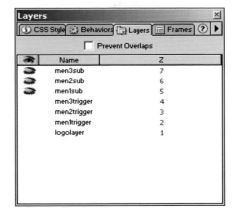

In the Layers panel, select each
submenu layer and click the left
column to hide the layer.

2 Create the four flyout menu layers:

- Insert four new layers onto the page.

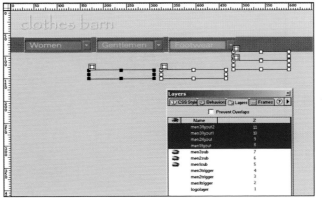

Create each flyout menu layer
and set its attributes.

- Use the property inspector to set the attributes
shown in the table.

Set the attributes of the four
flyout menu layers on the
property inspector, using this
table as a guide.

Name	L	T	W	H
men1flyout	169px	132px	140px	blank
men2flyout	325px	132px	140px	blank
men3flyout1	481px	92px	120px	blank
men3flyout2	481px	112px	120px	blank

3 Insert the flyout menu tables:

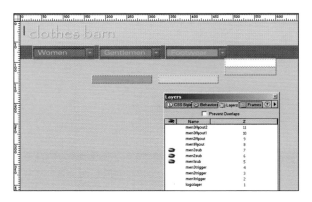

The flyout menus now have colorful table cells.

- Insert a single cell table in each of the four flyout menu layers, using the attributes shown in the table.

Using the Insert Table dialog, set the attributes of the table cells in four flyout menu layers.

Table in Layer	Rows	Col	Width	Border	Padding	Spacing
men1flyout	1	1	140px	0	0	0
men2flyout	1	1	140px	0	0	0
men3flyout1	1	1	120px	0	0	0
men3flyout2	1	1	120px	0	0	0

4 Set the background color of the table cells:

- Set the background color of the table cells, using the information in the table.

Use the information in this table as you set the background color of the table cells.

Table Cell in Layer	Set Color to
men1flyout	#CC9999
men2flyout	#DEE3D6
men3flyout1	#FFFFFF
men3flyout2	#E2C5C5

5 Apply the DW4 W3C Object Color Changer behavior to the flyout menu table cells:

- Use the same technique we used in Step 6 of the previous section to apply the DW4 W3C Object Color Changer behavior to the submenu cells. That is, click inside the table cell so that the **<td>** tag is highlighted, open the Behaviors panel, click the + button, and select the DW4 W3C Object Color Changer from the Studio VII flyout menu.

- Use the table as a guide.

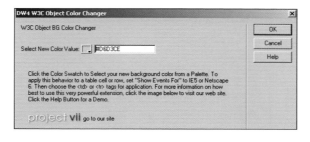

Set the Background Color Changer behavior of each submenu cell.

Table Cell in Layer	onMouseOver Color	onMouseOut Color
men1flyout	#D6D3CE	#CC9999
men2flyout	#D6D3CE	#DEE3D6
men3flyout1	#D6D3CE	#FFFFFF
men3flyout2	#D6D3CE	#E2C5C5

This table shows the color numbers to insert into the Select New Color Value field on the DW4 W3C Object Color Changer dialog for both the onMouseOver and onMouseOut events.

6 Add the remaining necessary table cells to each table in the four flyout menu layers:

- Click inside the table cell in each flyout layer and use the Tab key to complete the following steps:

  Add seven cells to the table in men1flyout.
  Add four cells to the table in men2flyout.
  Add two cells to the table in men3flyout1.
  Add two cells to the table in men3flyout2.

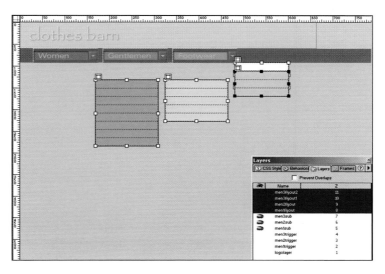

Add the additional table cells to flyout menu layers.

USING THE ASSETS PANEL TO INSERT IMAGES INTO MENU LAYERS

We're going to use the Assets panel to quickly populate the table cells in all the submenu and flyout menu layers. Use this table as a guide:

These two use the same images

men1sub	men2sub	men3sub	men1flyout	men2flyout	men3flyout	men3flyout2
ch2iface4men1a.gif	ch2iface4men2a.gif	ch2iface4men3a.gif	ch2iface4men1sub1a.gif	ch2iface4men2sub1a.gif	ch2iface4men3sub1.gif	ch2iface4men3sub1.gif
ch2iface4men1b.gif	ch2iface4men2b.gif	ch2iface4men3b.gif	ch2iface4men1sub1b.gif	ch2iface4men2sub1b.gif	ch2iface4men3sub2.gif	ch2iface4men3sub2.gif
ch2iface4men1c.gif	ch2iface4men2c.gif		ch2iface4men1sub1c.gif	ch2iface4men2sub1c.gif	ch2iface4men3sub2.gif	ch2iface4men3sub2.gif
ch2iface4men1d.gif	ch2iface4men2d.gif		ch2iface4men1sub1d.gif	ch2iface4men2sub1d.gif		
ch2iface4men1e.gif	ch2iface4men2e.gif		ch2iface4men1sub1e.gif	ch2iface4men2sub1e.gif		
ch2iface4men1f.gif			ch2iface4men1sub1f.gif			
ch2iface4men1g.gif			ch2iface4men1sub1g.gif			
ch2iface4men1h.gif			ch2iface4men1sub1h.gif			

1   Insert the images into the three main submenus:

- For a clearer view of your task, hide all the menus except for men1sub, men2sub, and men3sub.
- Open the Assets panel to insert the images into the table cells.
- Drag the images into the cells, using the table as a guide.

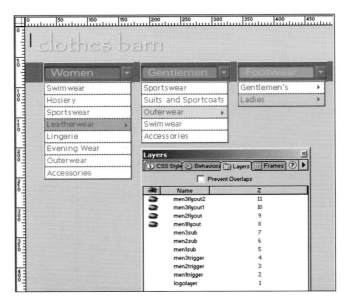

Insert the images into the main submenus.

2 Insert the images into the four flyout menus:

- For a clearer view of your task, now hide the three main submenus:

    men1sub
    men2sub
    men3sub

- Open the Assets panel to insert the images into all the table cells. Use our image table as a guide.

- Drag the images into the cells using the previous table as a guide.

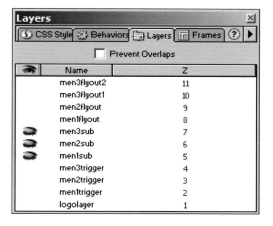

In the Layers panel, hide the three main submenus and set the previously hidden menus to default visability.

Adding Hotspots to Menu Trigger Down Arrows

When users access the menu system, we want them to use the down arrow buttons to activate the drop-down submenus. Rather than slicing the trigger images into complex segments, we're going to assign hotspots to the areas over the arrows, creating client–side image maps. We're going to be working with the three trigger layers, so make sure that they are set to visible.

1 Hide all the submenu and flyout layers in preparation for applying the behaviors that control the menu system.

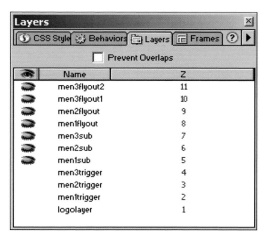

Hide all the submenu and fly-out layers and make sure that the three trigger layers are now set to default visability.

2 Apply the hotspots:

- Click on the first trigger image.
- Select the Rectangular Hotspot tool on the property inspector.
- Draw a box around the down arrow button in the first trigger layer (men1trigger).
- Repeat to draw hotspots around the arrows in the other two trigger layers.

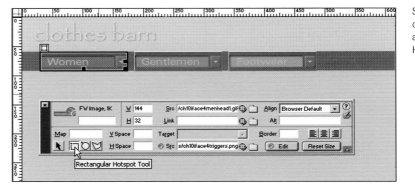

Select the first trigger image, open the property inspector, and click on the Rectangular Hotspot tool.

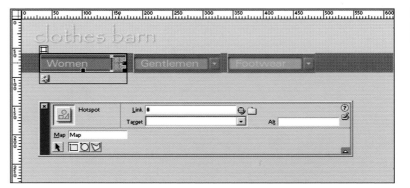

Draw a rectangle around the down arrow button in the first trigger image.

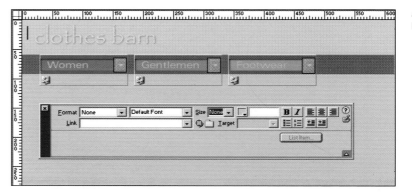

All three hotspots have been added.

ADDING THE LAYER THAT CONTROLS THE CLOSING OF ALL OPEN MENUS

When we click or mouse over buttons and links to open our menu layers, we need to make sure of two things—that the menus stay open to allow users to select items and that the menus are hidden when not needed. The easiest way to do this is to create a special layer that sits underneath the menu layers and that contains a JavaScript behavior to hide the menus. The JavaScript is applied to a transparent GIF that lives inside the layer. When the arrow buttons are clicked to open a menu, the menucloser layer is also made visible. But because it only contains a transparent image, we really can't see it. However, our mouse can "feel" it. So, when we mouse out of a menu and into the open areas between menus, above menus, and below menus, we come into contact with the menucloser layer. As soon as we "touch" it, our menus are closed.

Tip: The secret is that touching the menucloser layer not only hides the menus, it hides itself, as well. Then it lies dormant and hidden until we click on one of the arrow buttons again.

1   Insert the menucloser layer:

  • Insert a new layer.

  • Using the property inspector, set these attributes:

   Name: **menucloser**
   Tag: **DIV**
   L: **0px**
   T: **0px**
   W: **98%**
   H: **400px**

   Leave all other fields in their default states.

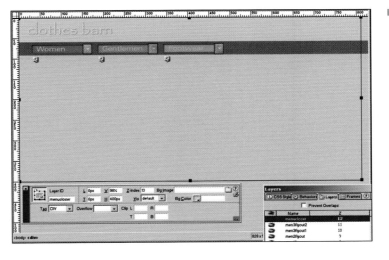

Insert the menucloser layer.

2   Insert the image into the menucloser layer:

  • Click inside the layer.

  • Use the Assets panel to find and insert the image called shim.gif.

  • Before you move your cursor one millimeter, use the property inspector to set the width and height of shim.gif to the following:

   W: **100%**
   H: **400**

3 Move the menucloser layer to its proper z-index:

For menucloser to function properly, it must be placed behind the menu layers but in front of the logolayer.

- Open the Layers panel.

- Drag menucloser down so that it comes to rest at the third position in the z-index, between men1trigger and logolayer.

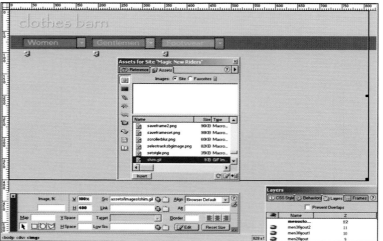

Insert shim.gif into the menucloser layer.

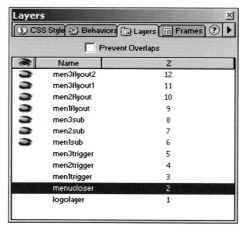

Drag the menucloser layer to the second from bottom position in the Layers panel.

APPLYING PVII AUTO LAYER BEHAVIOR

The PVII Auto Layer behavior was created by DHTML wizard (and my partner) Gerry Jacobsen to make the showing and hiding of multiple layers a snap. You activate a layer by simply selecting it in the Auto Layer dialog and clicking the Show Layer button. Clicking a trigger button shows its associated layer. As you click another trigger, Auto Layer shows that button's associated layer but remembers the first layer and hides it.

Each time you click a trigger that fires the Auto Layer script, it keeps adding the previous layers to a sort of list called an *array*. So Auto Layers actually knows to hide all the layers it previously had made visible—each time you click a button. You use this awesome script on the menucloser layer first.

1 Apply Auto Layer to menucloser:

   • Select the shim.gif image inside menucloser by selecting the menucloser layer and then gently clicking inside.

   • To make sure that you've got hold of the image, take a quick peek at the property inspector. You should also see the **<IMG>** tag in bold on the status bar.

   • Open the Behaviors panel.

   • Click the + button and then choose Studio VII/ Auto Layers by PVII.

   • Click OK. It sounds odd, but you do not actually select any layers here. You simply open the Auto Layer window and click OK. We are telling Auto Layer to hide all layers in its memory.

   • Choose (onMouseOver) as the event.

   Remember! No layers are set to show in this step because we want all Auto Layers to hide, including menucloser itself.

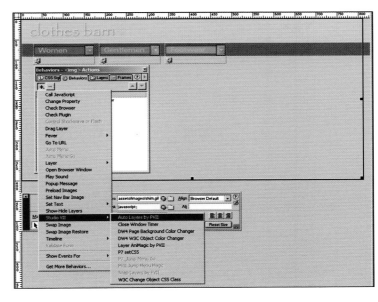

In the Behaviors list, choose Studio VII/Auto Layers by PVII.

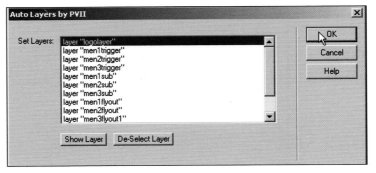

In the Auto Layers window, all you need to do is click OK. We don't select any layers in this step.

2   Apply Auto Layer to the men1trigger trigger images:

   • Select the hotspot over the arrow button in men1trigger.

   • Open the Behaviors panel and choose Studio VII/Auto Layers by PVII.

   • Select layer men1sub and click the Show Layer button.

   • Select layer menucloser and click the Show Layer button.

   • Click OK and ensure that the event is onClick.

     This action causes men1sub and menucloser to become visible and all other auto layers to hide.

3   Select the hotspot over the arrow button in men2trigger:

   • Open the Behaviors panel and choose Studio VII/Auto Layers by PVII.

   • Select layer men2sub and click the Show Layer button.

   • Select layer menucloser and click the Show Layer button.

   • Click OK and ensure that the event is onClick.

     This action will cause men2sub and menucloser to become visible and all other auto layers to hide.

4   Repeat this procedure for the arrow button over the third trigger menu, men3trigger, but select men3sub and menucloser.

5   Apply Auto Layers by PVII to the submenu images that open the flyout menus:

   • Select the image labeled Leatherwear in men1sub.

   • Open the Behaviors panel and choose Studio VII/ Auto Layers by PVII.

   • Select layer men1flyout and click the Show Layer button; and then repeat for the following:

        men1sub

        menucloser

   • Click OK and ensure that the event is onMouseOver.

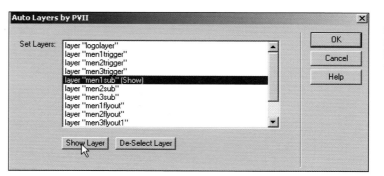

In the Auto Layers dialog, select men1sub and click the Show Layer button. Then select menucloser and click the Show Layer button.

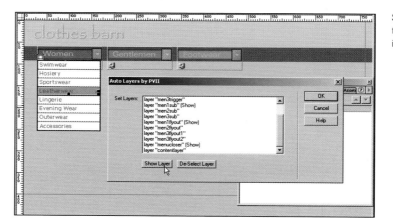

Select Leatherwear and apply the Auto Layers behavior to its flyout menus.

- Select the image labeled Outerwear in men2sub.

- Open the Behaviors panel and choose Studio VII/ Auto Layers by PVII.

- Select layer men2flyout and click the Show Layer button; and then repeat for the following:

   men2sub

   menucloser

- Click OK and ensure that the event is onMouseOver.

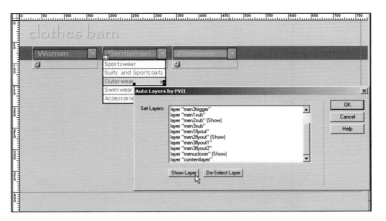

Select Outerwear and apply the Auto Layers behavior to its flyout menus.

- Select the image labeled Gentlemen's in men3sub.

Tip: When setting events on images, if Show Events For is set to IE5, you will see two versions of the same event listed above and below a separator line. The bottom events have parentheses. These are the ones to pick from because they insert an **<a>** tag around the event instead of placing the event directly within the **<img>** tag. This would not be an issue, except that Netscape 4 will not fire events from **<img>** tags.

- Open the Behaviors panel and choose Studio VII/ Auto Layers by PVII.

- Select layer men3flyout1 and click the Show Layer button; then repeat for the following:

   men3sub
   menucloser

- Click OK and ensure that the event is onMouseOver.

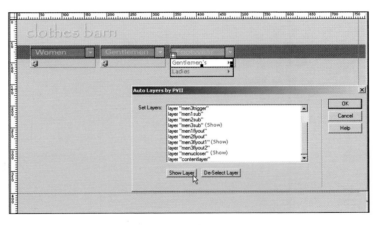

Select Gentlemen's and apply the Auto Layers behavior to its flyout menus.

- Select the image labeled Ladies in men3sub.

- Open the Behaviors panel and choose Studio VII/ Auto Layers by PVII.

- Select layer men3flyout2 and click the Show Layer button; and then repeat for the following:

  men3sub
  menucloser

- Click OK and ensure that the event is onMouseOver.

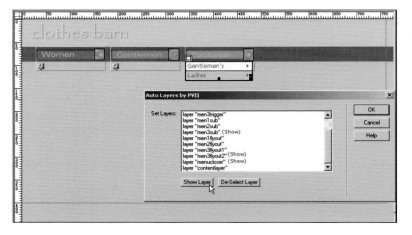

Select Ladies and apply the Auto Layers behavior to its flyout menus.

6 Apply Auto Layers to submenu images adjacent to the flyouts:

When a user mouses over a flyout link (Leatherwear in mensub1, for example), the flyout opens. But what if the user is just *passing through* and mouses off Leatherware and onto Sportswear or Lingerie? We want the flyout to close. So we need to add the Auto Layers behavior to those links adjacent to the flyout links.

- Use the table as a guide to apply the last instances of Auto Layers to the menu items in the men1sub and men2sub layers.

In Layer	Menu Item	Layers to Show	Event
men1sub	Sportswear	men1sub; menucloser	onMouseOver
men1sub	Lingerie	men1sub; menucloser	onMouseOver
men2sub	Suits and Sportcoats	men2sub; menucloser	onMouseOver
men2sub	Swimwear	men2sub; menucloser	onMouseOver

Use this table as you apply the last instances of Auto Layers.

CORRECTING BROWSER-SPECIFIC PROBLEMS

To make our menu system foolproof and smooth, we need to add a few simple JavaScripts. The Netscape Resize Fix keeps our layers in place when Netscape 4 users resize their browser window. The NN4 Return False Fix, searches for onClick events with null links and adds return false at the end to stop Netscape 4 from displaying the hourglass cursor. The IE Link Scrubber eliminates the dotted lines that appear around clicked links in IE4 and 5.

1 Apply the Netscape Resize Fix:

   • Choose Commands and Add/Remove Netscape Resize Fix.

   • Click the Add button.

2 Apply the NN4 Return False Fix:

   • Choose Commands/Studio VII/Apply N4 Return False Fix.

   • Click the Apply button.

3 Apply the IE link Scrubber:

   • Choose Commands/Studio VII/IE Link Scrubber.

   • Click the Scrub Em! button.

Tip: If your preferences are set to apply the Netscape fix whenever you place a layer on your page, you don't need to reapply it. Actually, if you try to add it again, the Add button will say Remove. (But don't remove it!)

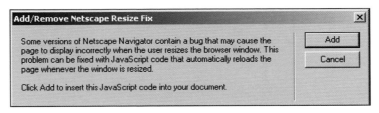

In the Add/Remove Netscape Resize Fix dialog, click Add to keep layers in place in Netscape 4.

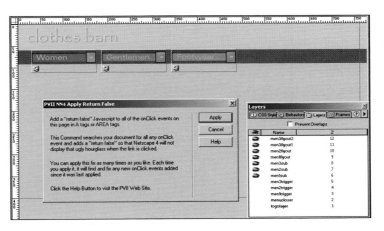

In the PVII NN4 Apply Return False dialog, click Apply to keep Netscape 4 from displaying the hourglass when someone clicks a link.

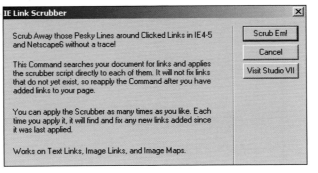

In the IE link Scrubber dialog, click Scrub Em! Remove the lines around clicked links.

ADDING PLACEHOLDER CONTENT
TO THE PAGE

To give your project a finished look, let's add a little content to the page.

1 Insert a contentlayer:

- Insert a new layer on the page and use the property inspector to assign the following attributes:

  Name: **contentlayer**
  Tag: **DIV**
  L: **0px**
  T: **109px**
  W: **100%**
  H: **Leave Blank**

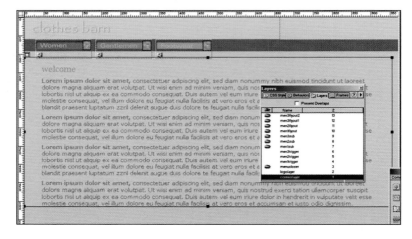

The page looks much more finished with our placeholder content.

2 Insert some text into the contentlayer:

- Insert a few paragraphs of text into the layer and assign it CSS styles from the externally linked style sheet.

- Use .heading to style a paragraph containing a heading.

- Use .mainparagraph to style the main body of text Or you can create your own styles.

3 Using the Layers palette, drag the contentlayer to the bottom of the stack.

4 View your work by using Dreamweaver's Preview in Browser function. Don't forget to check your work in many different browsers.

MODIFICATIONS

The menu we just created is extremely versatile. The layers can be moved around, images edited, menus added, or text substituted for the menus. You can even turn it sideways to create a vertically oriented flyout menu.

You are limited only by your imagination. The techniques covered in this project are all you need to create any type of drop-down, flyout, or popup menu.

If you're into animation, you could use the PVII Layer AniMagic behavior to make your menus slide open and closed like a window shade. Or you could create more complex images than we used to accomplish some interesting metaphorical effects, such as a file drawer opening and closing, for example.

As a matter of fact, the next project will show you how to take this menu and turn it sideways!

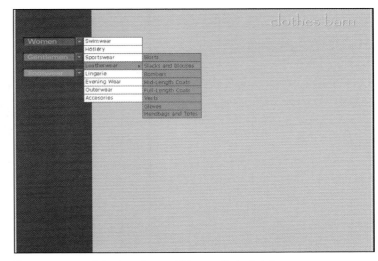

Our menu can easily be turned around into a vertical orientation.

BUILDING A DHTML FLYOUT MENU

"Give a man a fish and you feed him

for a day. Teach a man to fish, and

you feed him for a lifetime."

—CHINESE WEB DEVELOPMENT PROVERB

A DHTML Flyout Menu

Popup-flyout menus are cool, save space, and, if properly designed, make extremely intuitive navigation systems. So what's with the silly fishing quotation-parable? Well, the technique used to create this menu (as well as the drop-down menu in the previous project) is so surprisingly simple that we want to make sure that it really sinks in.

If you master this technique, you'll be able to pop up, fly out, or drop down anything you want, whenever you feel the urge.

The secret is that all the hard work has been done for you through the magic of Dreamweaver extensions. As you work through this project, you're really part of a team. Beside you, in spirit, are developers Gerry Jacobsen, Massimo Foti, and Al Sparber.

Building a DHTML Flyout Menu

by Al Sparber

In the finished menu, rolling over the side-pointing arrows reveals submenus. The menus close automatically when you move your mouse off.

IT WORKS LIKE THIS

Just like in the drop-down menu project, we have menu triggers, and some of the triggers have arrows. The purpose is the same except that these arrows point to the right, and mousing over an arrow produces a submenu next to it. The other obvious difference is that our trigger images (the main menu headings) are oriented down the page, instead of across. Once again, the objective is to create an attractive menu with a clear and unambiguous purpose.

Our project menu has eight headings. Two of the headings have a flyout arrow indicating that—you guessed it—another related menu flies open when you do something to the arrow with your mouse. In this case, you simply point at it.

The mission was to create a menu that is so obviously a menu that no user in his right mind would think otherwise. I think we succeeded.

Our project menu has two flyouts. It's easy to make more.

We use transparent images for the menu items, as we did in the previous project. Remember, each menu image is around 200 bytes, so the overhead and download times are negligible versus plain text—especially considering that we'd need additional JavaScript code to achieve the same effect. We haven't done precise measuring, but the image method may, in fact, take up less code than plain text.

> **Note:** The images used in this project are made with un-anti-aliased text and are alpha transparent. When using this project's technique, do not get fancy with your images, or you run the risk of substantially increasing download times.

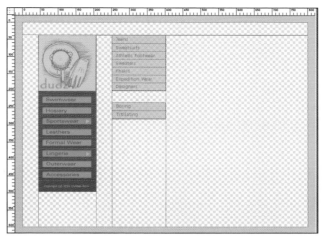

The images in this project are a snap to make in Fireworks 4. This is the main image as seen in Fireworks with slices turned on and is included in the Assets/Fireworks folder of the project folder.

PREPARING TO WORK

Let's go through the routine. You need to install some extensions, copy the project folder from the CD to your hard drive, and then fire up Dreamweaver and define a new site using your copied project folder as the target. If you've already completed the previous project, you can skip to Step 3 of this section.

> **Note:** Remember, if you want to see how the completed site looks in either Dreamweaver or your browser, you can find all the files in the finished_project folder.

1 Install the PVII Auto Layers behavior (if you haven't already done so) and the DW4 W3C Object Color Changer behavior:

- Browse to the Extensions folder on the CD.
- Open the Behaviors/Actions subfolder.
- Double-click P7_autoLayers.mxp to install the behavior.
- Repeat to install DW4w3ccolorchanger.mxp.

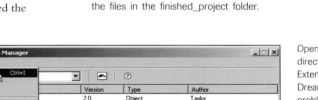

Open the Extension Manager directly via the Manage Extensions command in Dreamweaver if you have any problems installing an extension.

2 Install the NN4 Return False Fix and the Scrubber commands:

The Project VII NN4 Return False Fix command eliminates Netscape showing the hourglass cursor when clicking a null link to fire a JavaScript.

- Browse to the Extensions folder on the CD.
- Open the Commands subfolder.
- Double-click the file called N4 Return False Fix.mxp to install the command.
- Repeat to install scrubber.mxp.

3 Copy the projects Folder:

- Browse to the projects folder on the CD.
- Copy the project_three folder to a convenient location on your hard drive.

4 Define a new Dreamweaver site using the project_three copy as your local root folder.

Note: I've set up the work page with CSS styles so you can get right to heart of the project.

THE MAIN MENU

The main menu is contained by a table inside a layer. The layer can be positioned to pixel-level precision thereby ensuring that all our submenus align with the main one.

1 Build the main menu layer:

This layer will house the main menu headings.

- Open index.htm from the root of your project_three site.
- Insert a layer on your page via the Objects panel or the Insert menu and give it these attributes:

> Layer Id: **menumain**
> L: **12px**
> T: **24px**
> W: **162px**

Leave the Height blank and all other fields in their default state.

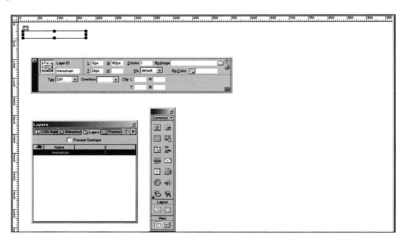

Insert the main menu layer on your page.

64

2 Insert a table into the main menu layer to house your menu images:

The table is used to lend structure to your images.

- Use the Objects panel or the Insert menu to place a table inside the menumain layer and set its attributes accordingly:

  Rows: **10**
  Columns: **1**
  Width: **162 Pixels**
  Border: **0**
  Cell Padding: **0**
  Cell Spacing: **0**

  Leave all other settings on the property inspector at their defaults.

Tip: Never, ever drag table borders. The capability to resize table parts by dragging is usually a recipe for disaster. Use the entry fields on the property inspector to configure tables. And it's usually a good idea to refrain from setting heights unless you have a specific reason to.

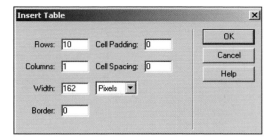

Insert a ten-row, single-column table inside the menu main layer.

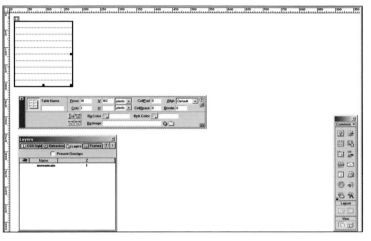

The table fits snugly inside the layer.

3 Populate the table with the main menu images:

Use the Assets panel to find images and quickly insert them into the table. The image that goes into the table's first row is proj3iface_top.gif.

- Scroll down the Assets list until you find proj3iface_top.gif and select it.
- Click inside the first table row.
- Click the Assets panel's Insert button to place the image in the row.

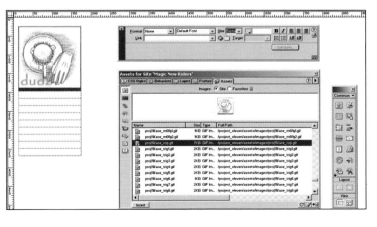

Use the Assets panel to find and insert images quickly into your table, as is done with the first image in this figure.

- Insert the following images into the remaining nine table rows:

  Row 2   proj3iface_trig1.gif

  Row 3   proj3iface_trig2.gif

  Row 4   proj3iface_trig3.gif

  Row 5   proj3iface_trig4.gif

  Row 6   proj3iface_trig5.gif

  Row 7   proj3iface_trig6.gif

  Row 8   proj3iface_trig7.gif

  Row 9   proj3iface_trig8.gif

  Row 10   proj3iface_bottom.gif

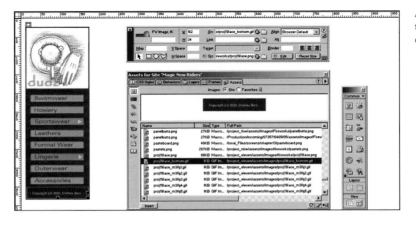

All images are inserted into the table, and the menu looks complete.

Tip: Remember to save your work frequently. The quickest method is to simply press Ctrl+S (Command+S).

CREATING THE FIRST FLYOUT LAYER AND ITS SUBMENU ITEMS

The flyouts are constructed the same way as the main menu. We'll start by adding a new layer. The first flyout layer will house the submenu that flies out from the Sportswear heading on the main menu.

1 Insert a new layer:

Insert a layer on your page via the Objects panel or the Insert menu.

- Set these attributes:

  Layer Id: **men3flyout** (because it's flying out from the third menu listing on the main menu)

  L: **173px**

  T: **263px**

  W: **151px**

  Leave the Height blank and all other fields in their default state.

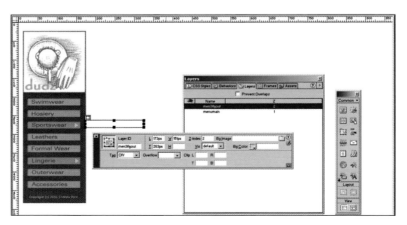

Insert the first flyout menu layer on your page.

2 Insert a table into the first flyout layer to house the menu images:

- Use the Objects panel or the Insert menu to place a table inside the menumain layer and set its attributes accordingly:

  Rows: **1**
  Columns: **1**
  Width: **151 Pixels**
  Border: **0**
  Cell Padding:
  Cell Spacing: **0**

  Leave all other settings on the property inspector at their defaults.

- Click inside the lone cell of the new table and set its background color to **#F0C600**.

We want the flyout menu to match the background color of its parent heading on the main menu. It's not an exact match—we want the flyout to be a tad brighter.

Before we add the remaining rows to this table, we will apply a JavaScript behavior that causes the table cell to change onMouseOver and then change back onMouseOut. Conventional Web designers would use a second image and apply a swap image JavaScript. Because we are by no means conventional, we will save precious bandwidth and simply change the color beneath each of our transparent images.

Tip: A table cell is the same as a table row in a single column table. In a two-column table, each row has two cells.

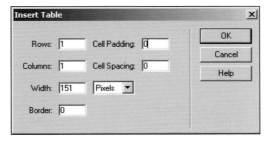

Insert a single-row, single-column table inside the men3flyout layer.

Tip: It's easy to determine the left position of men3flyout because we know that menumain's left position is 12, and its width is 162. So at left 174 both layers would make a perfect join. However, we backed it to the left by one pixel to ensure that there is no chance of a gap. So the final left position is 173! Of course, we preview often just to make sure that all our browsers are getting the math correct.

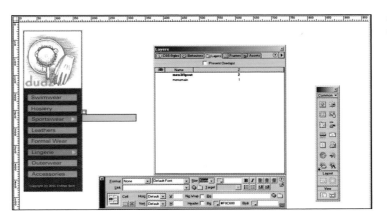

Apply a background color to the **<td>**.

3 Apply the behavior that changes the background color onMouseOver:

- Make sure that your Behaviors panel is set to Show Events For IE 5.0 (although it doesn't say so, this also includes Netscape 6). This setting is made by opening the Behaviors menu and selecting Show Events For on the next-to-last line. The IE5 setting opens up the W3C DOM (Document Object Model) and allows JavaScripts to be applied to virtually any element on your page.

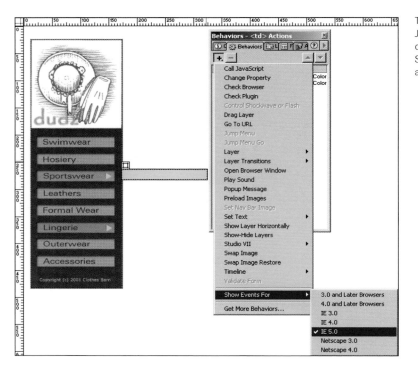

To permit application of JavaScript behaviors to a table cell (**<td>**), we must opt to Show Event For IE5 (which also includes Netscape 6).

- Click inside the flyout table cell.
- Open the Behaviors menu again.
- Choose Studio VII/DW4 W3C Object Color Changer.

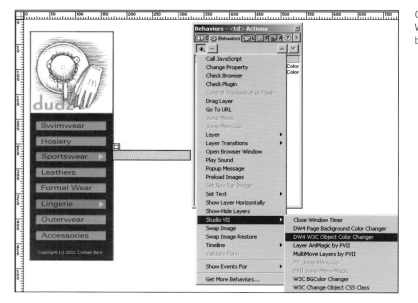

Choose the Studio VII DW4 W3C Object Color Changer behavior.

68

- Enter **#D6D3CE** in the Select New Color Value field and click OK.

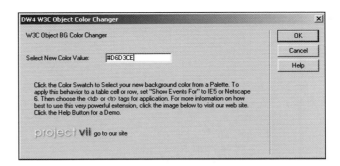

Set the onMouseOver color to **#D6D3CE** in the DW4 W3C Object Color Changer dialog.

- Make sure that OnMouseOver is selected in the Events column. If it's not, select the listed event and click the down arrow to open the events menu and select onMouseOver.

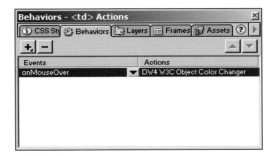

Make sure that the event is set to onMouseOver.

4 Apply the behavior that changes the color back to yellow onMouseOut:

- Click inside the flyout table cell again.
- Open the DW4 W3C Object Color Changer behavior.
- Enter **#F7C700** into the Select New Color Value field and click OK.
- Set the event to onMouseOut.

Set the onMouseOut color to **#F7C700** in the DW4 W3C Object Color Changer dialog.

Now we're ready to add the remaining table rows to our flyout menu. By adding the rows now, after having applied the Color Changer behavior, we can use the Tab key to create the new rows and automatically copy the JavaScript behaviors.

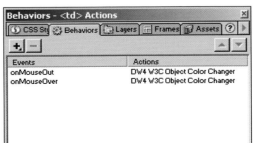

The Behaviors panel shows both events entered on the **<td>** of the flyout table.

5 Add the remaining rows to our flyout menu table:

- Click inside the lone flyout menu table row and press the Tab key six times to add six new rows.

  We now have seven rows, and each contains the DW4 W3C Object Color Changer behavior.

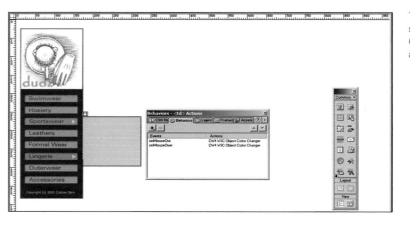

The flyout menu now contains seven rows, each with the Color Changer behavior applied.

6 Populate the table with the flyout menu images:

- Open the Assets panel to insert the proper images into the table.
- Scroll down the Assets list until you find proj3iface_m3fly1.gif, the first row image.
- Click inside the table row.
- Click the Assets panel's Insert button to place the image inside the row.
- Insert the following images into the remaining six table rows:

Row 2	proj3iface_m3fly2.gif
Row 3	proj3iface_m3fly3.gif
Row 4	proj3iface_m3fly4.gif
Row 5	proj3iface_m3fly5.gif
Row 6	proj3iface_m3fly6.gif
Row 7	proj3iface_m3fly7.gif

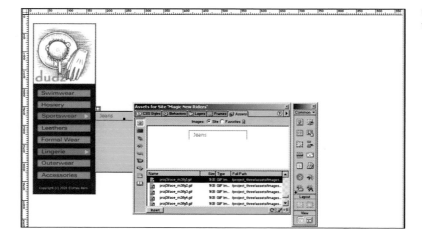

Use the Assets panel to insert the flyout menu images.

7 Set the men3flyout layer to hidden:

The flyout menus need to be hidden and appear only when we mouse over the corresponding main menu heading. So let's hide our flyout now.

- Open the Layers panel.
- Select men3flyout.
- Click to the left of its name to hide it. (It's hidden when a closed eye icon appears.)

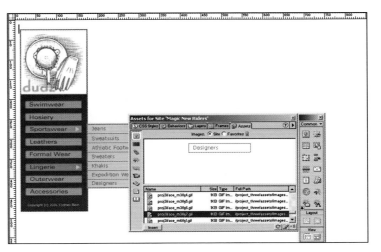

The first flyout with all its images inserted.

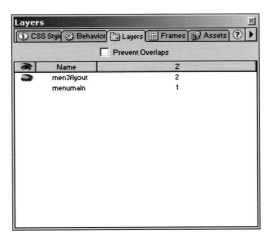

Set the men3flyout layer to hidden.

SETTING UP THE REMAINING FLYOUT MENU LAYER

Now we'll set up the second and final flyout menu that pops out to the right of the Lingerie heading.

1 Insert the second flyout menu layer:

- Insert a new layer.
- Set these attributes:

    Layer Id: **men6flyout** (because it's flying out from the sixth heading on the main menu)

    L: **173px**

    T: **360px**

    W: **151px**

- Remove any value from the height field and leave it blank. Leave all other fields in their default state.

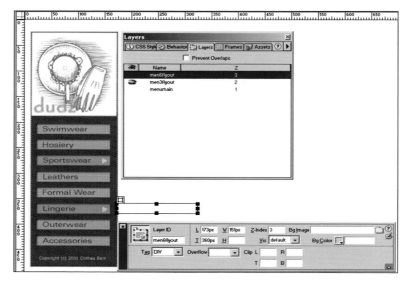

Insert the second flyout menu layer.

2 Insert a table into the second flyout layer:

- Use the Objects panel or the Insert menu to place a table inside the menumain layer and set its attributes accordingly:

    Rows: **1**

    Columns: **1**

    Width: **151 Pixels**

    Border: **0**

    Cell Padding: **0**

    Cell Spacing: **0**

    Leave all other settings on the property inspector at their defaults.

- Click inside the lone cell of the new table.
- Set its background color to **#99CC99**.

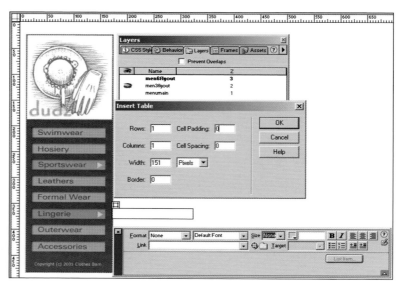

Insert a single-row, single-column table inside the men6flyout layer.

We want the flyout menu to match the green background color of its parent heading on the main menu. Before we add the remaining row to this table, we'll apply the Object Color Changer behavior, just like we did on the first flyout.

Apply a background color to the **\<td\>**.

3 Apply the behavior that changes the color back to yellow onMouseOver:

   • Click inside the flyout table cell.

   • Open the Behaviors menu.

   • Choose Studio VII/DW4 W3C Object Color Changer.

   • Enter **#D6D3CE** in the Select New Color Value field and click OK.

   • Make sure that the event is set to onMouseOver.

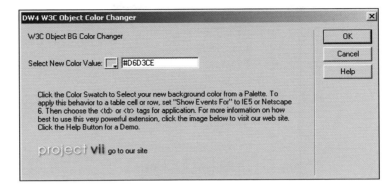

Set the onMouseOver over color to **#D6D3CE** in the DW4 W3C Object Color Changer dialog.

4 Apply the behavior that changes the color back to yellow onMouseOut:

   • Click inside the flyout table cell.

   • Open up the DW4 W3C Object Color Changer behavior.

   • Enter **#99CC99** into the Select New Color Value field and click OK.

   • Set the event to onMouseOut.

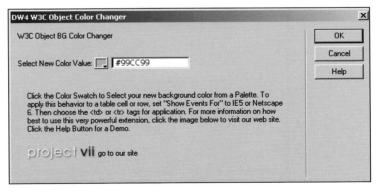

Set the onMouseOut color to **#99CC99** in the DW4 W3C Object Color Changer dialog.

5 Add a new table row:

- Press the Tab key to add one additional table row.

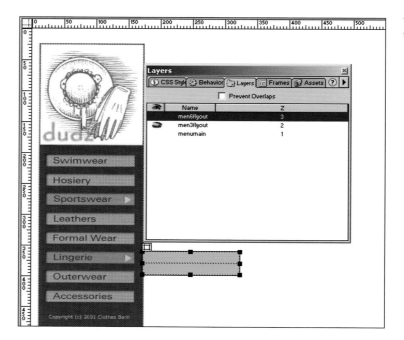

The men6flyout table has two table rows.

6 Populate the table with the flyout menu images:

Use the Assets panel to insert the proper images into the table.

- Click inside the first table row.
- Scroll down the Assets list until you find proj3iface_m6fly1.gif and select it.
- Click the Assets panel's Insert button to place it inside the table row.
- Repeat the preceding steps to insert proj3iface_m6fly2.gif into the second table row.

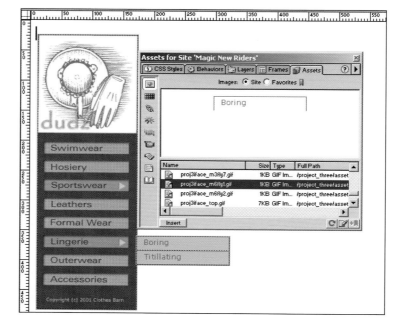

Use the Assets panel to insert both of the menu images into the second flyout.

7 Set the men6flyout layer to hidden:

- Open the Layers panel.
- Select men6flyout.
- Click to the left of its name to hide it. (It's hidden when a closed eye icon appears.)

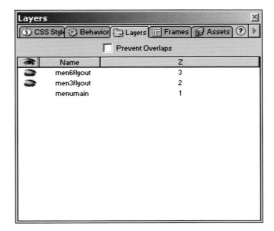

Use the Layers panel to set men6flyout to hidden.

Creating the menucloser Layer and Applying the PVII Auto Layers Behavior

As you learned in the previous project, the menucloser layer contains a transparent image that controls the closing of all open submenus.

The process is simple. When we mouse over a heading that controls a submenu flyout, the menucloser layer is also made visible. The menucloser sits below the menus, and its transparent image contains a PVII Auto Layers behavior that hides all submenus onMouseOver. When our mouse leaves the submenu, it touches the menucloser layer, and the submenu snaps shut. This action also hides the menucloser layer until it is needed again.

1 Insert the menucloser layer:

- Insert a new layer with these attributes:

    Name: **menucloser**
    L: **0px**
    T: **0px**
    W: **500px**
    H: **500px**

- Leave all other fields in their default states.

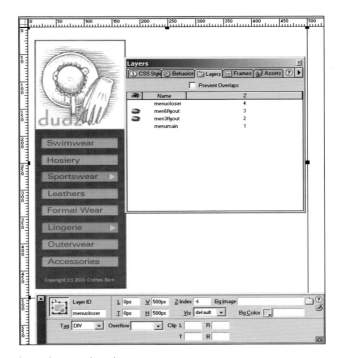

Insert the menucloser layer.

2 Insert a transparent GIF inside menucloser:

- Temporarily hide the menumain layer to get a clear view of your page.
- Click inside the menucloser layer.
- Use the Assets panel to find and insert the image called shim.gif.
- Before you move your cursor one millimeter, use the property inspector to set the width and height settings of shim.gif:

    W: **500**
    H: **500**

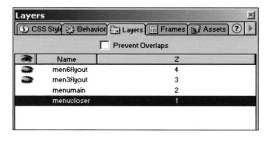

Insert shim.gif inside the menucloser layer.

3 Move the menucloser layer to its proper z-index:

For menucloser to function properly, it must be placed behind the menu layers.

- Use the Layers panel to drag menucloser down so that it comes to rest at the bottom of the panel. Dreamweaver automatically renumbers the z-indices and sets menucloser to 1.
- Set the menumain layer back to visible.

Use the Layers panel to move menucloser below the menu layers in the z-index.

APPLYING THE PVII AUTO LAYERS BEHAVIOR

If you've completed Project 2, "Building a DHTML Drop-Down Menu," you'll remember that you use Auto Layers to activate (make visible) a layer by simply select-ing it in the Auto Layers dialog and clicking the Show Layer button. Clicking a trigger button shows its associated layer. As you click another trigger, Auto Layer shows that button's associated layer, but remembers the first layer and hides it. Each time you click a trigger that fires the Auto Layer script, it keeps adding the previous layers to a sort of list called an *array*. So, each time you click a button, Auto Layers actually knows to hide all the layers it previously had made visible.

1 Apply PVII Auto Layers to menucloser:

- Select the shim.gif image inside menucloser by selecting the menucloser layer and then gently clicking inside.

- You'll know that you've got hold of the image by taking a quick peek at the property inspector. You'll also see the **<IMG>** tag in bold on the status bar.

- Open the Behaviors panel.

- Click the + button, and then choose Studio VII/Auto Layers by PVII.

- Click OK. It sounds odd, but you do not actually select any layers here. You simply open the Auto Layers dialog and click OK. We are telling Auto Layers to hide all layers in its memory.

- Choose (onMouseOver) as the event.

Remember! No layers are set to show in this step because we want all Auto Layers to hide, including menucloser itself.

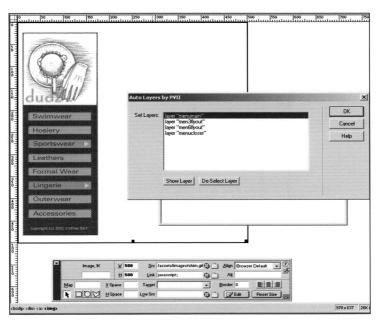

Click OK without selecting any layers to apply Auto Layers to the menucloser layer.

2 Apply PVII Auto Layers to the menumain heading images:

- Select the Hosiery image in the main menu.

- Open the Behaviors panel.

- Choose Studio VII/Auto Layers by PVII. Don't set any layers to Show because we're only hiding layers, not showing layers onMouseOver for this menu item.

- Click OK and set the event to onMouseOver.

  This action causes all Auto Layers to hide. It sounds wrong, but you do not have to actually select anything.

- Click OK, and all layers in Auto Layers memory will hide.

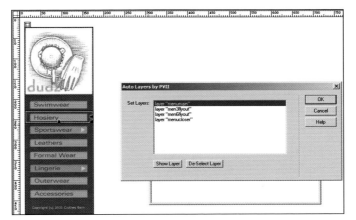

Apply PVII Auto Layers to the main menu images. In this figure, we are applying the behavior to the Hosiery image.

This step ensures that the main menu headings adjacent to the ones that invoke the flyouts are set to close the flyouts. That is, mousing over Sportswear opens the Sportswear flyout menu, but if you move your mouse over Hosiery or Leathers, the flyout closes.

Note: Remember, you do not select any layers in this step.

- Repeat this step and apply the PVII Auto Layers behavior to each of the following images in the same manner as we did to the Hosiery image:

  Leathers
  Formal Wear
  Outerwear

3 Apply PVII Auto Layers to the images that open the flyout menus:

  - Select the image labeled Sportswear in the main menu.

Note: Remember! Setting a layer to Show (in the auto Layers dialog) means that it will be shown while all other layers in Auto Layers memory are hidden.

  - Open the Behaviors panel.
  - Choose Studio VII/Auto Layers by PVII.
  - Select the men3flyout and menucloser layers and click the Show Layer button.
  - Click OK and ensure that the event is onMouseOver.

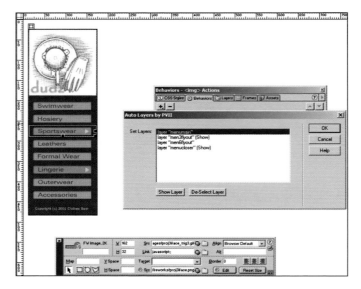

Apply the PVII Auto Layers behavior to the Sportswear image.

  - Select the image labeled Lingerie in the main menu.
  - Open the Behaviors panel.
  - Choose Studio VII/Auto Layers by PVII.
  - Select the men6flyout and menucloser layers and click the Show button:
  - Click OK and ensure that the event is onMouseOver.

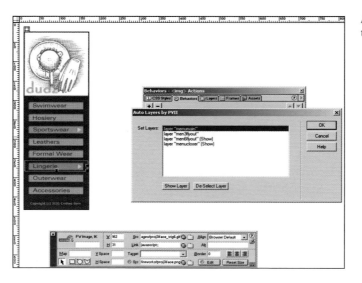

Apply the PVII Auto Layers behavior to the Lingerie image.

CORRECTING BROWSER-SPECIFIC PROBLEMS

To make our menu system foolproof and smooth, we need to add a few simple JavaScripts. The Netscape Resize Fix keeps our layers in place when Netscape 4 users resize their browser window. The NN4 Return False Fix, searches for onClick events with null links and adds Return False at the end to stop Netscape 4 from displaying the hourglass cursor. The IE Link Scrubber eliminates the dotted lines that appear around clicked links in IE4 and 5.

1   Apply the Netscape Resize Fix:

   • Choose Commands and Add/Remove Netscape Resize Fix.

   • Click the Add button.

     If the button reads Remove, select Cancel. The resize fix has been added automatically because your Dreamweaver preferences have been set to do so.

2   Apply the NN4 Return False Fix:

   • Choose Commands/Studio VII Flyout/Add N4 Return False Fix.

   • Click the Apply button.

3   Apply the IE link Scrubber:

   • Choose Commands/Studio VII/IE Link Scrubber.

   • Click the Scrub Em! button.

Start Recording	Ctrl+Shift+X
Play Recorded Command	Ctrl+P
Edit Command List...	
Get More Commands...	
Manage Extensions...	
Apply Source Formatting	
Clean Up HTML...	
Clean Up Word HTML...	
Add/Remove Netscape Resize Fix...	
Optimize Image in Fireworks...	
Create Web Photo Album...	
Set Color Scheme...	
Format Table...	
Sort Table...	
Fixed Background	
StudioVII	▶
Layer2style	
Back to my Frame	
NetscapeLayerFix	

You can find all the Netscape 4 fixes on the Commands menu.

ADD SOME PLACEHOLDER CONTENT TO THE PAGE

To give your project a finished look, let's add a little content to the page. We need to shim the first and third columns. We'll be using the image called shim.gif in the assets/images folder. The first column is shimmed to make sure that we have a "dead zone" so that the main menu layer does not obscure the text in the table. The third column is shimmed down to a width of 2 pixels and given a background color to create a vertical rule to the left of the last column.

1   Use the Layers panel to temporarily hide all layers.

    menumain should be the only visible layer on your page when the project is completed.

   • In the Layers panel, click to the left of menumain to hide it.

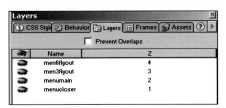

Hide all layers.

2   Insert a content table:

- Use the Objects panel or the Insert menu to place a one-row by four-column table on your page that has these settings:

  Width: **100%**
  Border: **0**
  Cell Padding: **0**
  Cell Spacing: **36**

- Use the property inspector to set the Vertical Alignment of the second and fourth columns to Top.

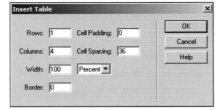

Insert the content table into your page.

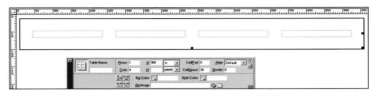

Make the table 100% wide and give it four columns.

3   Insert shims (transparent GIFs) and set the table's cell (column) widths.

- Click inside the first column.
- Open the Assets panel to find and insert shim.gif.

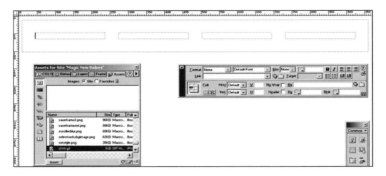

A shim is inserted in the first column to ensure that the main menu is not covering the page content.

- Set the shim's width to **140** pixels and its height to **12** pixels.
- Click off to the right of the shim (or select the **<td>** tag on the status bar).
- Use the property inspector to set the cell width of the first column to **180** pixels.
- Leave the second column without a width setting.
- Insert a shim in the third column and set its width to **2** pixels and its height to **12** pixels.
- Click off to the right of the shim.
- Using the property inspector, set these attributes for the table cell:

  Background color: **#666666**
  Width: **2 pixels**

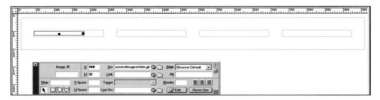

Size the shim to 140 pixels by 12 pixels.

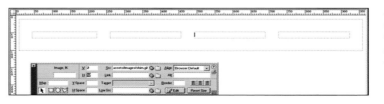

Add a shim to the third column and set it to 2 pixels wide. Color the cell to create a vertical rule between the third and fourth columns.

- Click in the fourth cell and set its width to **200**.

- Type a heading and a few paragraphs of placeholder text into both the second and fourth columns.

  Notice how the content is taking shape. Our vertical rule is now clearly identifiable between the third and fourth columns.

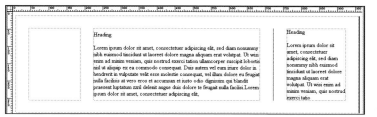

Enter placeholder text into the second and fourth columns. The vertical rule is now apparent.

USING CSS TO STYLE THE PLACEHOLDER TEXT

We've included a style sheet in the project page to get you started. To edit the styles, use Dreamweaver's CSS Editor or your favorite third-party editor.

1. Apply a class to the table text:

   - Start with the second column.
   - Click inside the column.
   - Select the **<td>** tag on the Dreamweaver status bar.

> **Note:** You may notice that the code in this book sometimes wraps to the next line. That wrapping is caused by the narrowness of the column within this book. Dreamweaver does not restrict the length of the line; the code appears on one line.

   - Right-click (Ctrl+click) the tag and choose Set Class.
   - Select tabledtext as your class.

```
.tabledtext {  font-family: Verdana, Arial, Helvetica,
sans-serif; font-size: 12px; color: #FF9900}

.sidebartable {  font-family: Verdana, Arial, Helvetica,
sans-serif; font-size: 11px; color: #666666}

h1 {  font-family: Georgia, "Times New Roman", Times,
serif; font-size: 36px; font-weight: normal; color:
#999999}

h2 {  font-family: Georgia, "Times New Roman", Times,
serif; font-size: 14px; color: #FF9900}

.emphatic {  font-family: Verdana, Arial, Helvetica,
sans-serif; font-size: 14px; color: #999999}
```

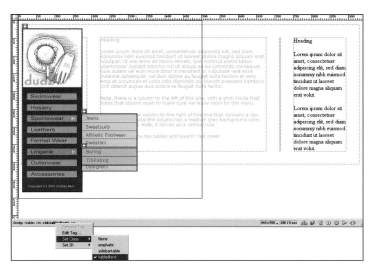

Assign CSS styles by selecting a tag on the status bar and right-click (Ctrl+click) to access the Set Class menu.

81

2 Apply a class to each heading:

- Click to the right of the first heading.
- Open the format menu on the property inspector.
- Select Heading1 as your format.
- Click inside the fourth column.
- Select the **<td>** tag on the Dreamweaver status bar.
- Right-click (Ctrl+click) the tag and choose Set Class.
- Select sidebartable as your class.
- Click to the right of the heading in the fourth column.

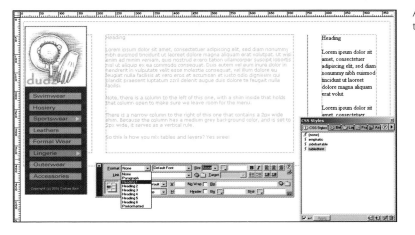

Assign the Heading1 format to the first heading.

- Choose Heading2 from the format menu on the property inspector.

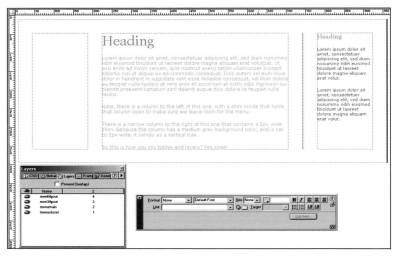

The placeholder text is now styled.

3 Make the menu visible:

Now that our placeholder text is styled, we can once again make our menu visible.

- Use the Layers panel to set menumain to visible by setting its closed eye to open.
- Preview your work in the browser using the Preview in Browser function in Dreamweaver.

  Violá! You've made flyout menus!

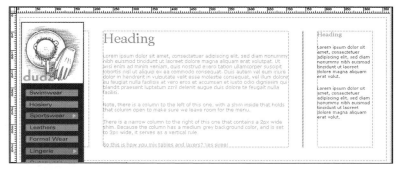

With our menu revealed, notice how the table structure leaves plenty of room.

Tip: Remember, you can compare your work to the author's by opening the index file in the finished_project folder.

ADDING HYPERLINKS TO MENU ITEMS

When your menu is finished, you can add hyperlinks to the menu items to make a navigable site. The best ways to add new pages are

1. Use the File/Save As command to save your new project file with a new name, thereby creating one or more cloned pages.

2. Create a new page corresponding to each of the menu items. Leave the pages blank. Then set up all your hyperlinks in the index page using your newly created blank pages as the targets.

When you have the hyperlinks in place, save the index page. With the index still open, use the File/ Save As command to overwrite each of the blank pages.

If you want to have a template rather than an ordinary page, you can use Craig Foster's Project 12, "Taking Control with Templates and Library Items," as a guide and save your completed project page as a Dreamweaver template file.

MODIFICATIONS

Now that you have mastered the fine art of popping out, flying out, and dropping down, you can do some really cool things. You can create menus with multiple flyouts. Drop-down submenus can have one or more flyouts. Of course, menus aren't the only use for this technique. You can use it to hide and show images, or pop up descriptive text to expound on a simple link. The uses are, in fact, limitless!

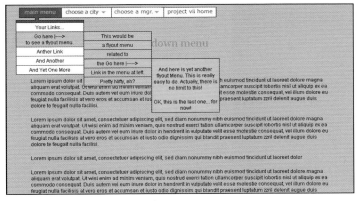

A drop-down menu with a double flyout.

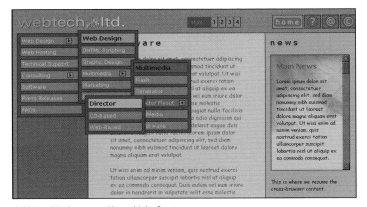

A hierarchical menu with multiple flyouts.

USING CSS TO MAKE NAVIGATION IMAGES

"There is nothing more difficult for a truly

creative painter than to paint a rose,

because before he can do so he has first to

forget all the roses that were ever painted."

—HENRI MATISSE

IMAGE-LESS ROLLOVER BUTTONS

CSS can empower you to create Web pages that are exciting, unique, and highly economical in regard to the Internet's precious bandwidth. Success is contingent on being able to think outside the box. Ingenuity rules the day.

When we think about Web page buttons, we think about GIFs or JPGs made with programs like Macromedia Fireworks or Adobe ImageReady. We think in terms of *images*. In fact, every browser has the ability to use Operating System buttons—those plain gray rectangles that are used to submit Web forms.

Look beyond the box a bit, and you will discover that form buttons can be styled. You can give them color; you can change type; you can change borders; you can use Dreamweaver Extensions to swap different styles onMouseOver. In effect, you can make them look and behave like image buttons. Because browsers draw these buttons on-the-fly, they require no server download. You can achieve all these miracles simply by using Cascading Style Sheets.

Project 4

Using CSS to Make Navigation Images

by Al Sparber

The finished page with image-less rollover buttons across the top.

IT WORKS LIKE THIS

Internet Explorer 4+ and Netscape Navigator 6 support styled forms. Opera swears they will be supported as well in an update to version 5. Degradation is totally graceful in all unsupporting browsers, except my old nemesis: Netscape Navigator 4. If Navigator 4 catches on to what I'm attempting to do with buttons, it will start retching like a cat about to expel a monster hairball.

So, we're going to have to employ a little bit of skullduggery. We will deceive Navigator 4 into believing that he (don't ask me to explain now, but I know for a fact that Navigator is a boy) should render perfectly ordinary, unstyled form buttons. In addition, we will plant a second style sheet in a place where he can't find it.

The Sting…

Although Netscape 4 supports externally linked CSS files, it does not support external CSS files that are imported. I made a master sheet called nn.css, which contains all the styles we need *except* for the ones that style the buttons, and I linked it to our page. Then I made a second CSS file called W3csheet.css that contains only those styles that affect the buttons. I used the **@import** technique to hide the button styles from Netscape 4 browsers. Now Netscape 4 sees only the linked style sheet, which contains friendly styles. Linking and importing of style sheets can be done via the DW CSS panel. Don't worry if you feel a bit lost right now. Coming up is a thoroughly enlightening step-by-step tutorial!

> **Note:** If you are not familiar with CSS, we strongly suggest that you acquire our favorite CSS book: *Cascading Style Sheets—The Definitive Source* by Eric Meyer (O'Reilly).

Linking and Importing CSS Files

Because we discuss how to link style sheets elsewhere in the book, I took the liberty of setting this one up for you. This is how it all looks in the **<head>** of the document:

```
<link rel="stylesheet" href="assets/style_sheets/
nn.css" type="text/css">

<style type="text/css">
<!--
@import url(assets/style_sheets/w3csheet.css);
body {  background-image: url(assets/images/
spring.jpg); background-repeat: repeat-x;
background-color: #FFFFFF}
-->
</style>
```

The linked CSS is inserted first. All CSS-aware browsers (including Navigator 4) will understand this.

The imported CSS is inserted next. Internet Explorer and Netscape 6 will use all styles in the linked sheet and all styles in the imported sheet. Because the imported sheet is lower down in the source code, its styles will take precedence over similarly named styles in the linked sheet.

So the styles that determine what the buttons look like can safely be declared in the imported sheet. And Navigator 4 will be blissfully unaware!

Netscape 4 also has problems with background images declared in externally linked CSS files. It cannot solve the path to the image unless the CSS file is in the same folder as the page linking to it. The W3C-recommended workaround is to make the image path absolute. That is, if your domain was **www.elmerfudd.com**, and the image was in a folder called images, the images folder was in the root of your site, and the image was named wabbit.gif, the path would be as follows:

http://www.elmerfudd.com/images/wabbit.gif

However, when this is done, you will not be able to see the background when you preview the page locally. To enable you to see the background locally, I embedded a duplicate body style into the page itself. It's on the line directly below the **@import** code.

Preparing to Work

Before we begin, you'll need to install an extension and set up a working Dreamweaver site. The necessary files are all stored on the *Dreamweaver 4 Magic* CD.

1 Install the PVII W3C Change CSS Class Behavior:

- If Dreamweaver is open, close it now. When the extension is installed, Dreamweaver will need to initialize the new behavior, so you'll have to restart it.
- Browse to the Extensions folder on the CD.
- Open the Actions subfolder.
- Double-click the file called w3cChangeClass.mxp to install the behavior.

Browser Compatibility

We have tested this interface and found that it is fully functional in the following browsers:

MSIE 4 (Windows and Mac)

MSIE 5 (Windows and Mac)

MSIE 5.5 (Windows)

NN4.08–4.76 (Windows)

NN4.5 (Mac)

Opera 5.01 (Windows)

Netscape 6 (Windows and Mac)

2 Copy the projects folder:

- Browse to the projects folder on the CD.
- Copy the project_four folder to a convenient location on your hard drive.

3 Define a new Dreamweaver site using the project_four copy as your local root folder.

Note: Remember, if you want to see how the completed site looks in either Dreamweaver or your browser, you can find all the files in the finished_project folder.

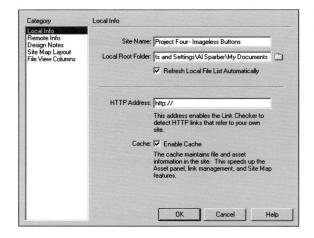

Use the site definition window to define the site for this project.

INVESTIGATING THE CASCADING STYLE SHEETS (CSS)

You'll find two style sheets in the assets folder of the site nn.css and W3csheet.css. The style sheets are completely set up and are already attached to the worksheet document you'll use to build your new page. (If you want to learn more about attaching style sheets, please see Project 1, "Using Cascading Style Sheets to Make Selectable Themes.")

1 Open index.htm:

- Open the file called index.htm in the root of your project_four defined site.
- Notice the image spanning the top of a blank page. It is the page background image and is set via the redefined body style in the nn.css file, which you will look at later.

The image itself is 540 pixels wide by only 32 pixels high. Its source is defined by the background–image url, which is set to images/spring.jpg. By setting the repeat attribute of the background to repeat-x, we cause the image to situate itself at the top-left corner of the page, and it keeps repeating to the right until all available space is taken up. Because the background color is set to white (#FFFFFF), all space around the image is also set to white.

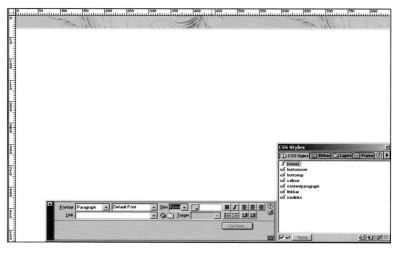

Open the index.htm file and look at the image spanning the page and the other elements that are displayed automatically.

2 Look at nn.css.

The main CSS is called nn.css, and it is used by all CSS-aware browsers because it is linked to our page. The code to the right is inside.

Note: To view the CSS files, select one or the other in the Dreamweaver Site window and double-click. The file will open in whatever application you have chosen as your default Style Sheet Editor. If you haven't chosen a default editor, you can use the Dreamweaver Preferences utility to define one, or you can open the file directly in a plain text editor.

Note: For additional CSS insight, drop by the Project VII Web site (**www.projectseven.com**). We're always adding CSS-related tutorials.

```
h1 { font-family: Georgia, "Times New Roman", Times,
serif; font-size: 28px; color: #CCCCCC; font-weight: normal;
margin-top: 12px; margin-right: 0px; margin-bottom: 12px;
margin-left: 36px}

.linkbar { font-family: Verdana, Arial, Helvetica, sans-serif;
font-size: 10px; color: #666666; width: 100%; padding-top:
3px; padding-right: 3px; padding-bottom: 3px; padding-left:
3px; border: #999999 solid; text-align: center; border-width:
1px 0px 0px; clear: right; margin-top: 16px; margin-right:
60px; margin-bottom: 0px; margin-left: 60px}

.contentparagraph { font-family: Arial, Helvetica, sans-
serif; font-size: 13px; color: #8C8684; margin-top: 12px;
margin-right: 60px; margin-bottom: 0px; margin-left: 60px;
text-align: justify; line-height: 20px}

.navlinks { font-family: Arial, Helvetica, sans-serif; font-
size: 12px; color: #666666; text-align: center; margin-top:
24px; margin-right: 60px; margin-bottom: 12px; margin-left:
60px; border: #666666; border-style: solid; border-top-
width: 1px; border-right-width: 0px; border-bottom-width:
0px; border-left-width: 0px; clear: left}

body {background-color: #FFFFFF; background-image:
url(images/spring.jpg); background-repeat: repeat-x}

.navlinks a:link { color: #D6D7A5; text-decoration: none}

.navlinks a:visited { color: #8C928C; text-decoration: none}

.navlinks a:hover { color: #C6C394; text-decoration: none}

.navlinks a:active { color: #666666; text-decoration: none}

a:link { color: #666666; text-decoration: none}

a:visited { color: #999999; text-decoration: none}

a:hover { color: #D6CF73; text-decoration: none}

a:active { color: #666666; text-decoration: none}

b { color: #848A7B}

.callout { font-family: Arial, Helvetica, sans-serif; font-size:
16px; color: #D1CD76; margin-top: 12px; margin-right: 60px;
margin-bottom: 0px; margin-left: 60px; text-align: justify;
line-height: 20px }
```

This HMTL file, which will be linked to the page, is the master sheet called nn.css; it contains all the styles you need except the ones that style the buttons.

Note: You may notice that the code in this book sometimes wraps to the next line. That wrapping is caused by the narrowness of the column within this book. Dreamweaver does not restrict the length of the line; the code appears on one line.

3 Look at W3sheet.css.

The second CSS is called W3csheet.css and is used by Internet Explorer and Navigator 6, but it is ignored by Navigator 4. It contains only those styles that define what the buttons look like. The code to the right is inside.

.buttonup { font-family: Arial, Helvetica, sans-serif; font-size: 12px; color: #D6D3CE; background-color: #A7A998; border: 1px #333333 solid; height: 24px; width: 86px; margin-top: 0px; margin-right: 1px; margin-bottom: 0px; margin-left: 0px ; cursor: hand; font-weight: bold}

.buttonover { font-family: Arial, Helvetica, sans-serif; font-size: 12px; color: #847D84; background-color: #DEDB9C; border: 1px #333333 solid; height: 24px; width: 86px; margin-top: 0px; margin-right: 1px; margin-bottom: 0px; margin-left: 0px; cursor: hand; font-weight: bold}

W3csheet contains but two styles: the styles used by the W3C Change CSS Class behavior to create the rollover effect on the styled form buttons.

When you inspect the CSS panel in Dreamweaver, you'll notice that the listed styles are an amalgamation of both sheets. Of course, only custom styles appear in the CSS panel. Redefined styles are automatically applied as needed and, therefore, would serve no purpose taking space in the list.

Use the CSS Styles panel to check the custom styles in every CSS file associated with the current document. The Pencil icon at the bottom of the panel opens the CSS Editor.

If you want to edit a style, select one of the two CSS files and click the Edit button.

90

WORKING THE PAGE

Now you're going to make your page come to life with color and interaction. You'll add a logo, style your buttons (and add CSS rollover effects to them), create supporting pages, set up links, add some content, and create a library-driven text navbar.

1 Add a logo:

First add a logo to identify this page.

- Choose Insert/Image.
- Browse to the Images folder of your defined site and select the image called logo.gif. Then click the Select button.
- Make sure your cursor is to the right of the logo and press the Enter or Return key to create a new paragraph.
- The logo image is now in the top left on your worksheet page, and you are ready to insert some form buttons.

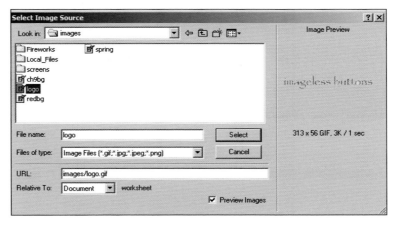

Use the Select Image Source dialog to select the logo.gif.

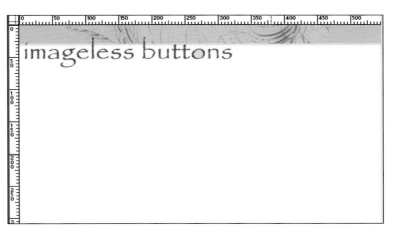

The logo image inserted on your page.

2 Add the buttons:

You're going to add a form and six form buttons to your page. The form is necessary to maintain support for Netscape Navigator 4, so please follow each step!

- Choose Insert/Form Objects/Button.
- Click Yes when Dreamweaver asks if you'd like to insert a form.

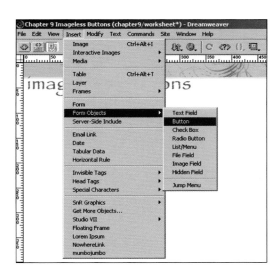

Use the Insert menu commands to insert six buttons on the page.

- Dreamweaver will automatically add **\<form\>** tags around your buttons. This is important because Navigator 4 will not render the buttons unless it first sees the **\<form\>** tags. As a point of reference, check the source code to make sure it contains a **\<form\>** tag pair of **\<form\>** and **\</form\>** surrounding your buttons; they should look like the code to the right.
- Place your cursor to the right of the first button and repeat the process to add a second button.
- Repeat again, four more times, for a total of six buttons.

```
<body bgcolor="#FFFFFF">
<p><img src="images/logo.gif" width="313" height="56"></p>
<form name="form1" method="post" action="">
<input type="button" name="Button"  value="Button">
<input type="button" name="Submit2" value="Button">
<input type="button" name="Submit3" value="Button">
<input type="button" name="Submit4" value="Button">
<input type="button" name="Submit5" value="Button">
<input type="button" name="Submit6" value="Button">
</form>
<p> </p>
</body>
</html>
```

Make certain that the code has the **\<form\>** tags.

3 Set the properties of the buttons:

- You need to set two properties for the buttons: Actions and Name.
- Select each button and set its Action to None on your property inspector so that the button's label changes from Submit to Button.

Use the property inspector to set Action to None for each of the six buttons.

- Select each button and type a meaningful name into the Label field on the property inspector, using these six names (from left to right):

  Home
  Information
  Products
  Press
  Clients
  Contact

4   Apply the buttonup style to the buttons:

- Select the Home button and then select its input tag on the Dreamweaver status bar (at the bottom-left border of your Dreamweaver window).

- Right-click (Ctrl+click) the input tag.

- Select Set Class.

- Select the buttonup style from the flyout menu.

- Repeat these actions for all buttons.

- As you set the style, you'll notice the button will resize. Don't worry. This is normal behavior in Dreamweaver. The buttons will look fine once you preview the page in your browser.

Use the input tag popup menu to set the class to the buttonup style.

5   Apply the Change Class Behavior:

Breathe some life into your buttons with the PVII CSS Change Class behavior. (First make sure you've installed it!)

- Select the Home button.

- Open the Behaviors panel and click the + sign to open its menu.

- Select Studio VII.

- Select W3C Change Object CSS Class from the flyout menu.

- In the W3C Change Object CSS Class dialog, select buttonover from the list of available styles and then click OK.

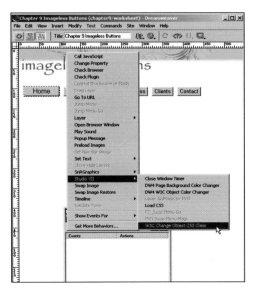

Select the button and use the Behaviors panel to apply the W3 Change Object CSS Class behavior.

- Make sure that onMouseOver is the event listed on the left side of the Behaviors panel.

- Select the Home button again and apply a second instance of the W3C Change Object CSS Class behavior.

- This time you are going to reverse the process and select buttonup as the style to change to. Set this event to fire onMouseOut.

- Repeat these actions for the remaining five buttons.

Note: If the proper event is not available in the Behaviors panel list, open the Behavior menu (by clicking the panel's + sign) and check to make sure that IE5 is the selected browser under Show Events For.

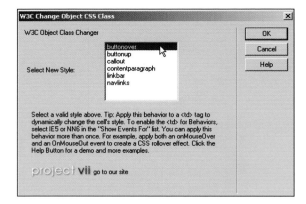

In the W3 Change Object CSS Class dialog, select buttonover.

6 Link the buttons:

You are going to set up your site by quickly creating the pages that relate to each of the buttons. Then you'll link the buttons to other pages. To do so, you'll use the Dreamweaver Go To URL behavior feature.

- Choose File/New.
- Leave the page blank.
- Choose File/Save.
- Enter the file name **information.htm**.
- Using this process, create all the pages that relate to the buttons. Here are the files you need to create:

    information.htm
    products.htm
    press.htm
    clients.htm
    contact.htm

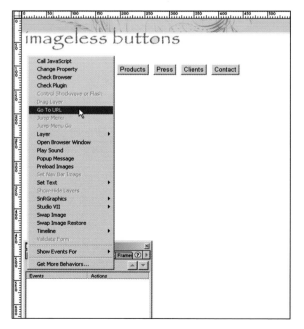

Open the Behaviors panel and click + to access the Go To URL option.

- Select the Home button.

- Open the Behaviors panel and click the + sign to open its menu.

- Select Go To URL.

- Click the Browse button and in the subsequent file selection dialog, pick index.htm.

- Repeat this process for the remaining buttons so they all are linked to their respective pages. Note that the default event is onClick, so there's no need to change that event.

So why did you create these new pages and leave them blank? Because you have all your scripts and links working properly on the index.htm page, you can use File/Save As to overwrite the files you just created. The overwritten files will all have the correct links and behaviors applied.

- Open index.htm.

- Choose File/Save As.

- Highlight information.htm.

- Click the Save button.

- Choose Yes when Dreamweaver asks if you'd like to overwrite the existing file.

- Repeat to overwrite the remaining files:

  products.htm
  press.htm
  clients.htm
  contact.htm

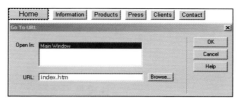

Click the Browse button to navigate to the file.

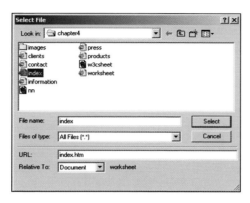

Select index.htm.

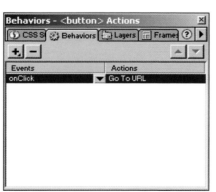

The Behaviors panel shows the event and the action after the Go To URL behavior is applied to the Home button.

7 Add the content:

Now you're ready to add content to your pages. You'll get a good feel for using CSS to style your pages without using tables. Of course, at this point, you can do whatever you want to personalize the project.

- Open the index.htm page.

- Insert your cursor just to the right of the last button and press Enter (Return) to create a new paragraph.

- Select Heading 1 from the Format drop-down on your property inspector.

- Type in a heading for your page.

- Press Enter (Return) again to create a new line after the Heading.

- Select Paragraph from the Format drop-down on your property inspector.

- Right-click (Ctrl+click) the **\<p\>** tag on the Dreamweaver status bar and select Set Class.

- Select the contentparagraph style from the flyout menu.

- Type some text or use the Corporate Mumbo Jumbo Object (included on the CD) to enter some placeholder text.

Note: If you prefer to use tables, you can add a table below the buttons and enter your content into the table as described above.

Use the Format drop-down on the property inspector to select Heading 1.

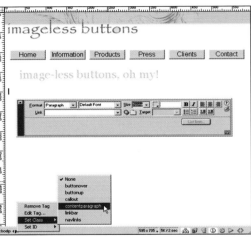

Right-click (Ctrl+click) the **\<p\>** tag on the Dreamweaver status bar to access the Set Class flyout menu.

8 Add a Text Navbar to the bottom of the page:

Use a Dreamweaver library item to place text links at the bottom of your pages. It's always a good idea to place text links at the bottom of a page, and it's especially helpful to visitors who've reached the bottom of a page and can no longer see the navigation buttons at the top!

- Create a new paragraph below your content. Then select the **\<p\>** tag on the Dreamweaver status bar, choose Set Class, and apply the linkbar class.

- Open the Assets panel and choose the Library icon on the panel's icon bar. Because we've included the library for you, you will see it in the window. It's called Navlinks.

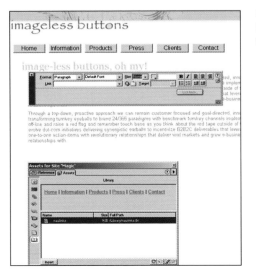

Use the Assets panel to insert the library item in a new paragraph.

- Click the Insert button on the Assets panel's bottom border to insert the library item in your new paragraph. Note that the library item inherits the formatting of the paragraph, which is determined by the CSS Class applied to the **<p>** tag. The library item itself contains absolutely no styling. Ah, the power of CSS!

9 Preview your work using the Dreamweaver Preview in Browser function.

Note: Library items are powerful tools that can make Web site maintenance a snap. The Dreamweaver documentation does a wonderful job of discussing this feature. If you're not yet familiar with Dreamweaver library items, I strongly recommend that you read about them and put them to work for you!

MODIFICATIONS

You can easily change the position of the buttons to run vertically down the left side of the page. This would be especially handy if you needed a large number of buttons but wanted to keep your design viewable at 640×480 without the need for horizontal scrollbars.

Once again, let your imagination be your guide.

The buttons can easily be made to run vertically down the page.

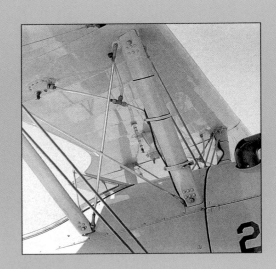

CREATING AN HTML FRAMES-BASED INTERFACE

"People who like this sort of thing will

find this the sort of thing they like."

—ABRAHAM LINCOLN

MODAL WINDOWS

What are modal windows? Well, most modern software applications live inside windows. Windows organize a program into logical and navigable spaces. The idea of using HTML frames to divide a browser into logical, navigable spaces is not new. When Netscape invented frames, they were the rage—for about two weeks. Then the gurus (we won't mention names) went on a search and destroy mission to rid the Web of this most useful tool. Why? Well, I think it's because they simply lacked imagination.

Frames have always intrigued me. The most valid reason I've heard for not using frames is that some older browsers don't support them. So if your audience tends to favor Netscape Navigator version 1.0 or MS Internet Explorer version 2.0, please do yourself a favor and skip to the next chapter. However, if you are an *outside-the-box* thinker, please do read on!

Project 5

Creating an HTML Frames-Based Interface

by Al Sparber

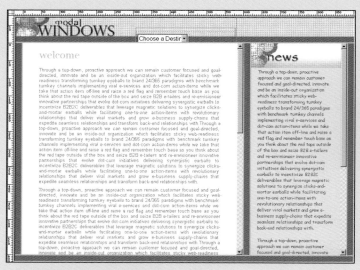

The Modal Windows finished project.

IT WORKS LIKE THIS

This project involves the creation of a frames-based Web site that is, well, just a lit-tle bit unique. The most complex aspect is building the frameset itself. So, to make my life easier, I wrote a special little extension that builds it for me. Oh, and you get to use that, too!

Our frameset is a complex one that employs seven separate frames. This is a lot more reasonable than it sounds because four of the seven frames use the same exact source file and exist solely to create the border effects of an application interface. A fifth frame, the header, contains a logo and a stylized jump menu. That frame loads just once. The sixth and seventh frames contain the main content and the sidebar. The main content frame is the only frame that changes as users surf the site.

Starting now, forget all the negatives you've heard about frames. You're going to make this baby very attractive to the search engines! After you create the frameset, you'll learn how to enter appropriate **<noframes>** content, where to put your Meta tags, and how to ensure that no page can be opened outside the frameset.

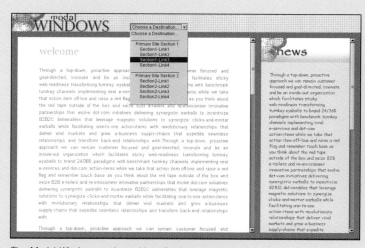

The Modal Windows project with stylized jump menu magic.

PREPARING TO WORK

Preparing for a *Dreamweaver 4 Magic* project is probably pretty much a routine for you now. Install the requisite extensions, copy the project folder from the CD to your hard drive, fire up Dreamweaver, and then define a new site using your copied project folder as the target.

1 Install the ModalWindows, Corporate Mumbo-Jumbo, and PVII Jump Menu Magic objects:

   • Browse to the Extensions folder on the CD.

   • Open the Objects subfolder.

   • Double-click the file ModalWindows.mxp to install the object.

   • Repeat these actions for the files P7Jump Menu.mxp and MX16753_MumboJumbo.mxp.

2 Install the TMT_Back to My Frame command:

   • Browse to the Extensions folder on the CD.

   • Open the Commands subfolder.

   • Double-click the file back_to_my_frame.mxp to install it.

3 Copy the projects folder:

   • Browse to the projects folder on the CD.

   • Copy the project_five folder to a convenient location on your hard drive.

4 Define a new Dreamweaver site using the project_five copy as your local root folder.

Note: Remember, if you want to see how the completed site looks in either Dreamweaver or your browser, you can find all the files in the finished_project folder.

Note: You'll find the style sheet (main.css) in the style_sheets folder of the assets directory. The style sheet is completely set up and is already attached to the worksheet document you'll use to build your site.

BROWSER COMPATIBILITY

We have tested this interface and found that it is fully functional in the following browsers:

   MSIE 4 (Windows and Mac)

   MSIE 5 (Windows and Mac)

   MSIE 5.5 (Windows)

   NN4.08–4.76 (Windows)

   NN4.5 (Mac)

   Opera 5.01 (Windows)

   Netscape 6 (Windows and Mac)

CREATING THE FRAMESET

Dreamweaver makes it easy for you to create framesets by offering several predefined sets on the Frames section of the Objects panel (you can also access these from the Frames flyout on the Insert menu). In addition, a new object developed especially for this book allows you to insert a Modal Windows frameset with one click of the mouse.

1 Insert the Modal Windows Object into the main page:

- Open the single file in the root of the project folder; it's called main.htm.

- Open the Objects panel.

- Select the Frames section.

- Click the Insert Modal Windows Frameset icon— the red and blue colored affair.

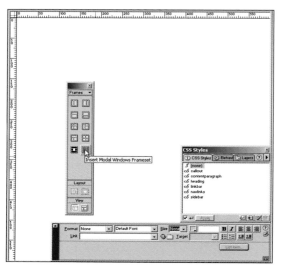

Use the Insert Modal Windows Frameset icon in the Frames section of the Objects panel to create the frameset.

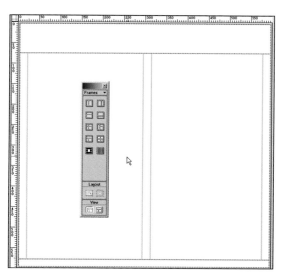

As soon as you click to insert the Modal Windows Frameset icon, you see the outlines of the frames.

102

2 Create the source files and then save everything:

After you insert the frameset, you see a representation of the frames. The only actual file in use is main.htm, which is sitting in the large frame on the left side of the window. Dreamweaver is holding a spot for the other files until you name and save them.

• Choose File/Save All Frames.

Dreamweaver highlights the entire frameset and prompts you to save the frameset file. The Save File dialog should be pointing to the root of your project folder. If it's not, browse to it before saving.

• Determine that you're in the proper folder.

• Type **index** in the filename field.

• Click Save.

Dreamweaver saves the frameset as index.htm and then begins highlighting the individual frames so you can create and save the files that comprise the frameset. The next frame to be highlighted should be the bottom border.

• Name the file **borders.htm**.

• Click Save. Use the filename **borders** for all the files that comprise the three tall, narrow frame columns and also the short, wide row at the bottom.

• When Dreamweaver prompts you to overwrite the file, choose Yes. (The idea is that you are reusing a single little file as the source file for four of your seven frames. This is a complex but frugal frameset!)

• Name the file for the topmost frame **header.htm**.

• Name the file for the large right frame **sidebar.htm**.

The remaining frame is already occupied by the file main.htm because the Modal Window object is programmed to place whatever file was open when you inserted the object into that frame. Dreamweaver, therefore, will not prompt you to save it.

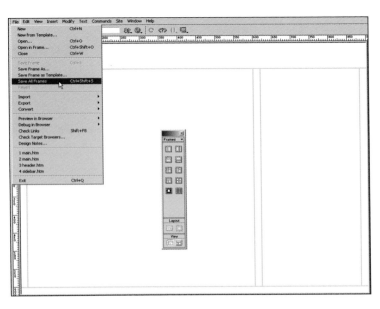

Select the Save All Frames command from the File menu.

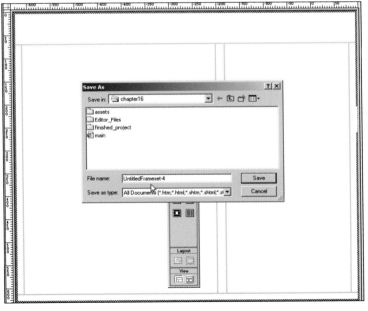

After you select Save All Frames, Dreamweaver asks you to name and save the frameset file.

So the frameset has been saved as index.htm, the top frame contains header.htm, the left central frame contains main.htm, the right central frame contains sidebar.htm, and the remaining four frames all contain borders.htm. If you haven't already noticed, you do not have to enter any settings for the frameset or the frames. All that has been taken care of for you by the Modal Windows object! Now you can concentrate on tidying up and optimizing things.

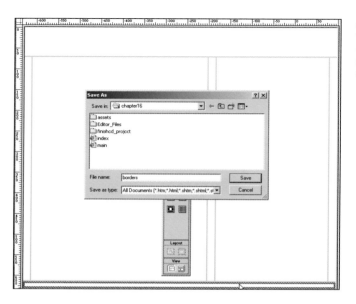

After you save the frameset file, Dreamweaver creates each of the individual frames and prompts you to save each one.

3 Title all your pages. Dreamweaver 4 makes this task very easy:

- Open index.htm. Note that you see nothing but a big white expanse (unless frame borders are turned on). Where are the frames?
- Choose View/Visual Aids and turn on Frame Borders.
- Click inside the top frame and then replace Untitled Document (in the title field of the button bar) with your title. When you're working with a frameset, it's usually okay to use the same title for all your pages because users will see the title of the frameset only in the browser's title bar.
- Click inside the main and sidebar frames and enter titles for those pages.
- Click inside one of the border frames and enter its title. (Remember, you're reusing this page four times, so you need to title only one instance of it!)

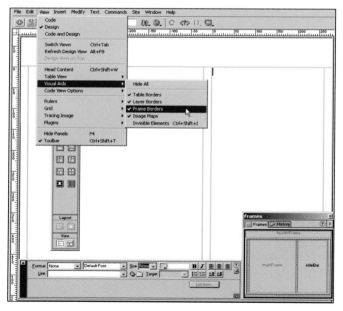

Turn on Frame Borders to see the outline of the border of each frame.

Type over Untitled Document to provide a title for the frame in the Title field on the button bar.

4 Add **<noframes>** content:

- Choose Modify/Frameset/Edit NoFrames Content.
- Type any content you want onto the page.

Dreamweaver makes it easy for you to enter **<noframes>** content, the stuff seen by browsers that don't support frames, so you want to insert a couple of paragraphs here that nicely describe the site. Use some keywords and phrases to make your point. When you finish your site, you should come back here to enter a hyperlink to every page of your site that you want the search engine spiders to index.

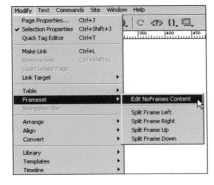

Choose Modify/Frameset/Edit NoFrames Content to access the NoFrames Editor window.

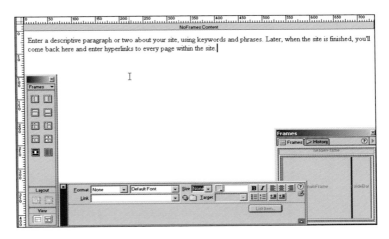

Enter content for the page in the NoFrames Editor window.

5 Add **<meta>** tags:

- While you're in the NoFrames editor window, switch to Code View.
- Enter any **<meta>** tags you might want to use.

In case you're not sure what Meta tags are, there is a good discussion of the topic in the Dreamweaver Help files, as well as in the printed manual.

While in NoFrames Editor, you can switch to Code View and enter or edit **<meta>** tags.

```
1 <html>
2 <head>
3 <title>Dreamweaver Magic- Modal Windows</title>
4 <meta http-equiv="Content-Type" content="text/html; charset=iso-8859-1">
5 <meta NAME="Classification" CONTENT="dreamweaver,templates,resource,experts,themes,extensions,
  tutorials,tips">
6 <meta NAME="KeyWords" CONTENT="dreamweaver templates,tutorials, web design themes,fireworks
  dreamweaver studio,design packs,dropdown menus,dhtml,javascript,macromedia resources,dreamweaver
  resources,dreamweaver behaviors,commands,objects">
7 <meta NAME="Description" CONTENT="Templates and Tutorials to Harness the full power of
  Macromedia Dreamweaver and Fireworks">
8 <meta name="copyright" content="2000 Project VII Development">
9 <meta name="robots" content="INDEX, FOLLOW">
10 <meta name="document-classification" content="Web Programming">
11 <meta name="document-rating" content="General">
12 </head>
13 <frameset rows="69,*,16" border=0 frameborder="no">
14     <frame name= "headerFrame" noresize scrolling="no" marginwidth=0 marginheight=0
  frameborder="NO" src="header.htm">
15     <frameset cols="16,1*,16,260,16" border=0 frameborder="no">
16         <frame name="leftBorder" scrolling="no" noresize marginwidth=0 marginheight=0
  src="borders.htm">
17         <frame name= "mainFrame" noresize marginwidth=0 marginheight=0 frameborder="no"
  src="main.htm" scrolling="AUTO">
```

The finished index page for this project contains the actual Meta tags from the Project VII Web site for reference.

Note: For those who prefer a visual environment, Dreamweaver has a feature to facilitate entry of Meta tags. To open the Meta tag window, choose Insert/Head Tags/Meta. Also, a very powerful Meta Manager command (by Massimo Foti) is available on the Dreamweaver Exchange.

6 Add the Back to My Frame command:

With the measures you've taken so far, your site will do well with the search engines. To make sure indexed pages cannot be opened independently of your frameset, you'll apply Massimo Foti's Back to my Frame command. That command loads the entire frameset whenever a user attempts to open one of the pages that comprise it. Massimo was thoughtful enough to have made this command able to take care of multiple pages with a single insertion.

- Open all the files that will have the command applied: main.htm, sidebar.htm, header.htm, and borders.htm.
- From within any one of those pages, choose Commands/Back to my Frame.
- Select the All Open Documents option.
- Browse to (or type) **index.htm**.
- Click Insert.
- Dreamweaver inserts this simple code:

```
<script language="javascript">
//tmtC_backToFrame
if(top==self) {
self.location.href='index.htm';}
//tmtC_backToFrameEnd
</script>
```

Now if any of those pages is launched, the parent frameset (index.htm) will be loaded instead.

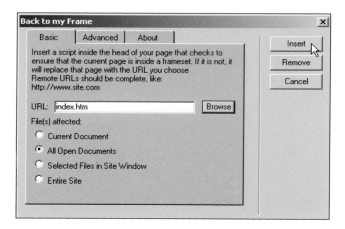

Open all the pages that require the Back to my Frame command, go to one of those pages, choose Commands/Back to my Frame, select the All Open Documents option, and insert the command.

Note: You may notice that the code in this book sometimes wraps to the next line. That wrapping is caused by the narrowness of the column within this book. Dreamweaver does not restrict the length of the line; the code appears on one line.

Designing the Component Pages
of the Frameset

When your frameset is created, configured, and saved, you are ready to work on the interface's design aspects, including the insertion of a very special jump menu. You'll start by adding color to your border pages.

1   Style the Border page:

Note: I used Fireworks 4 for all the images. Stock styles were used with various brushes and strokes, but no other images were used.

- Make sure that borders.htm is open.
- Choose Modify/Page Properties.
- Click the Browse button next to the Background Image field.
- Browse to and select graylines.gif from the assets/images folder.
- Click Apply to make the background image visible on your page.
- Click the color flyout square labeled Background and use the Eyedropper tool to pick up the dominant color in the background image. This is important so that there will be some color on the page during the time it takes for the image to download.
- Save the page.
- Open the frameset (index.htm) to see the changes.

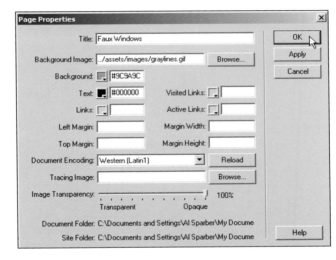

Choose Modify/Page Properties and browse to locate the image file you will use as the background on the page.

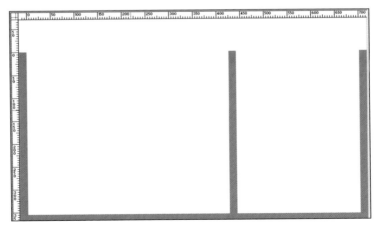

You can see the shapes of the frames after you apply the background images to the border panes.

2 Redefine the **<body>** in the Header page:

- Open header.htm. You're going to redefine the body tag in the CSS Editor.

- Open the CSS panel and click the Pencil icon on the panel's lower right border to open the Edit CSS window.

- Click the New button to open the New Style window, and then select the Redefine HTML Tag radio button.

- Select body from the drop-down list of tags (it may already be selected depending upon where your cursor was when you started).

- Make sure the option labeled This Document Only is selected because you want the style to be embedded in this particular page only.

- Click OK.

- In the Style Definitions window, select the Background category.

- Set the Background Color to white (**#FFFFFF**).

- Click the Browse button.

- Browse to and select assets/images/tracksbg.gif to define the Background Image.

- Select repeat-x from the Repeat drop-down list.

- Select the Box category and set all margin attributes to **0**.

- Click OK to complete the style, and then click Done to exit the Edit Style Sheet window.

- Netscape 4 will not reliably support CSS page margin settings. To work around this, open the Page Properties window and set Margin Width and Margin Height to **0**.

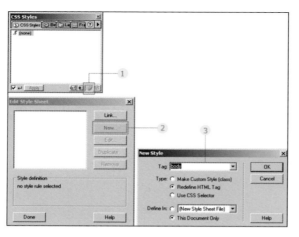

Access the Edit CSS window to redefine the body of the header page.

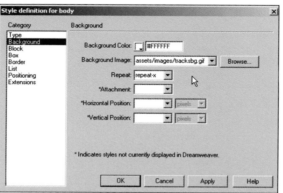

Set the style of the background in the **<body>** tag.

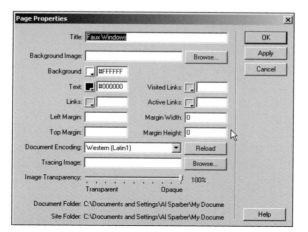

Set the HTML margins to **0** for Netscape 4 compatibility.

108

3 Prepare the page to accept the jump menu in
header.htm:

For the jump menu to work in Netscape 4, you must
insert it inside a pair of **\<form\>** tags. Because you'll
be using a table to position your logo and the jump
menu, it's best to place the table inside the form.

- Choose Insert/Form.
- Choose View and select the Invisible Elements
  option so you can see the red outline of the form's
  borders.

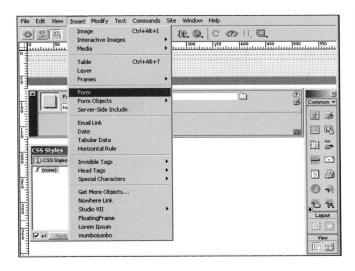

Choose Insert/Form and watch
as Dreamweaver inserts the
new form, outlining it in red.

4 Insert the logo image in the Header page:

Note: In case you're wondering what fonts we used in
the logo and the news header, they're Papyrus and
Emancipation.

- Position your cursor inside the form (you'll see the
  form tag on the status bar turn bold) and insert a
  1-row by 2-column table. The table must be inside
  the form.
- Set cell spacing, padding, and border to **0**.
- Set table width to **100 pixels**.
- Click inside the first column and use the Assets
  panel to insert the image assets/images/tlogo.gif.
- Type some placeholder text into the second column so it doesn't collapse on you. You'll be
  putting your jump menu in there in a minute!
- Notice that things do not appear to line up correctly. Choose View/Visual Aids/Invisible Elements
  to toggle off the Invisible Elements option, and
  things will fall into place.

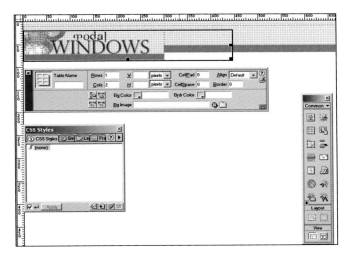

Make sure you insert the table
inside the form and set the
table's properties.

When you edit the jump menu, it's easier working from within the frameset page. That way, all frame names will be available from the target drop-down list in the PVII Jump Menu Magic Interface. However, one of the enhanced features of the PVII jump menu is that you can also type a target in at any time—whether or not you are within the frameset.

5 Insert the drop-down jump menu:

The PVII Jump Menu was chosen for this project because it is an enhanced version of the Dreamweaver Jump Menu object and it provides a little more flexibility and power.

- Insert your cursor in the second table column.

- Backspace over the placeholder text to remove it.

- Choose Insert/Studio VII/PVII Jump Menu Magic. The first menu item becomes selected.

- Type over unnamed1 with a nice lead-in phrase for your menu, such as **Choose a Destination**.

- Leave the menu name alone, or change it to a more descriptive name if you like.

- Because the first menu item is a descriptive phrase, set Page to Load to header.htm and the Target to headerFrame to render the link essentially null.

- Choose an option that suits you from the three available:

  - Insert Go Button After Menu: Both the Go button and selecting menu items operate the menu.

  - Require Go Button: Only the Go button operates the menu.

  - Select First Item After URL Change: After a menu item is selected, the menu resets itself to show the first item. (We chose to turn this option on in the finished project.)

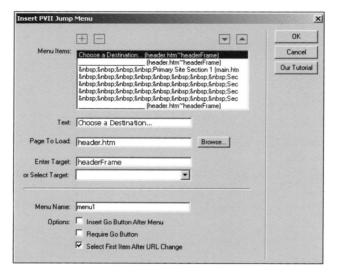

Choose Insert/Studio VII/PVII Jump Menu Magic and complete the dialog to insert the interface.

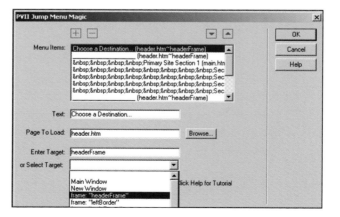

If you use Jump Menu Magic with the frameset open, you can choose the frame targets from a convenient drop-down menu.

6 Look at this example. Obviously, you can enter your own links, but to illustrate the hierarchical design used to set up this menu, I've listed out the code.

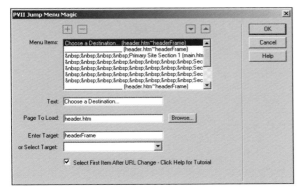

The Choose a Destination... option is a simple description. The Page To Load is set to the header.htm page in the headerFrame target. So if a visitor inadvertently selects it, the header page will simply reload itself.

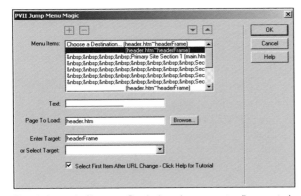

Directly beneath Choose a Destinaion... is a separator line created with underscore characters typed into the Jump Menu Magic Text field. The Page To Load and Targets are likewise set to reload the header page.

```
<option value="header.htm~headerFrame" selected>Choose a Destintion...</option>
<option value="header.htm~headerFrame">_____</option>
<option value="header.htm~headerFrame">    Primary Site
Section 1</option>
<option value="test.htm~mainFrame">       
 Section1-Link1</option>
<option value="test.htm~mainFrame">       
 Section1-Link2</option>
<option value="test.htm~mainFrame">       
 Section1-Link3</option>
<option value="test.htm~mainFrame">       
 Section1-Link4</option>
<option value="header.htm~headerFrame">_____</option>
<option value="header.htm~headerFrame">    Primary Site
Section 2</option>
<option value="test.htm~mainFrame">       
 Section2-Link1</option>
<option value="test.htm~mainFrame">       
 Section2-Link2</option>
<option value="test.htm~mainFrame">       
 Section2-Link3</option>
<option value="test.htm~mainFrame">       
 Section2-Link4</option>
<option value="header.htm~headerFrame">      
 </option>
```

The underscore characters are used to simulate separator lines. Notice that the link and target are header and headerFrame. You do not want the selection of a separator line to change a page! The non-breaking spaces ( ) are used to create indents. (We show you the code here for illustrative purposes only!) Everything you see in Step 6 was entered through the PVII Jump Menu Magic interface. To see how it was done, follow these steps:

- Open index.htm in the finished_project folder.

- Open the Behaviors panel.

- Select the jump menu in the header frame and double-click the onChange event in the Behaviors panel to open the Jump Menu Magic window.

- Compare the entries in the Jump Menu Magic window line-by-line, with the earlier code sample to see how the indents and descriptive lines were entered.

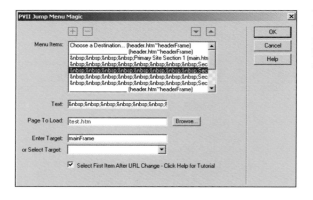

The first actual link opens test.htm in the mainFrame. To make the link Section1-Link1 indented, you type ** ** eight times.

CREATING A CUSTOM STYLE

Notice that the menu is white. Well, you can make it look pretty in MS Internet Explorer or Netscape 6 by creating a custom style and applying it to the **<select>** tag of your menu.

Note: Instead of setting the section headings and separator lines to reload the header page into the header frame, you can set the links to a null JavaScript by typing **java.script:;** and leaving the target blank. This may cause errors in some older browsers, so do this only if you are sure of a version 4 or higher browser target audience.

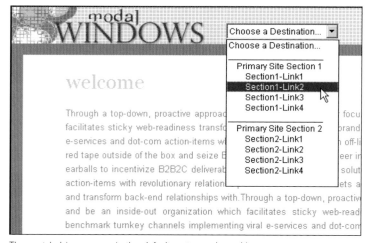

The unstyled jump menu is the default system color—white.

1 Create the link between the page and the main.css, in which the new style will appear:

- Open the CSS panel.
- Click the Pencil icon on the panel's lower-right border to open the Edit CSS window.
- Click the Link button.
- Click Browse.
- Browse to and select the CSS file assets/style_sheets/main.css.
- Click OK to link it to your page.

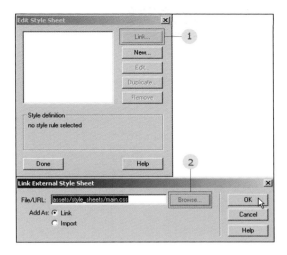

Open the Edit Style Sheet window, click Link, and specify the CSS file you want to use.

2 Create a custom style to colorize your menu:

- Select main.css and click Edit.
- In the main.css window, click New.
- Choose Make Custom Style (class), make sure Define In: main.css is selected, and type **.mainmenu** as the name of the new style. Click OK and the Editor opens.
- Set these Type properties:

  Font: **Arial**
  Font Size: **12pixels**
  Font Color: **#333333**

- Set this Background property:

  Background Color: **#D6D7D6**

- Click OK, and then click Save. Finally, click Done.
- Select the menu.
- Make sure the **<select>** tag is bold on the status bar and use either the status bar contextual menu or the CSS Panel to apply the .mainmenu class to the **<select>** tag of the menu.

In the Edit Style Sheet window, click Edit to access the main.css window so that you can create a new style.

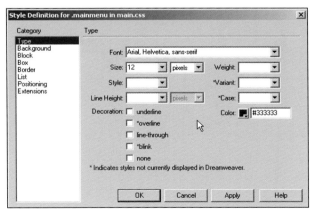

Enter the Type attributes for your newly created style, called .mainmenu.

3 Check your work:

Now you're in the home stretch. Preview your work in either MSIE or Netscape 6, and you'll see a nicely styled menu. The menu will look perfectly fine in older browsers, but it will be shown in the default system color.

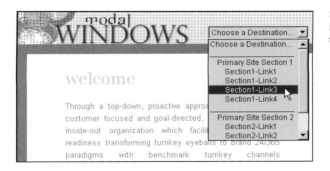

Preview with MSIE or Netscape 6, and you'll see that the menu is now styled.

ADDING THE FINISHING TOUCHES

The sidebar frame contains the page sidebar.htm, and because it is a separate frame, its content remains fixed while the main frame is scrolled. If its content requires scrolling, it can be scrolled independently of the main frame. After you finish the sidebar page, you'll turn to the main page (main.htm). This is the easiest page you have to work with. Because it plays host to your main content, you kept it plain white for easy reading. The pre-linked style sheet is set to define how the text looks. That's it!

1 Link the sidebar page to the main style sheet and redefine its **\<body\>** tag:

- Open sidebar.htm.
- Open the CSS Editor.
- Link the page to main.css like you did for the header page.
- Click the New button to open the New Style window, and then select the Redefine HTML Tag radio button.
- Select body from the drop-down list of tags.
- Make sure the This Document Only option is selected. Click OK.

- In the Style Definitions window, select from the Background list Category.
- Set the Background Color to **#FFE7C6**.
- Click the Browse button.
- Browse to and select assets/images/sidebg.gif to define the background image.
- Select repeat-x from the Repeat drop-down list.
- Don't close the window because you're not quite finished yet!

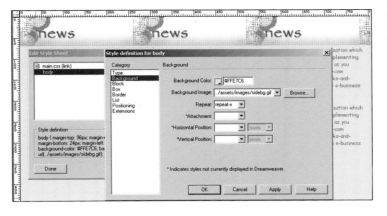

Select Background from the Category list and enter the Background attributes.

2   Add margins to the body:

Add some margins to the body to fit the text below the background image and also to provide a little white space.

- Select the Box category.
- Set these margin settings:

    Top: **96 pixels**
    Right: **24 pixels**
    Bottom: **24 pixels**
    Left: **24 pixels**

- Click OK and then Done to close the CSS window. The background image and color are now in place, and you're ready to enter some content.

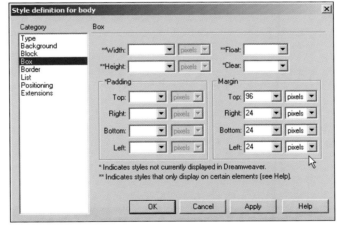

Select the Box category and enter the margins.

3   Add the content to the sidebar page:

- Type a few paragraphs of boilerplate text for effect.

Note: To facilitate entering boilerplate (placeholder) text, you can use the Corporate Mumbo-Jumbo object to automatically insert some interesting gibberish into your page. To use Corporate Mumbo-Jumbo, choose Insert, mumbojumbo.

Notice that the background image tiles left to right (repeat-x). Because the frame that houses this page is 260 pixels wide, you'll see only one instance of the image when you view the entire frameset. Setting the image as a background as opposed to simply inserting it on the page will ensure a snug fit in all browsers.

4 Check your work. To see how setting an image as a background looks in the frameset, save your changes, open the index.htm page, and preview it in your browser.

The margins add white space, making the text in the page easier to read and more attractive, as well as making sure the top margin contains adequate room for the background image.

LOOKING AT THE CASCADING STYLE SHEET

What you'll find conspicuously missing from the main pages (main.htm and sidebar.htm) are HTML tables. I am a big proponent of CSS and tend to use tables only when they are absolutely necessary. In addition to the styling flexibility of using block elements (mainly paragraphs and DIVs), the code economy is amazing. Have a look under the hood and compare the source code to a traditional page (of like content) done with tables.

Remember that, in addition to the styles in main.css, you can set up a few page-specific styles.

Note: You should take the time to familiarize yourself with CSS. It's an easy study, and some excellent books are available. At the very least, thoroughly read the Dreamweaver manual or CSS topics in the Help documentation. The time investment is well worth it.

The main.css.

```
h1 { font-family: Georgia, "Times New Roman",
Times, serif; font-size: 28px; color: #CCCCCC;
font-weight: normal; margin-top: 12px; margin-right:
0px; margin-bottom: 12px; margin-left: 0px}

.contentparagraph { font-family: Arial, Helvetica,
sans-serif; font-size: 13px; color: #8C8684;
margin-top: 12px; margin-right: 0px; margin-bottom:
12px; margin-left: 0px; text-align: justify; line-height:
20px}

b { color: #848A7B}

a:link { color: #666666}

a:visited { color: #666666}

a:hover { color: #333333}

a:active { color: #666666}.heading { font-family:
Georgia, "Times New Roman", Times, serif; font-size:
28px; color: #CCCCCC}

.mainmenu{ font-family: Arial, Helvetica, sans-serif;
font-size: 12px; color: #333333; background-color:
#D6D7D6}

.sidebar { font-family: "Comic Sans MS", Arial,
sans-serif; font-size: 12px; color: #666666}
```

MODIFICATIONS

Let your imagination be your guide! The most significant modifications you can make to this particular project involve the style sheets, the images, and the frame sizes. If you would like to modify the frame sizes, I recommend that you do it in the source code. That method is very easy and eliminates the danger of inadvertently moving a border and having Dreamweaver rewrite the frameset. All other frame modifications can be safely and efficiently performed using the Frames panel and Property Inspector in tandem. The following steps show you how you can modify the frameset in the source code.

1 Choose Modify/Frameset and select Edit NoFrames Content.

2 Choose View/Code to view the frameset code.

   • The first line sets the height of the frame rows by using these settings:

      The header frame is 69px.

      The main frame (*)—a lone asterisk (*)—sets a frame to dynamically resize based on the available window size minus the sum of any frames set to a fixed dimension.

      The bottom border frame is 16px.

   • The third line sets the width of the columns:

      The outermost left border is 16px.

      The main frame (*)... * sets a frame to dynamically resize based on the available window size minus the sum of any frames set to a fixed dimension.

      The border frame that butts up against the right side of the main frame is 16px.

      The sidebar frame is 260px.

      The rightmost border frame is 16px.

The frameset code.

```
<frameset rows="69,*,16" border=0 frameborder="no">
<frame name= "headerFrame" noresize scrolling="no" marginwidth=0 marginheight=0 frameborder="NO" src="header.htm">
<frameset cols="16,*,16,260,16" border=0 frameborder="no">
<framename="leftBorder" scrolling="no" noresize marginwidth=0 marginheight=0 src="borders.htm">
<frame  name= "mainFrame" noresize marginwidth=0 marginheight=0 frameborder="no" src="main.htm" scrolling="AUTO">
<frame name="midBorder" scrolling="NO" frameborder="NO" noresize marginwidth="0" marginheight="0" src="borders.htm">
<frame src="sidebar.htm" marginwidth="0" marginheight="0" scrolling="AUTO" noresize frameborder="no" name="sideBar">
<frame src="borders.htm" name="riteBorder" scrolling="NO" marginwidth="0" marginheight="0" noresize frameborder="NO">
</frameset>
<frame name="bottomBorder" scrolling="no" noresize marginwidth=0 marginheight=0 frameborder="NO" src="borders.htm">
</frameset>
```

Note: When changing frame sizes, watch your asterisks. Preview the file often if you're using Netscape 4 because it has several mathematical bugs in its programming that render certain dimensions inaccurately. Netscape 6 has fixed these problems.

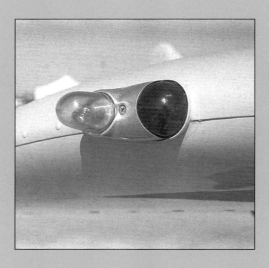

CREATING A CLICKABLE DHTML TABBED INTERFACE

"Much of what's taught is actually teaching how

to be a certain variety of stylist. That's not a

long-term skill. A Web-designer is someone who

creates useful networked interfaces, and I

see that need continuing to increase."

—JOHN DOWDELL

A User-Friendly Tabbed Interface

Real-world metaphors are an excellent means of conducting viewers through your Web site. A study done by Microsoft showed that tabbed interfaces are one of the best real-world metaphors. Literally every testee recognized what the tabs were and how to use them. Other advantages to tabbed interfaces are that they allow you to present a lot of information without requiring the viewer to scroll, they allow the viewer to keep track of the information he has already accessed, and they are visually pleasing. So why aren't they used on more Web sites? One reason may be that the tabs commonly used on Web sites do not behave the way the viewer expects them to. They are static. Nothing happens to the tabs when the viewer clicks on them.

This project shows you how to create a tabbed interface that perfectly mimics the natural action of folder tabs. Whether used as the basis of a navigation system or to create small, interactive elements, this dynamic combination of image swaps and show/hide layers may be just what you are looking for to make your Web site sparkle.

Project 6

Creating a Clickable DHTML Tabbed Interface

by Linda Rathgeber

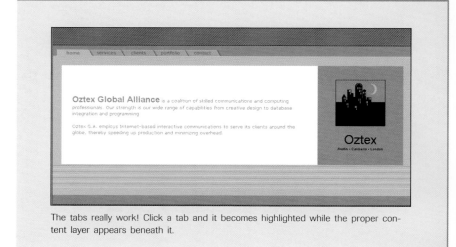

The tabs really work! Click a tab and it becomes highlighted while the proper content layer appears beneath it.

IT WORKS LIKE THIS

An image of five tabs is converted to an image map with Dreamweaver 4's rectangular hotspot tool. A series of Swap Image behaviors is assigned to the hotspots. These behaviors are used to swap each of the up (normal state) tab images with its corresponding down (highlighted state) image, restore each of the other up images, show a content layer, and hide each of the other content layers.

PREPARING TO WORK

Preparing for a Dreamweaver 4 Magic project is pretty much a routine. Install the requisite extensions, copy the project folder from the accompanying CD-ROM to your hard drive, and then fire up Dreamweaver and define a new site using your copied project folder as the target.

1 Install the N4 Return False Fix command:

This Project VII command eliminates Netscape showing the hourglass cursor when clicking a null link to fire a JavaScript.

- Browse to the Extensions folder on the CD.
- Open the Commands subfolder.

Dreamweaver behaviors allow visitors to interact with a Web page to change the page in various ways or to cause certain tasks to be performed. A behavior is a combination of an event, such as the viewer clicking on a link, with an action triggered by that event through the magic of JavaScript.

Note: Remember, if you want to see how the completed site looks in either Dreamweaver or your browser, you can find all the files in the finished_project folder.

120

- Double-click the file called: N4 Return False Fix.mxp to install the command.

2   Install the Scrubber command:

This Project VII command eliminates the dotted outline around clicked links in Microsoft Internet Explorer.

- Browse to the Extensions folder on the CD.

- Open the Commands subfolder.

- Double-click the file named scrubber.mxp to install the command.

3   Copy the projects folder:

- Browse to the projects folder on the CD.

- Copy the project_six folder to a convenient location on your hard drive.

4   Define a new Dreamweaver site using the project_six copy as your site root.

SETTING THE PAGE PROPERTIES

The carved look of our page is accomplished by using a cleverly designed background image.

The image is a mere 40 pixels wide by 2000 pixels tall and weighs in at a slim 2.48KB.

1   Set up the Page Properties:

- Open the index.htm page in the site's root.

- Choose Modify/Page Properties.

- Type #**CCCC99** for the background color.

- Type **assets/newbackgroundb.gif** into the background image field.

Note: You can also use the Browse button to insert an image, as well as the Assets panel.

- Click OK to apply your settings.

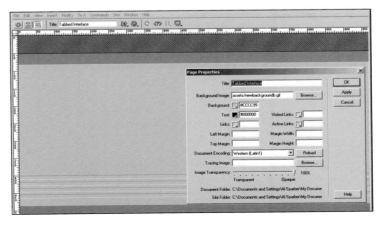

Use the Page Properties dialog to set background color and image.

2 Set up the page margins:

We've presupplied and linked an external style sheet to the index page. It's called tabby.css and is located in the assets/style_sheets folder. Let's open the style sheet and inspect the body style to see how we have set the page margins.

- Click the Pencil icon on the bottom of the CSS Styles panel.

- Double-click tabby.css and then double-click body.

- Select the Box category on the left side of the Style Definition dialog and notice that all four margins are set to 0.

Note: To support all new browsers, including Navigator 6 and Opera 5, always set page margins in a style sheet. Never in the Page Properties dialog!

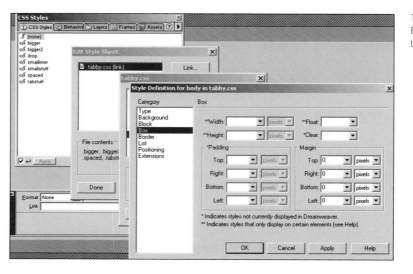

Take a peek inside the CSS Editor to see how we set the body margins.

INSERTING THE TAB LAYER

The tabs are contained in a layer that is positioned to vertically align with the topmost green band in our background image. We know that the green band begins 50 pixels from the top of the image, so you need to place the layer 50 pixels from the top of the window.

1 Insert the tab layer:

- Insert a layer on your page.

- Use the property inspector to set its attributes:

    Layer ID: **triggers1**
    Left: **0**
    Top: **50**
    Width: **540px**
    Height: **45px**

- Leave all other settings alone.

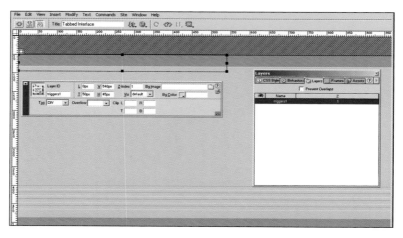

Insert the triggers1 layer and set its attributes on the property inspector.

2 Insert the tab image inside the layer:

- Use the Assets panel to find and insert the image called assets/tab_f01.gif, and insert it inside the layer.
- Use the property inspector to name this image object **tabimg1**.

  The image fits perfectly inside the channel created by the band in the background image. That's the power of pixel-perfect positioning with Dreamweaver and CSS layers!

Note: My Assets panel contains duplicate images because I have several backup and prototype folders in my site. Your panel will only contain one of each image!

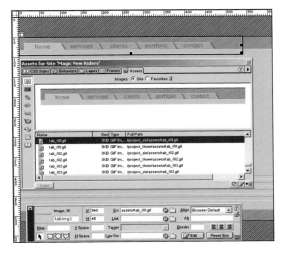

Insert the tab image inside the new layer.

CREATING IMAGE MAP HOTSPOTS AND SETTING SWAP IMAGE BEHAVIORS

Hotspots are simple to create in Dreamweaver and can be used to create dozens of interesting effects. Hotspots enable you to define multiple clickable areas in a single image to which you can apply JavaScript behaviors. You'll use them in this exercise to perform two operations at the same time: moving the tab images forward and backward; and switching the content layers.

1 Draw the hotspots:

Draw a rectangular hotspot over each tab in the image.

- Click on the Rectangular Hotspot tool in the lower left of the property inspector panel.
- After the cursor changes from an arrow to a crosshair, place the crosshair at the top left of the first tab and drag diagonally to create a small, rectangular hotspot.
- Carefully drag hotspots over each of the four remaining tabs, making sure that there are no overlaps.

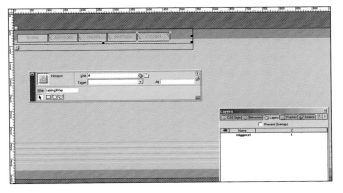

Create an image map by drawing rectangular hotspots over each tab.

Tip: Hotspots can be resized by grabbing and dragging one of the four corners, and they can be nudged using your keyboard arrow keys.

2 Swap the first image:

Use Swap Image behaviors to set each hotspot to change the source image of the image object named tabimg1. We have five tab images in our Assets folder, and each one represents the highlighted state of a particular tab.

- Click on the hotspot over tab 1 to select it.
- Open the Behaviors panel and click on the Add Action (+) button.
- Choose Swap Image from the Behaviors panel to begin building the dynamic tab set.
- In the Swap Image dialog, click the Browse button, browse to the Assets folder, and select tab_f01.gif. That's right! You want it to swap itself.
- Click the Select button.
- Back in the Swap Image dialog, leave the Preload Images box checked, but uncheck Restore Images onMouseOut.
- Click OK and set the event to onClick.

3 Apply Swap Image to the remaining four hotspots:

- Select the hotspot over the second tab.
- Click on the + button on the Behaviors panel.
- Choose Swap Image from the pop-up menu.
- Click on the Browse button.
- Select tab_f02.gif.
- Leave Preload Images checked.
- Uncheck Restore Images onMouseOut.
- Again, change the default onMouseOver to onClick.
- Repeat these actions for the hotspots on tabs three, four, and five, using tab_f03.gif, tab_f04.gif, and tab_f05.gif, respectively.
- Preview in your browser, and you'll see the magic has begun!

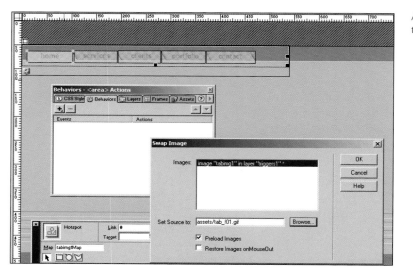

Apply Swap Image behaviors to each hotspot.

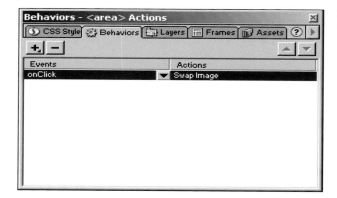

Set the swap image events to onClick.

INSERT THE CONTENT LAYERS

The next order of business is to use the Draw Layer technique to create five layers below the tabs. You'll add fixed width tables to each of the layers to hold the content for that layer. This content can be text, images, or a combination of both.

1   Set up the first layer:

- Click on the Draw Layer button on the Object panel.

- When the cursor changes to a crosshair, click near the left edge of the program window, just under your tabs, and drag diagonally to draw a layer.

- Use the property inspector to set its attributes as follows:

    LayerID: **content1**
    Left: **0px**
    Top: **109px**
    Width: **100%**
    Height: **288px**

2   Insert a table in the layer:

- Place your cursor inside the layer.

- Insert a table with the following attributes:

    Rows: **1**
    Columns: **2**
    Width: **95%**
    Padding: **0**
    Spacing: **0**
    Border: **0**

- Click OK to insert the table.

- Select the table, and in the property inspector, set these additional attributes:

    Height: **288px**
    Align: **Center**

    Centering a table makes it float in the middle of the page no matter what the size of the browser window.

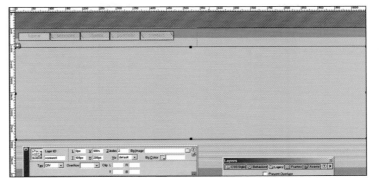

Draw the first content layer and use the property inspector to set its attributes.

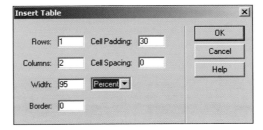

Insert a table inside the new layer.

- Click inside the left column and use the property inspector to assign a background color of **#FFFFFF** and a width of **75%**.

- Click inside the right column and assign a background color of **#999966** and a width of **25%**.

- Use the Assets panel to insert graphic.gif inside the right column.

- Place your cursor in the padding area of the cell next to the image and use the property inspector to set the cell's Horizontal alignment attribute to Center.

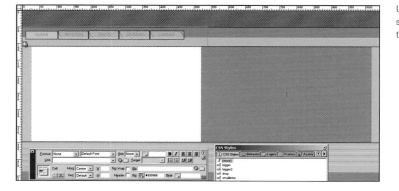

Use the property inspector to set additional attributes for the table.

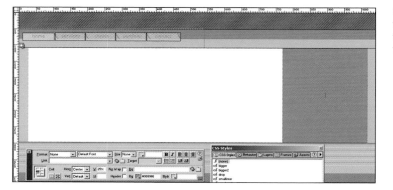

Use the property inspector to set attributes for each of the two cells (columns) in the table.

- With cursor to the right of the image, press Enter to create a new paragraph.

- Type the heading **Oztex**, and press Enter again.

- Type the subheading **Austin – Canberra – London**.

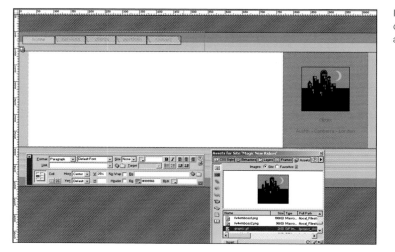

Insert an image in the right column and type a heading and subheading.

126

- Place your cursor on the same line as Oztex and use the property inspector to set its format to Heading 1.
- Place your cursor on the subheading line and right-click (Ctrl+click) the **<p>** tag on the status bar (bottom-left edge of the Dreamweaver window) and choose Set Class/smallstuff.

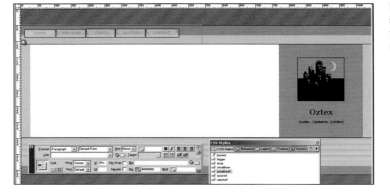

Use the property inspector to set the Oztex to Heading 1 format and set the subheading's CSS class to smallstuff.

3 Set up the remaining four content layers:

Tip: At this point, you can use copy and paste to make four copies of your original content1 layer. Each time you paste a copy, use the property inspector to correctly name it.

- Select the content1 layer in the Layers panel.
- Choose Edit/Copy.
- Choose Edit/Paste four successive times to paste four copies of content1. Because they are duplicates, you will have five layers all named content1.
- Use the Layers panel to rename the newly pasted layers as follows:

  content2
  content3
  content4
  content5

- Then set the preceding layers to Hidden. Only content1 and triggers1 should be set to visible.

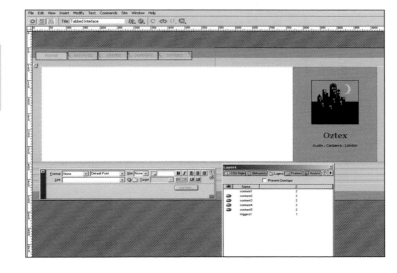

After pasting four copies of content1, use the Layers panel to rename the copies and set the visibility attributes for all layers.

Note: We have included an alternate background image if you want your layers to include a lot of content. To see an example, open the file called indexlong.htm in the finished_project folder.

4 Add content to the tables:

- Add whatever content you want to the content1 table. Use the finished_project index page as a guide. Add text, graphic content, or both to your tables. If you copy the content from the finished_project, the CSS classes will already be applied. If you type your own content, use the CSS classes included to style your text.

- To add your own content, hide all the content layers except for the one you want to edit.

- Type in your text.

- Use the tag selector on the status bar to assign custom CSS classes as you see fit.

- Keep the content to an amount that comfortably fits the assigned height of the content layers (288 pixels).

We've pasted content from the finished_project page into our working page. You can, of course, type in your own content.

SHOWING AND HIDING LAYERS

Here's where the real fun starts. We're going to make the same hotspots, to which we attached the tab Swap Image behaviors, perform double duty by attaching the Show-Hide Layers behavior to them.

1 Apply Show-Hide Layers to the Tab1 hotspot:

- Select the hotspot on the first tab.

- Click the + button on the Behaviors panel and choose Show-Hide Layers.

- In the Show-Hide Layers dialog set the following layer properties:

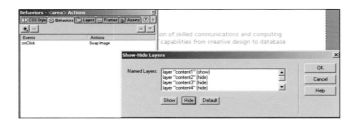

Set content layer visibility properties in the Show-Hide Layers dialog.

Content1:	**Show**
Content2:	**Hide**
Content3:	**Hide**
Content4:	**Hide**
Content5:	**Hide**
Triggers1:	**Don't Set!**

- Click OK.

- Change the event to onClick.

128

2 Apply Show-Hide Layers to the remaining four hotspots:

- Use the technique in Step 1 to apply the Show-Hide Layers behavior to the remaining four hotspots. Use the table as a guide.
- Remember to set the events to onClick.

Named Layer	Hotspot1	Hotspot2	Hotspot3	Hotspot4	Hotspot5
Content1	Show	Hide	Hide	Hide	Hide
Content2	Hide	Show	Hide	Hide	Hide
Content3	Hide	Hide	Show	Hide	Hide
Content4	Hide	Hide	Hide	Show	Hide
Content5	Hide	Hide	Hide	Hide	Show
Triggers1	Don't Set!	Don't Set!	Don't Set!	Don't Set!	Don't Set!

Use this table as a guide in applying the Show-Hide behaviors.

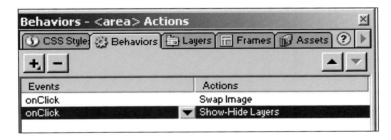

Don't forget to set the events to onClick.

WRAPPING THINGS UP

There are a few last tasks to do before your tabbed interface is complete.

1 Install the Netscape Resize Fix.

- Choose Commands and then Add/Remove Netscape Resize Fix.
- Click on the Add button to insert a JavaScript to correct a bug in some versions of Netscape Navigator, which causes the page to display incorrectly if the viewer resizes the browser window.

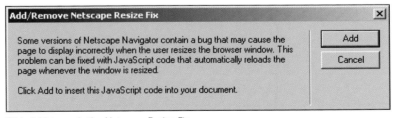

Click Add to apply the Netscape Resize Fix.

Note: If your preferences are set to automatically insert the Resize fix whenever you insert a layer, the fix is already in your page, and instead of an Add button, you will see a Remove button. If you see the Remove button, just click Cancel.

2 Add the Studio VII N4 Return False Fix and Link Scrubber commands.

- To do this, select each command from the Command menu, and in the dialog that opens for each, click Apply (or Scrub Em!) to insert the commands.

Note: Both the N4 Fix and Scrubber are cumulative fixes. That is, they can be reapplied over and over and will only fix new links added since the last application.

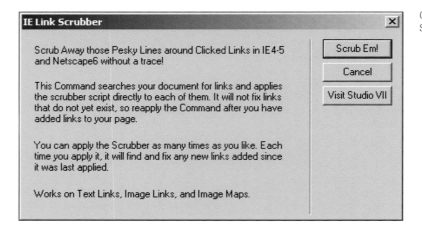

Click Scrub Em! to apply the Scrubber command.

IE Link Scrubber

Scrub Away those Pesky Lines around Clicked Links in IE4-5 and Netscape6 without a trace!

This Command searches your document for links and applies the scrubber script directly to each of them. It will not fix links that do not yet exist, so reapply the Command after you have added links to your page.

You can apply the Scrubber as many times as you like. Each time you apply it, it will find and fix any new links added since it was last applied.

Works on Text Links, Image Links, and Image Maps.

Scrub Em!
Cancel
Visit Studio VII

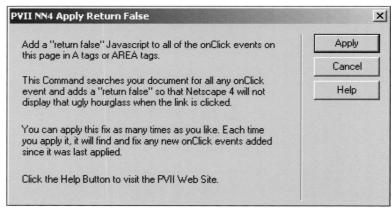

Click Apply to insert the NN4 Return False Fix.

PVII NN4 Apply Return False

Add a "return false" Javascript to all of the onClick events on this page in A tags or AREA tags.

This Command searches your document for all any onClick event and adds a "return false" so that Netscape 4 will not display that ugly hourglass when the link is clicked.

You can apply this fix as many times as you like. Each time you apply it, it will find and fix any new onClick events added since it was last applied.

Click the Help Button to visit the PVII Web Site.

Apply
Cancel
Help

MODIFICATIONS

We've included the graphical elements needed to complete this project on the accompanying CD, but before you begin your own tabbed interface project, you'll need to do some planning and create your own graphics.

Determine the number of tabs your interface will need. For each tab needed, create a separate image that displays the full set of tabs. In image one, position the first tab in front of the other tabs. In image two, position the second tab in front of the others.

Continue rotating the positions of the tabs in this manner for the full number of tabbed images your design requires.

The techniques used in creating this tabbed interface can be employed with other kinds of images too. Examples might be the half-moon tabs you find in an old dictionary or the vertical tabs you might find in a loose-leaf binder. On the CD, you will find an example of a small tabbed interface (textlinks.html) that could be inserted on a normal page to add an interactive element such as a menu or series of images. Have fun!

CONSTRUCTING A DHTML COLLAPSIBLE LAYER MENU

"Intuitive navigation is the

Holy Grail of Web design.

Drink from the cup, and your site will

have life…and lots of repeat visitors."

—AL SPARBER

DHTML COLLAPSIBLE LAYER MENU

The menu you create in this project is a study in getting folks from here to there with a subtle, intuitive elegance. We've packed 19 hyperlinks into a space that would normally fit just five. Every Web designer should keep one of these babies in the supply bin for quick deployment. It's one of our favorite Dreamweaver potions.

Project 7

Constructing a DHTML Collapsible Layer Menu

by Al Sparber

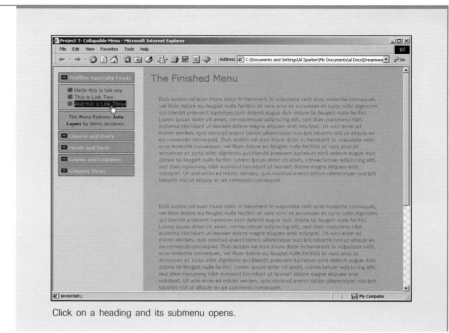

Click on a heading and its submenu opens.

IT WORKS LIKE THIS

The collapsible menu works by manipulating the visibility of multiple layers. Five visible hyperlinks are on the menu. Each link has a corresponding submenu. Including the closed-state menu, there are six menus in all, representing all possible states.

The six menus are in six separate layers. The layers are stacked one atop the other. When you click a link on the opening menu, the appropriate submenu layer is made visible while all other menus are hidden.

PREPARING TO WORK

Preparing for a *Dreamweaver 4 Magic* project is pretty much a routine. Install the requisite extensions, copy the project folder from the CD to your hard drive, and then fire up Dreamweaver and define a new site using your copied project folder as the local root folder.

1 Install the PVII Auto Layers behavior (if you haven't already done so):

   Dreamweaver makes our menu easy to construct. With assistance from PVII extension author Gerry Jacobsen, it's going to be easier still.

   • Browse to the Extensions folder on the CD.

   • Open the Behaviors/Actions subfolder.

   • Double-click P7_autoLayers.mxp to install the behavior.

BROWSER COMPATIBILITY

We have tested this interface and found that it is fully functional in the following browsers:

- MSIE 4 (Windows and Mac)
- MSIE 5 (Windows and Mac)
- MSIE 5.5 (Windows)
- NN4.08–4.76 (Windows)
- NN4.5 (Mac)
- Opera 5.01 (Windows)
- Netscape 6 (Windows and Mac)

2 Install the NN4 Return False Fix command:

This PVII command eliminates Netscape's showing the hourglass cursor when clicking a null link to fire a JavaScript.

- Browse to the Extensions folder on the CD.
- Open the Commands subfolder.
- Double-click the file named N4 Return False Fix.mxp to install the command.

3 Copy the projects folder:

- Browse to the projects folder on the CD.
- Copy the project_seven folder to a convenient location on your hard drive.

4 Define a new Dreamweaver site using the project_seven copy as your local root folder.

Note: Remember, any time you want to see how the completed site looks in either Dreamweaver or your browser, you can find all the files in the finished_project folder.

BUILDING THE CLOSED-STATE MENU LAYER

The closed-state menu is the default menu that appears when the page first loads. CSS is central to this design. Our style sheet project7.css is in the root of the working project site that you have defined and is already linked to your work page.

1 Open the file called index.htm in the root of your project_seven defined site.

2 Create a new layer on the page:

- Insert a layer on the page.
- Name the layer **menumain**.
- Assign these attributes:

     ID: **menumain**
     Tag: **DIV**
     L: **10px**
     T: **15px**
     W: **200px**
     H: (blank)
     Vis: **default**

Assign the attributes for the menumain layer.

- All other fields should be blank, with the exception of z-index.

- Leave z-index set to the value Dreamweaver inserted. We will change that later.

Note: z-index determines the stacking order of layers on the page. The higher the number, the closer to the top of the stack.

3 Create a table in the new layer:

- Click inside the menumain layer.

- Insert a table.

- Assign these attributes:

  Rows: **5**
  Cell Padding: **6**
  Columns: **1**
  Cell Spacing: **3**
  Width: **200 Pixels**
  Border: **0**

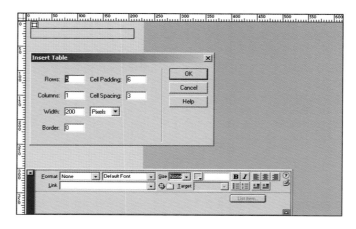

Insert a table into the menumain layer.

4 Apply the styles to the each row:

- Open the CSS Styles panel.

- Click inside the top row of your new table.

- Select the **<td>** tag on the Dreamweaver status bar on the bottom-left border of the editor window.

- Open the CSS panel.

- With the **<td>** tag still selected, choose the menu-header style from the list of available styles.

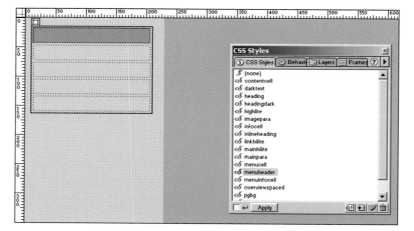

Make sure that the **<td>** tag is selected and then apply the menuheader style to each row in the table.

Tip: Another way of applying a style is to right-click (Ctrl+click) the tag name on the status bar and choose Set Class from the menu that pops up.

- If the check box to the left of the Apply button is checked (default), the style will automatically be applied. If the box isn't checked, click the button to apply the style.

- Apply the menuheader style to the remaining four table rows.

136

5 Insert the down arrows into each table row:

- Open the Assets panel (F11).
- Click inside the top table row.
- Select the down.gif image in the lower window of the panel.
- Click the Insert button at the panel's bottom-left corner.
- Repeat the preceding steps to insert the image into the remaining rows.

6 Insert the main text headings in each of the table rows to the right of the down arrow images:

- Insert a space to the right of the down arrow in the first row.
- Type the heading **Truffles Specialty Foods**.
- Continue inserting a space and typing the heading for each row, using these headings:

  Cheese and Dairy

  Meats and Such

  Grains and Legumes

  Grocery Items

7 Enter a null link for the text and the arrow image:

- Select the first heading by placing your cursor to the right of the last character in the text string.
- Drag your mouse left to select all the text and the down arrow image, as well.
- With the text and image still selected, enter a null link into the Link field of your property inspector by typing **javascript:;** (include the colon and the semicolon).

This selection technique later enables us to apply a single JavaScript event that encompasses both the text and the arrow image.

Repeat the preceding steps to apply a null link to the text headings and down arrows in the remaining rows.

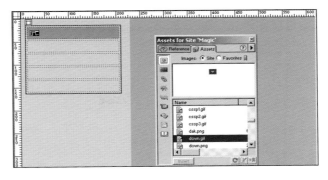

Use the Assets panel to select and insert a copy of down.gif in each table row.

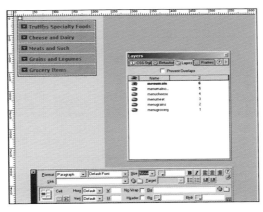

Type the five main headings into the table rows to the right of the arrow image.

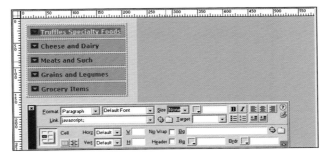

Use the property inspector Link field to enter a null link to enable application of JavaScript behaviors.

Note: If you see a border around the images, after you've applied the null link, select the image and use the property inspector to set its border to **0**. We've encountered this on some test systems.

CREATING THE SUBMENU LAYERS

The submenu layers contain the contextual menus related to each main heading and appear when the related heading is clicked.

1 Copy and paste to create a duplicate menumain layer:

Note: I used the Layers panel to make the layer invisible to help me see the icon.

- Choose View and make sure that the Invisible Elements option is selected.
- Turn on the Layers panel (F2) and highlight menumain.

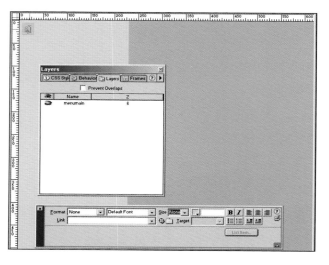

Choose View/Visual Aids/Invisible Elements to make sure that your invisible items are set to show. Click to the right of the yellow icon and then paste the layer copy.

- Copy the layer to your Clipboard.
- Click to the right of the yellow layer icon at the top-left corner of your window.
- Paste a copy of menumain on your page so that you have a duplicate that occupies the same position.
- Highlight the second instance of menumain on your Layers panel.
- Click the name twice to make it editable and change it to menumainopen.
- Click the z-number twice to make it editable and change the z-index of menumainopen to **5**.
- We renumbered the z-index of menumainopen because we're going to be stacking layers atop each other and menumain needs to be on top of all the others. The layer with the highest z-index is the top layer.

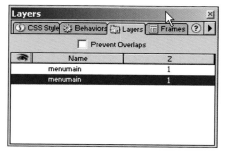

You now have two instances of menumain—the original and a copy.

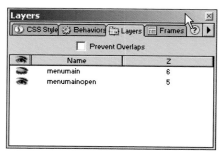

Duplicate the layer, change the name of the duplicate menumain layer to menumainopen, and then change its z-index to **5**.

138

2 Insert two new cells inside the table within the menumainopen layer:

- Because we're going to be editing the menumainopen layer, set menumain to invisible to get it out of our way (we'll make it visible again later).

- Right-click (Ctrl+click) inside the top row of the table inside the menumainopen layer.

- Select Table from the popup menu.

- Select Insert Rows or Columns from the Table fly-out menu.

- Insert two new rows and select the Below the Selection option.

Now that we have our two new rows, we need to style and populate them. The first row will contain the submenu links that pertain to the first heading, Truffles Specialty Foods.

3 Replace the down arrow image with the up arrow image:

- Select the down arrow image to the left of the Truffles Specialty Foods heading.

- Open the Assets panel and browse to the image called up.gif.

- Click the Insert button to insert the up arrow.

- Delete the down arrow.

4 Apply the styles to the two new rows:

- Insert your cursor in the first new row.

- Select the **<td>** tag on the Dreamweaver status bar.

- Open the CSS panel.

- Select the Style called menucell.

- If the check box to the left of the Apply button is checked (default), the style will automatically be applied. If it's not checked, click the button to apply the style.

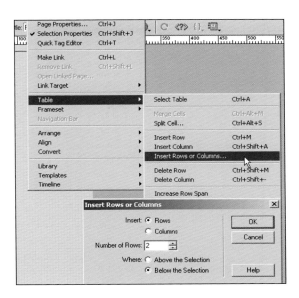

Insert two new table rows below the first main link in the menumainopen layer.

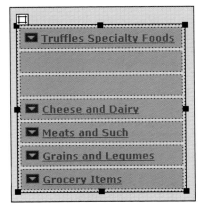

The table inside menumainopen should now look like this figure.

- Insert your cursor inside the second new row.

- Using the same procedure as for the first row, apply the style called menuinfocell.

- The second new row contains a little marketing information and so has a slightly different style.

5 Enter a hyperlink on the first row header and a marketing message in the second row:

- Place your cursor in the first new row.

- Open the Assets panel (F11) and insert the typebullet.gif image.

- Type **Hello this is link one** beside the bullet to create the first submenu text link.

- Select the text and the image together.

Use the Assets panel to quickly insert the typebullet.gif image into your document.

- Type **javascript:;** to enter a null link into the Link field of your property inspector.

Make sure to enter a null link to enable application of JavaScript behaviors.

Note: In this project, we're going to use a null link, but in your own project, you'll probably want to link to other pages.

- Place your cursor at the end of the line and insert a soft return by pressing Shift + Enter.

- Open the Assets panel (F11) and insert the typebullet.gif image.

- Type **This is Link Two** beside the bullet to create the second submenu text link.

- Insert a soft return by pressing Shift + Enter.

- Open the Assets panel (F11) and insert the typebullet.gif image.

- Type **And this is Link Three** beside the bullet to create the third submenu text link.

- Add null links (for this exercise) or links to content for your own project.

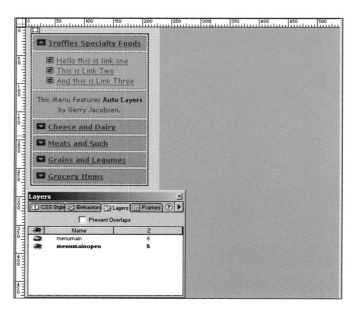

Add the submenu rows and the marketing message to menumainopen.

6 Place your cursor in the second new row:

- Type the marketing message **This Menu Features Auto Layers by Gerry Jacobsen**.

- Each of our five main menu headings (Truffles Specialty Foods, Cheese and Dairy, Meats and Such, Grains and Legumes, Grocery Items) requires a menu layer for its open (uncollapsed) state. Combined with the initial closed menu, we need six menu layers. So far we've created the first two menu layers—meunumain and menumainopen.

7 Use the same techniques employed to create the first two layers to construct the remaining layers—meunucheese, menumeat, menugrains, and menugrocery—remembering to replace the down arrow image with the up arrow image in all the headings of the submenu layers.

Create the remaining menu layers (from left to right): menumain, menumainopen, menucheese, menumeat, menugrains, and menugrocery.

8 Make sure that the layers are correctly positioned and have the correct settings:

- Open the property inspector.

- Make sure that the properties of each layer match those in the figure.

- Open the Layers panel.

- Make sure that the Layer IDs and z-index match those in the figure.

menumain	6
menumainopen	5
menucheese	4
menumeat	3
menugrains	2
menugrocery	1

Each menu layer is positioned at the same coordinates and is exactly the same width.

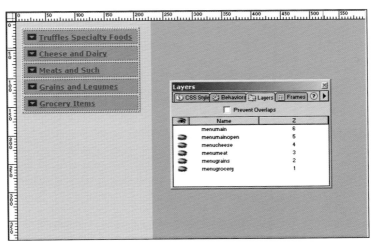

z-index determines the stacking order of the layers on your page.

APPLYING THE PVII AUTO LAYERS BEHAVIOR

The menu is powered by PVII's Auto Layers behavior, written by my partner, Gerry Jacobsen. It would take days to construct this menu without the help of Dreamweaver and PVII Auto Layers.

Our first step is to use an onLoad Auto Layers event on the body tag to initialize the menumain layer into Auto Layer's memory (otherwise, it won't hide when we open the other menus).

1 Apply PVII Auto Layers to the body tag to initialize the mainmenu layer into Auto Layer's memory.

- Select the **<body>** tag marker on the Dreamweaver status bar.
- Open the Behaviors panel (the title bar of the panel should now read Behaviors – <body> Actions).
- Click the + button to open the Behaviors menu and choose Studio VII/Auto Layers by PVII.
- When the dialog box opens, do absolutely nothing!
- Click OK.
- Make sure that the event is set to onLoad.

> **Note:** By doing absolutely nothing inside the Auto Layers dialog, except click OK, you are telling Auto Layers to place menumain into its memory.

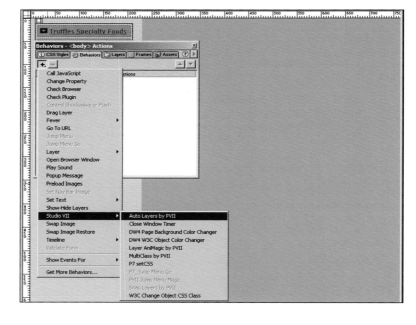

Select the **<body>** tag; and then choose Studio VII/Auto Layers by PVII from the Behaviors menu.

2 Check the null links:

Before we apply the behaviors to the hidden menus, let's do a little quality assurance check of our null links to make sure that both the text and the inline image (down.gif or typebullet.gif) for each link on each menu are wrapped together inside the **<a>** tags. We need this to be right because this will allow our users to click either the text or the image to activate a menu.

- Insert your cursor inside the text of a menu link.
- Select the **<a>** tag on the status bar.
- Choose View/Show Code and Design Views.
- Inspect the source code to make sure that the text and image are both inside the **<a>** tag pair.

Make sure that both the text link and the image are contained within the opening and closing anchor tags (**<a>** and **</a>**).

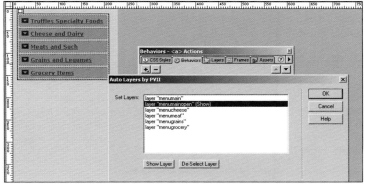

Select menumainopen to apply Auto Layers to make that layer visible while hiding all other menu layers.

3 Apply the PVII Auto Layers behavior to the hidden menus:

- Place your cursor inside the text link in the first row of the menumain layer, the link that reads Truffles Specialty Foods.
- Open the Behaviors panel and click the + button to open the Behaviors menu.
- Choose Studio VII/Auto Layers by PVII.
- In the Auto Layers dialog box, highlight layer menumainopen on the Main tab.
- Click the Show button.
- Click OK.

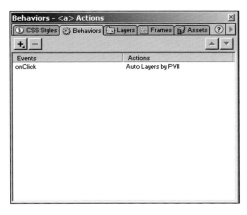

Make sure that onClick is the event that fires this behavior.

• Repeat Step 3 for all main links on all the menu layers so that each heading has an instance of PVII Auto Layers applied to it onClick. (Refer to this table for a complete matrix of how the behaviors are applied.)

Menu Layer	Main Link	Set this Layer to Show in the Auto Layers Behavior Window
Menumain	Truffles Specialty Foods	menumainopen
	Cheese and Dairy	menucheese
	Meats and Such	menumeat
	Grains and Legumes	menugrains
	Grocery Items	menugrocery
Menumainopen	Truffles Specialty Foods	menumain
	Cheese and Dairy	menucheese
	Meats and Such	menumeat
	Grains and Legumes	menugrains
	Grocery Items	menugrocery
Menucheese	Truffles Specialty Foods	menumainopen
	Cheese and Dairy	menumain
	Meats and Such	menumeat
	Grains and Legumes	menugrains
	Grocery Items	menugrocery
Menumeat	Truffles Specialty Foods	menumainopen
	Cheese and Dairy	menucheese
	Meats and Such	menumain
	Grains and Legumes	menugrains
	Grocery Items	menugrocery
Menugrains	Truffles Specialty Foods	menumainopen
	Cheese and Dairy	menucheese
	Meats and Such	menumeat
	Grains and Legumes	menumain
	Grocery Items	menugrocery
Menugrocery	Truffles Specialty Foods	menumainopen
	Cheese and Dairy	menucheese
	Meats and Such	menumeat
	Grains and Legumes	menugrains
	Grocery Items	menumain

Use this matrix in determining how to apply the behaviors to the menu layers.

Only the five main menu links in each layer have the PVII Auto Layers behavior applied. Remember, those five main links appear on all the layers, not just the menumain layer. The submenu links are simply hyperlinks to other pages.

The main links in the initial (menumain) menu layer open their respective submenus. The active links on the submenu layers open menumain. In other words, if menumeat is open, clicking the Meats and Such link shows menumain and hides all others. This technique gives the illusion of movement. Click Cheese and Dairy once, and its submenu seems to expand into view. Click again, and the submenu seems to collapse. What's really happening is that the first click makes the layer menucheese visible and hides all other layers. The second click makes menumain visible and hides all others (including, of course, menucheese!).

ADDING SOME CONTENT TO THE PAGE

Our menus are finished, but the page looks bare. Let's add some text to give it a finished look.

1 Clear the page:

- Hide all the layers and turn off Invisible Elements so that you can see the entire page.

2 Enter the content:

- Insert your cursor at the top of the page and type the heading **The Finished Menu**.

- Press Enter once to create a new paragraph.

- Type a sentence, but do not press Enter.

Change the first line of text from paragraph format to Heading1 format via the property inspector.

- With your cursor in the paragraph, select the **<p>** tag on the status bar and apply the mainpara CSS class to it.

- Press Enter and type in a few more paragraphs. They will retain the mainpara style automatically.

- Go back up to the heading and change the format on the property inspector from Paragraph to Heading1.

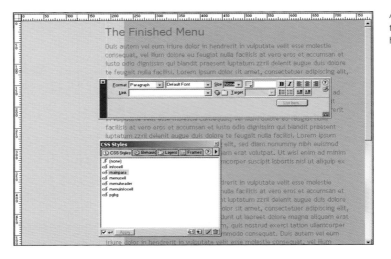

Apply the mainpara CSS class to the paragraph below the heading.

Note: Notice that the text does not seem to line up correctly and overlaps the gray part of the background image. This is simply a visual anomaly in Dreamweaver because of its rendering engine. The page will display correctly in your browser (even in Netscape 4!).

APPLYING THE NETSCAPE FIXES

The Netscape 4 Resize Fix keeps your page properly aligned when the browser window is resized. The NN4 Return False command eliminates the hourglass cursor when clicking the menu headers.

1 Insert the JavaScript code for the Netscape Resize Fix command:

- Open the Commands menu.
- Choose Add/Remove Netscape Resize Fix.

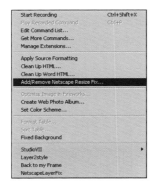

Find the Netscape Resize Fix on the Commands menu.

- Click the Add button.

> **Note:** If you have Dreamweaver configured (in user Preferences) to automatically insert the Netscape fix whenever you insert a layer, you can skip this step. If you are unsure, don't worry! If the fix is applied already, the Command window will show a Remove button instead of an Add button. Don't remove it!

2   Apply the N4 Return False Fix command:

- Choose Commands/Studio VII/Apply N4 Return False Fix.
- Click the Apply button.

Now you're finished. Make sure to set the menu main layter to visible so folks can see and use your nifty new layer.

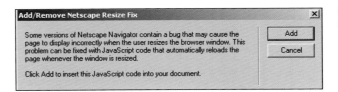

Click the Add button on the Netscape Resize Fix dialog.

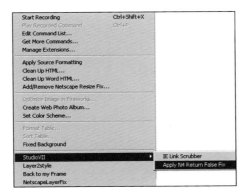

Find the Netscape Return False Fix on the Studio VII flyout of the Commands menu.

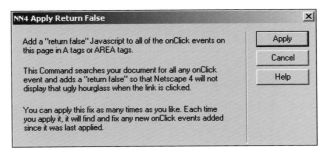

Click Apply in the Netscape Return False dialog to add the JavaScript.

Project 7 CSS

Use this page as a handy reference to the styles employed in the collapsible menu.

```
.menuheader { font-family: Verdana, Arial,
Helvetica, sans-serif; font-size: 12px; font-weight:
bold; color: #333333; border: 1px #333333 solid;
background-color: #999999}
```

```
.menucell { font-family: "Comic Sans MS",
"Trebuchet MS", Verdana, Arial, sans-serif;
font-size: 13px; font-weight: normal; color: #333333;
background-color: #9CBABD; border: 1px #333333
solid}
```

```
.menuinfocell { font-family: "Trebuchet MS",
Verdana, Arial, sans-serif; font-size: 12px;
font-weight: normal; color: #333333; background-
color: #CC9999; border: 1px #333333 solid }
```

```
.infocell a:link { font-family: Arial, Helvetica,
sans-serif; font-size: 12px; color: #CCCCCC}
```

```
h1 { font-family: Verdana, Arial, Helvetica,
sans-serif; font-size: 24px; font-weight: normal;
color: #666666}
```

```
h2 { font-family: Arial, Helvetica, sans-serif;
font-size: 12px; color: #FFCC00; font-weight: bold;
letter-spacing: 4px}
```

```
a:link { color: #333333; text-decoration: none}
```

```
a:visited { color: #333333; text-decoration: none}
```

```
a:hover { color: #CCCCCC; text-decoration: none}
```

```
a:active { color: #333333; text-decoration: none}
```

```
.pgbg { background-image:
url(images/bgliteteal.gif); background-color:
#9CBABD; background-repeat: repeat}
```

```
.mainpara { font-family: "Trebuchet MS", Arial,
sans-serif; font-size: 14px; color: #666666;
margin-top: 12px; margin-right: 36px;
margin-bottom: 12px; margin-left: 240px;
padding-top: 20px; padding-right: 20px;
padding-bottom: 20px; padding-left: 20px}
```

```
.menuheader a:link { color: #D6D3CE}
```

```
.menuheader a:visited { color: #D6D3CE}
```

```
.menuheader a:hover { color: #333333}
```

```
.menucell a:link { color: #333333}
```

```
.menucell a:visited { color: #333333}
```

```
.menucell a:hover { background-color: #333333;
color: #999999}
```

Our menu gets its look from the style sheets. Editing the styles numbers changes the look and feel of the menu instantly.

If you're not familiar with the awesome power of CSS, we suggest you visit the World Wide Web Consortium (W3C) at **http://www.w3.org**.

Notice that even though we have a Page Background style in the external project1.css file, we have a duplicate embedded in the head of the page as follows:

```
<style type="text/css">
<!--
.pgbg { background-image:
url(../images/bgliteteal.gif); background-color:
#9CBABD; background-repeat: repeat}
-->
</style>
```

Why? Because Netscape 4 cannot solve for the path of an image in a style sheet if the page and the style sheet are in different folders.

Note: You may notice that the code in this book sometimes wraps to the next line. That wrapping is caused by the narrowness of the column within this book. Dreamweaver does not restrict the length of the line; the code appears on one line.

MODIFICATIONS

The specific technique used to construct this menu by no means limits you to a single design. There are many approaches you can take. For example, you can create a menu comprised of a combination of text and images that furthers the illusion of animation. You can separate the menu headings and place each in its own layer with the submenus all hidden. Then you can use the PVII Layer AniMagic behavior to slide the headings up and down. As the headings slide, they create a space for the appropriate submenu, which can slide in from the left. Clicking another heading would cause the previous submenu to slide away while the headings glide into position to make room for the next submenu, which slides in from the left.

SIMULATING TREE-VIEW NAVIGATION

"I may not have gone where I intended

to go, but I think I have ended up

where I intended to be."

—DOUGLAS ADAMS

THE TREE-VIEW MENU

The tree-view menu system is designed to emulate the look and functionality of the tree-view navigation system found in many of today's operating systems. These tree-view objects are complicated and difficult to code and manage in an application API. There are also many "canned" tree-view scripts that use many complicated JavaScript routines to enable this type of menu on a Web site. Usually, these cannot be rendered in the Dreamweaver interface, which makes page design and layout difficult.

You are going to construct a visual representation of a tree-view menu system that you will be able to see and edit right in the Dreamweaver interface. You can easily assign new colors, link style properties, and add, delete, or change menu items and their page links just like you manage any other object in Dreamweaver. Because this menu system is vertical and each main menu item is usually closed, this menu style can easily accommodate many links—hundreds if you want.

Project 8

Simulating Tree-View Navigation

by Gerry Jacobsen

IT WORKS LIKE THIS

When users click on the plus (+) and minus (–) buttons of the finished tree-view menu, each menu level expands or contracts. The top of the menu also contains an Expand All and a Close All link to provide the user instant access to the entire menu or, when it gets too lengthy, a quick way to close all the menu items at once.

When the menu first opens, it is in the closed state. Only the main menu sections are showing. Each main menu section displays a plus sign on the left. When the user clicks on the plus sign, the detail section showing the menu choices for that section displays, pushing down all the stuff beneath it to make just the right amount of room. The plus sign also changes to a minus sign. When the user clicks the minus sign, that menu section closes up (collapses) back to its original state.

Each menu section is contained in a layer. Each layer contains a table that houses the images and actual menu names and links. When the user clicks on a plus or minus button, the appropriate layers are moved in just the right way to reveal or hide the menu section detail.

This menu can be used on any page; however, for ease of maintenance, the tree-view menu system is best deployed by placing it in a template or by placing it in the left frame of a frameset site so that you will only have one page to maintain.

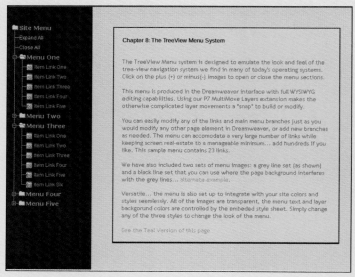

The finished tree-view menu.

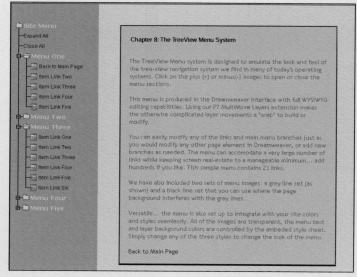

The alternate tree-view menu in teal.

PREPARING TO WORK

Preparing for a *Dreamweaver 4 Magic* project is routine. Install the requisite extensions, copy the project folder from the CD to your hard drive, and then fire up Dreamweaver and define a new site using your copied project folder as the local root folder.

1 Install the PVII MultiMove Layers behavior:

This Project VII behavior allows for setting multiple layer movements within one convenient, easy to manage interface. The capability to set both absolute and relative movements makes building and maintaining complicated layer movements much easier.

- Browse to the Extensions folder on the CD.
- Open the Behavior/Actions subfolder.
- Double-click the file called P7_MultiMove.mxp to install the behavior.

2 Install the NN4 Return False Fix command:

This Project VII command eliminates Netscape's showing the hourglass cursor when clicking a null link to fire a JavaScript.

- Browse to the Extensions folder on the CD.
- Open the Commands subfolder.
- Double-click the file called N4 Return False Fix.mxp to install the command.

3 Install the Scrubber command:

This Project VII command gets rid of those pesky little dotted lines that surround links in IE.

- Browse to the Extensions folder on the CD.
- Open the Commands subfolder.
- Double-click the file called Scrubber.mxp to install the command.

4 Install the Layer2Style command:

This extension by Jaro von Flocken corrects the inability to recognize more than one nested layer in Netscape 4x browsers. Applying this extension moves all the nested layer style tags from the body to the head of the document.

- Browse to the Extensions folder on the CD.
- Open the Commands subfolder.
- Double-click the file called Layer2style.mxp to install the command.

5 Install the PVII NowhereLink command:

This Project VII command allows you to easily create a JavaScript text link.

- Browse to the Extensions folder on the CD.
- Open the Objects subfolder.
- Double-click the file called NowhereLink.mxp to install the command.

6 Copy the projects folder

- Browse to the projects folder on the CD.
- Copy the project_eight folder to a convenient location on your hard drive.

7 Define a new Dreamweaver site using the project_eight copy as your local root folder.

Note: Remember, if you want to see how the completed site looks in either Dreamweaver or your browser, you can find all the files in the finished_project folder.

CREATING THE TOP MENU LAYER

In this section, you begin building the menu by creating the top navigation section of the menu. This includes the menu heading name and the Expand All and Collapse All links. These are contained in a separate layer that sits on top of the actual tree-view menu.

In this section and several following sections, we will be assembling the layers and sub-layers for the menu. Because it is difficult to work with layers and tables in certain color combinations, dark gray (#333333) being one of them, we always start out by assigning the new layer to our predefined temporary menulayer style before doing anything else. This temporary style sets the background color of the layer to light gray (#CCCCCC), which makes it much easier to work with. When we finish assembling the menu, we will change menulayer background color style to black so that all the layers will match the page background.

1 Open Dreamweaver and your new project_eight site:

In the root, you'll find two HTML files: index.htm and test_linkpage.htm, and three folders: assets, finished_project, and AlternateImageSets.

- In the site window, open the index.htm file.

   Notice that the page already has a title, and the background image has been defined in an internal style sheet. We have also included some predefined styles that will control the layers and menu item styles. Refer to the Styles listing for a complete reference on how these work.

2 Open the Layers panel:

We will be working with the Layers panel quite a bit, so this is the time to make sure that your Layers panel is open.

- Choose Window/Layers from the menu or press F2 to open the Layers panel.

- Make sure that the Layers tab is selected.

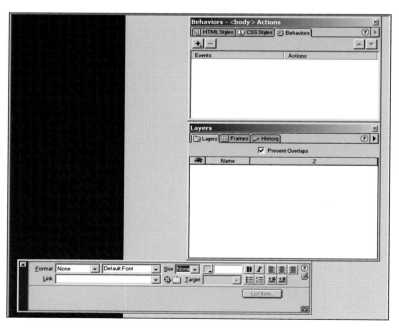

You may want to arrange the starting page and panel layout this way.

3 Open the Behaviors panel:

We will also be working with the Behaviors panel.

- Choose Window/Behaviors or press Shift+F3 to open the Behaviors panel.
- Make sure that the Behaviors tab is selected.

4 Make sure that the property inspector is open:

- Choose Windows/Properties or press Ctrl+F3 if you need to open the property inspector.

Your workspace should look similar to the one pictured in the figure next to Step 1.

Throughout this section we will be placing various layers on the page. The table summarizes all the layers, their style settings, and their purpose. Use this table as a reference guide when you add the settings for each layer:

Refer to this table as you add the settings for each layer.

Layer	Left	Top	Width	Height	z-index	Visibility	Notes
menutop	10	40	180	72	1	Default	The top part of the menu that contains the Expand All and Collapse All links.
menu1	10	112	180	144	2	Default	This layer contains Menu One items.
menu1open	0	0	36	18	2	Hidden	Nested layer containing the open images and close links for Menu One.
menu2	10	136	180	96	3	Default	This layer contains Menu Two items.
menu2open	0	0	36	18	3	Hidden	Nested layer containing the open images and close links for Menu Two.
menu3	10	160	180	168	4	Default	This layer contains Menu Three items.
menu3open	0	0	36	18	4	Hidden	Nested layer containing the open images and close links for Menu Three.
menu4	10	184	180	120	5	Default	This layer contains Menu Four items.
menu4open	0	0	36	18	5	Hidden	Nested layer containing the open images and close links for Menu Four.
menu5	10	208	180	144	6	Default	This layer contains Menu Five items.
menu5open	0	0	36	18	6	Hidden	Nested layer containing the open images and close links for Menu Five.
menucover	10	232	180	144	7	Default	The masking layer to cover the layer last menu when it is in closed position.

5 Insert the new top menu layer:

- Choose Insert/Layer from the menu.

- In the Layers panel, select the newly created layer (it should be named Layer1 at this point).

- Right-click (Ctrl+click) the **<div>** tag at the bottom left of the main window, and a listing of all the valid styles will appear in the Set Class submenu.

- Select the menulayers style to give the layer a gray background color.

Note: By default, the layer is transparent and, for our purposes, will be difficult to work with. That's why we immediately apply our predefined style to the layer.

Note: Setting the style using a predefined style, rather than using the Styles panel, helps ensure that you don't accidentally apply the style to another element on the page.

- Using the property inspector, set the following properties:

  Layer ID: **menutop**
  Left: **10**
  Top: **40**
  Width: **180**
  Height: **72**
  Z-Index: **1**
  Visibility: **default**

Enter the properties for menutop.

6 Insert the table:

- Click inside the new menutop layer.

- Choose Insert/Table.

- Set the following properties:

  Rows: **3**
  Columns: **2**
  Cell Padding: **0**
  Cell Spacing: **0**
  Width: **100%**

- Make sure that you have Cell Padding and Cell Spacing both set to 0 to ensure proper image alignment.

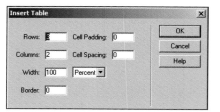

Insert the table, using these settings.

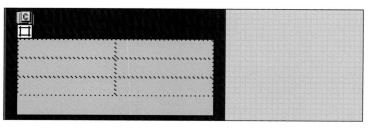

The table you created appears in the page.

7 Insert the image and text link in the first row of the table:

We're going to use the first column of this table to house the menu images and the second column to contain the menu name and links. We will apply our predefined style for the menu heading.

- Click inside the first column of the first row of the table.
- Choose Insert/Image from the menu.
- Navigate to the assets/images folder.
- Select the image named menu_folder_closedtop.gif and click Select.
- Click inside the second column of the first row of the table.
- Type **Site Menu** for the title of our menu.
- Make sure that your cursor is still inside the second column of the first row of the table and select the rightmost **<td>** tag marker on the Dreamweaver status bar (at the bottom left of the main window).
- Right-click (Ctrl+click) the tag and select Set Class-menuheading.

8 Insert the image and text link in the second row of the table:

- Click inside the first column of the second row of the table to set the insertion point.
- Choose Insert/Image from the menu and select the menu_tee.gif image.
- Click inside the second column and choose Insert/Nowhere Link from the menu.
- Enter **Expand All** as the link text and click OK.
- Select the rightmost **<td>** tag marker at the bottom of the main window (not the **<a>** tag).
- Right-click (Ctrl+click) the tag and select Set Class-menuitem.

Note: Don't worry about the images and text lining up just yet—we'll force the browser to do that later.

Enter the text for the first row in the table.

The cells should now be styled just like this.

9 Insert the image and text link in the third row of the table:

- Click inside the first column of the third row of the table to set the insertion point.
- Choose Insert/Image from the menu and select the menu_tee.gif image.
- Click inside the second column and choose Insert/Nowhere Link from the menu.
- Enter **Close All** as the link text and click OK.
- Select the rightmost **<td>** tag marker at the bottom of the main window (not the **<a>** tag).
- Right-click (Ctrl+click) the tag and select Set Class-menuitem.

10 Align the images and text:

> **Note:** To force the alignment of the images and text we will change the width property of the table. It's easier to do this after we have populated all the table cells.

- Click anywhere inside the table and select the **<table>** tag at the bottom left of the main window.
- In the property inspector, highlight the value in the width box and press the Delete button.
- Click anywhere on the page to see the change.
- Make absolutely sure that the width box is left blank by deleting the 100% value we entered. This is essential to allow the images to line up correctly in all browsers. That's it for the menutop layer.

Enter the text for the third row in the table.

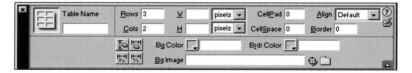

Delete the width setting of the table to force the alignment of the images and text.

Your finished menutop layer should look like this.

CREATING THE FIRST MENU SECTION LAYER

You will now build the first menu section. It includes the section title, which will be visible all the time, and all the detail page links for this section. After this first section is built, you will save time by doing a copy and paste to create the other sections.

1 Insert the new layer:

To keep things nicely arranged on the page, it is important to set your insertion point before creating a new layer.

- Click to the right of the yellow C icon at the top left of the window.
- Choose Insert/Layer.
- Right-click (Ctrl+click) the **<div>** at the bottom left of the window and select the CSS Style -menulayers.
- Using the property inspector, set the following properties:

  Layer ID: **menu1**
  Left: **10**
  Top: **112**
  Width: **180**
  Height: **144**
  Z-Index: **2**
  Visibility: **default**

Note: Maintaining a consistent insertion point at the top of the screen prevents accidental nesting of the layers when inserting them and keeps the layers visually aligned in the workspace.

Note: If you don't see the C icon, choose View/Visual Aids to turn on invisible elements.

Enter the properties for the new layer.

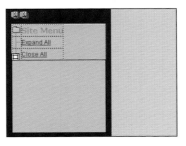

The newly created menu1 layer should look like this.

2 Insert the table:

- Click inside the new menu1 layer.
- Choose Insert/Table.
- Enter the following properties:

  Rows: **2**
  Cols: **4**
  Width: **100%**
  Cell Padding: **0**
  Cell Spacing: **0**

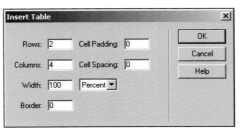

Insert a new table.

3   Insert the images in the first row:

> **Note:** Tables collapse while you're working on them if their cells are empty. To prevent this from happening, we take a round-about route to populating all the cells.

- Click inside the first column of the first row of the table.
- Choose Insert/Image.
- Select the menu_tee_plusmid.gif image.
- In the property inspector, type **javascript:;** in the Link box (include the colon and semicolon to create a null link).

> **Note:** A null link is a clickable link that doesn't load a page. We can apply events to a null link later.

- Click inside the second column.
- Choose Insert/Image.
- Select the menu_folder_closed.gif image.

  We will not finish this row right now. Instead we will start with the second row.

4   Insert the images and links in the second row:

- Click inside the first column of the second row of the table.
- Choose Insert/Image from the menu.
- Select the menu_bar.gif image.
- Click inside the second column.
- Choose Insert/Image.
- Select the menu_tee.gif image.
- Click inside the third column.
- Choose Insert/Image.
- Select the menu_link_default.gif image.

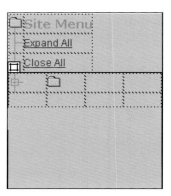

Insert images in the first and second columns in the first row in the table.

> **Note:** If you already have existing pages that you want to link to, you can enter the real name of the link and use the property inspector to browse to the actual html page to which you want to link. For the purpose of this example, we have assumed that you do not have any actual pages at this point and have supplied a dummy test page that we can link to instead. In a real-world implementation, these links would be to your actual pages.

- Click inside the fourth column, where we will enter our actual page links.

- Type **Item Link One** for the menu text.

- Select the text you just entered.

- Using the property inspector, click the Browse for File folder icon to browse to the actual page you want to link to or browse to our example page test_linkpage.htm.

- With the cursor still in this cell, right-click (Ctrl+click) the **<td>** on the bottom left of the window and select Set Class/menuitem.

  We're almost finished. Now we can go back to the first row, merge the two empty cells into one, and enter the menu name.

Populate the second row with appropriate images and a link.

5 Finish the first row:

- Click inside the third column of the first row.

- Hold down the Shift key and click inside the fourth column, selecting both cells by clicking twice in the fourth column, if necessary.

- Choose Modify/Table/Merge Cells to merge the two cells into one.

- Click inside this cell and type the menu name **Menu One**.

- With the cursor still in this cell, right-click (Ctrl+click) the **<td>** on the bottom left of the window and select Set Class/menuheading.

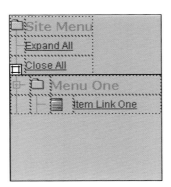

Set up the images and links for the first and second rows in the table.

6 Copy and paste the second row to create the rest of the menu items:

We are going to duplicate the work we just did to create the rest of the page links for this menu section.

Note: For our example, we add four more rows, but you can add as many as you want.

- Click inside one of the cells in the second row.
- Click on the **<tr>** tag on the bottom left of the main window so that the entire table row is selected.
- Hold down the Ctrl key and press C (Ctrl+C) to copy the table row.
- Click inside the fourth (last) column of this table row, making sure that your cursor is on the empty space after the link name.
- Hold down the Ctrl key and press V (Ctrl+V) to paste the row.

  A new table row is created, and it is an exact copy of the previous row.

- Click inside the last row you just created.
- Make sure that the cursor is on the empty space.
- Paste (Ctrl+V) the next table row.
- Repeat this copying and pasting process two more times to create the fourth and fifth rows so that your table looks like the one in the figure.

Note: It is crucial that the insertion point is to the right of the text link, not simply the last column, and that you use Ctrl+V and Ctrl+C (not Copy and Paste from the menu).

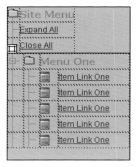

Paste four more rows into the table.

162

7 Change the links which are identical at this point, to the correct names:

- Click on the first row you copied (the second Item Link One).

- Change the text to **Item Link Two**.

- Browse to the file for your actual link or, if you're using our example, leave the test link that is already supplied.

- Repeat this for the rest of the links, naming them **Item Link Three**, **Item Link Four**, and **Item Link Five**.

8 Fix the last link:

- Click on the second image in the last row.

- Using the property inspector, click the Browse for File folder.

- Select the menu_bottom.gif image.

- Click the third image in the last row to change the third image to signify that this link (hypothetically) is an external link.

- Using the property inspector, click the Browse for File folder.

- Select the menu_link_external.gif image.

9 Align the images:

- Click anywhere inside the table.

- Select the **<table>** tag at the bottom left of the main window.

- In the property inspector, highlight the value in the Width box and press the Delete key.

Note: You can use your actual names and links or use our example names.

Note: To signify that this is the last item in this menu, we change the second image.

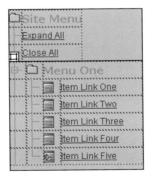

Make sure that your menu1 table has the last link image revised.

Note: Make absolutely sure that the Width box is left blank by deleting the pre-entered 100%. This is essential for allowing the images to line up correctly in all browsers.

- Click anywhere on the page to see the change.
- Save this page.

Believe it or not, the hard part is just about over. We will use copy and paste techniques to create the rest of the menu sections. But first, we are going to add the images and event triggers for the closing functionality of this menu section.

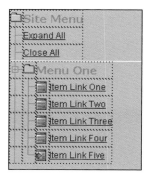

Your finished menu1 table should look like this.

10 Insert the nested trigger layer:

- Click inside the menu1 layer, making sure that your cursor is in the blank space to the right of the table and not in the table.
- Choose Insert/Layer.
- Right-click (Ctrl+click) the **<div>** at the bottom left of the window and select the CSS Style menu-layers.

USING A NESTED LAYER

So far, all we have in the menu is a plus image and the closed folder image. When a user clicks on the plus image, the menu expands to show all the menu items. However, unless we do something, we'll still have the plus image showing. We are going to create *a nested layer*—that is, a little layer housed inside the menu1 layer. This new nested layer will contain the minus and open folder images. Later, when we apply the JavaScript events, we will show this layer every time the plus image is clicked so that as the menu expands, the images also change accordingly. We are nesting this layer so that it will move in relation to its parent layer. In other words, we won't have to worry about positioning it when we move the menu layer around because a nested layer will move with its parent.

- Using the property inspector, enter the following properties:

    Layer ID: **menu1open**
    Left: **0**
    Top: **0**
    Width: **36**
    Height: **24**
    Z-Index: **2**
    Visibility: **hidden**

Enter the properties for the menu1open nested layer.

- Check that you have set the Visibility drop-down selection to hidden so that the layer is not visible when the page first loads.

  The nested layer, menu1open, is indented from and beneath its parent layer menu1. Also notice the closed eye icon to the left of the layer name. This indicates that the visibility is set to hidden. After we're finished editing this layer, it will become invisible. To view it for editing, select the layer in the Layers panel.

11 Insert the images into the nested layer:

- Make sure that the menu1open layer is selected by clicking on it in the Layers panel.
- Click inside the menu1open layer and choose Insert/Image.
- Browse to and select the menu_tee-minus.gif image.
- In the property inspector, type **javascript:;** into the Link box (don't forget to include the colon and semicolon).
- Click inside the layer to the right of the image, and choose Insert/Image.
- Browse to and select the menu_folder_open.gif image.

12 Save and preview (F12) this page.

- Notice the outline around the plus sign when you click on it. We'll remove that later with the Scrubber.
- Check the links to make sure that each one works.

  It's better to fix anything now because we are going to use this entire menu section as a template for creating the rest of the menu.

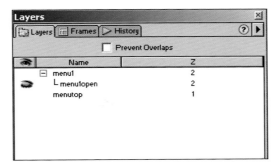

The Layers panel shows menu1 and its nested menu1open layer.

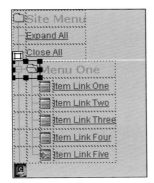

Your finished menu1open nested layer should look like this.

Note: You cannot see the nested layer yet. We'll apply some behaviors later to make it visible. The menu is expanded even though the closed image is showing, but it's a perfect time to make sure that everything lines up correctly and our actual page links are working.

USING AN EXISTING LAYER AS A TEMPLATE FOR A NEW ONE

Now that we have a fully formatted menu section, we can use this to serve as the template for the remaining sections. Each new menu section will be placed on top of the preceding menu section, with its top position set at 24 pixels more than the previous one to allow only the menu heading to show through. The process is to simply copy and paste this layer, rename it, position it, and change the link item names and page links.

1   Copy and paste the menu section layer:

- In the Layers panel, select the layer to copy, menu1 and copy (Ctrl+C) the layer.

- Click to the right of the last yellow C icon at the top of the page and paste (Ctrl+V) the copy to the page.

- Take a look at the Layers panel, and you will see the copied layer listed at the top with the same name as the source, menu1.

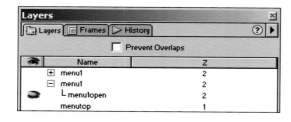

The Layers panel shows that the layer has been copied and pasted.

2   Redefine the new layer, along with its nested layer:

- Using the property inspector, enter the following properties:

  Layer ID: **menu2**
  Left: **10**
  Top: **136**
  Width: **180**
  Height: **96**
  Z-Index: **3**
  Visibility: **default**

Enter the properties for the menu2 layer.

Next you modify the nested layer that was also copied automatically.

- In the Layers panel, click the plus sign next to the layer you just copied to show the nested layer that was also copied.

- Use the property inspector to change only the name and the z-index:

  Layer ID: **menu2open**

  Z-Index: **3**

Enter the properties for the menu2open nested layer.

3 Modify the menu names:

Now we'll simply change the menu section name, link names, and if necessary, the page links contained in this menu section.

- Click inside the third cell of the first row.
- Change the menu section name to **Menu Two**.

4 Remove unwanted link rows:

- Click inside any cell of the last row.
- Click on the **<tr>** tag at the bottom left of the main window to select the entire row.
- Press the Delete key to delete this row.
- Repeat this procedure to remove the fourth row.

Note: For this example, we will need only three link items, so we remove the last two rows of the table.

Note: The layer shrunk to fit the height of the revised table because we set the height of this layer to 96 pixels (equal to one menu section name and three link items; each row is 24-pixels high, so 4×24=96). It will shrink to 96 pixels in height.

5 Change the menu bottom image:

- Click on the second image in the last row.
- Using the property inspector, click the Browse for File folder.
- Select the menu_bottom.gif image.

Note: For this example, we are not going to change the default link names and page links. If you were building an actual menu, you would change the names and page links now using the methods described previously.

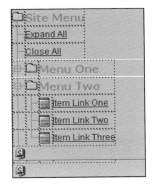

Your finished menu2 layer should look like this.

Adding Extra Page Links to a Menu

The Menu Three section contains six page links. We will cover the process of adding extra page links in this menu. First, we create the menu3 layer by using the same copy and paste technique we used for menu2. Then we change the formatting of the new layer.

1   Copy and paste using the menu1 layer as the source:

   • Because menu1 is still in the Clipboard, click to the right of the last yellow C icon at the top of the page.

   • Paste (Ctrl+V) the menu1 layer.

   In the Layers panel, the new layer will show directly above the source layer (menu1) with the same layer name.

2   Redefine the new layer, along with its nested layer:

   • Using the property inspector, enter the following settings:

   Layer ID: **menu3**
   Left: **10**
   Top: **160**
   Width: **180**
   Height: **168**
   Z-Index: **4**
   Visibility: **default**

   • Select the copied nested layer, still named menu1open, in the Layers panel.

   • Using the property inspector, enter the following settings for the nested layer:

   Layer ID: **menu3open**
   Z-Index: **4**

3   Modify the menu names:

   Now we'll simply change the menu section name, link names, and if necessary, the page links contained in this menu section.

   • Click inside the third cell of the first row.

   • Change the menu section name to **Menu Three**.

Enter the properties for menu3 layer.

Note: The height of this layer is set to accommodate one extra row.

4 Add new menu links:

- Using the copy technique described previously, click inside any cell of the last row of the table.
- Click on the **<tr>** tag on the bottom left of the main window.
- Press Ctrl+C to copy the row.
- Click inside the fourth (rightmost) cell of the last row and press Ctrl+V to paste the row.
- Change the item link name of the new row to **Item Link Six**.

  We now have two lines with the menu_bottom.gif image, so we'll need to correct this.
- Click on the image in the second column in the fifth row.
- Use the property inspector to browse to and select the menu_tee.gif image.

Note: You can also change the default or external image at this time to suit your needs.

Okay, we're done with the third menu section (at last!). The finished third menu section should look like the figure.

Note: We add one new row to the table to house the sixth menu item.

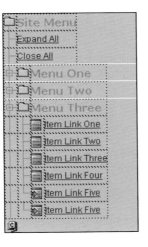

Copy the last row in the menu3 layer.

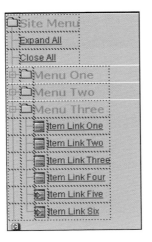

Your finished menu3 section layer should look like this.

4   Check the Layers panel to make sure it looks exactly
    like the figure.

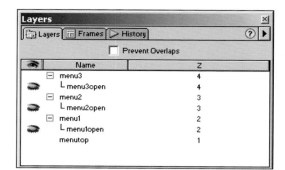

The Layers panel should
look like this when menu3
is completed.

CREATING ANOTHER MENU SECTION

Copying and pasting is a quick way to put together a menu. However, it can't be done
thoughtlessly, or you'll spend hours looking for a tiny error. Use the same method we
used for creating menu section three to create the fourth menu section.

1   Copy and paste the menu1 section.

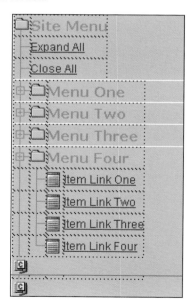

Your finished Menu Four section
should look like this.

Enter the properties for Menu
Four section.

170

2   Set the new menu layer and nested layer properties, referring to the table:

    • Delete the last link row using the same technique we used before, so that that there are only four items in this menu.

    • Change the second image in the last row to menu_bottom.gif.

    • Change the actual link names and page links if needed.

    • Change the menu section title to **Menu Four**.

Layer	Left	Top	Width	Height	z-index
menu4	10	184	180	120	5
menu4open	0	0	36	18	5

Refer to this table for the properties of the Menu Four section.

Note: Remember to set the nested layer name to menu4open and the z-index to 5, as well.

SETTING UP THE LAST SECTION IN A MENU

By now you've learned that not all menu sections are created equal. Because Menu Five is our last menu section, we will want to change the images in the first column to reflect the end of the menu, that is, we don't want to show any continuation lines in this column. Another change that we'll need to make is to the remaining rows. We will replace the bar images in those rows with a blank image (a placeholder).

1   Copy and paste the menu1 section.

Enter the properties for Menu Five section.

2   Set the new menu layer and nested layer properties, referring to the table.

Layer	Left	Top	Width	Height	z-index
menu5	10	208	180	144	6
menu5open	0	0	36	18	6

Refer to this chart for the properties for the Menu Five section.

Note: Remember to set the nested layer name to menu5open and the z-index to 6, as well.

In this example, Menu Five Section contains five link items, so we don't need to add or delete any.

Menu Five section before modifying images.

3   Modify the tee image in the first column.

•   Click on the image in the first column in the first row of Menu Five.

•   Use the property inspector to browse and select the menu_tee_plusbot.gif image.

4   Replace the menu_bar.gif images in each of the remaining rows of this menu section with shim.gif, a blank image that acts as a placeholder:

•   Click on the menu_bar.gif image in the first column in the second row of Menu Five.

•   Use the property inspector to browse to and select the shim.gif image, and then enter these properties:

    Width: **18**
    Height: **24**

Enter the properties for shim.gif.

5   Repeat this procedure for each of the remaining rows in Menu Five.

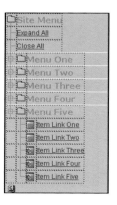

Your finished Menu Five section should look like this.

6 Change the actual link names and page links as needed.

7 Change the link icon to the external link as needed.

8 Change the menu section title to Menu Five.

9 In the nested layer menu5open, select the minus image and change it to menu_tee_minusbot.gif to reflect that it's the last menu in the hierarchy.

10 Review and double-check your work.

Now is a good time to check that all the layers are set up properly. Your Layers panel should look just like the figure. Double-check to make sure that your layer names and z-indexes are exactly like our example. Any duplicate layer names will cause script errors when you apply the movements to the menu.

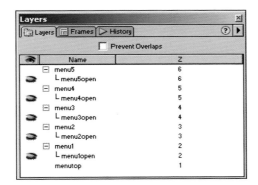

The Layers panel should look like this when all five menu sections are completed.

11 Save and preview (F12) this page.

Notice that all the menu sections are covered except for the last section; but you'll fix that next.

ADDING A MENU COVER

All the menu sections are automatically covered by the menu section above it except for the last section. You will now add the layer that covers the last menu section so that the detail is not visible when the menu first displays.

1 Insert a new layer:

- Set your insertion point at the top of the screen just to the right of the yellow C icons.
- Choose Insert/Layer.
- Right-click (Ctrl+click) the **<div>** tag in the status bar at the bottom left of the main window.
- Select the CSS Style-menulayers.

- Using the property inspector, enter the following properties:

  Layer ID: **menucover**
  Left: **10**
  Top: **232**
  Width: **180**
  Height: **144**
  Z-Index: **7**
  Visibility: **default**

2   Insert the shim.gif:

Because this cover layer has no real content, we will insert a transparent image to fill the space.

- Click inside the menucover layer.
- Choose Insert/Image.
- Select shim.gif.
- Using the property inspector, enter these properties:

  Width: **180**
  Height: **144**

We're done! The menu is now completely built (although is doesn't move yet!)

3   Save and preview (F12) this page to make sure that your layout looks exactly like the finished example.

Enter the properties for menucover.

Note: The height should always be enough to cover the last menu section, although you can set the height larger for a safety margin.

Note: Using a transparent image to fill the space ensures that Netscape 4 will render the cover layer correctly.

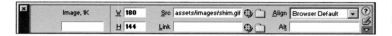

Enter the properties for the menucover shim.gif image.

Compare your completed tree-view menu system with this one.

4   Check your Layers panel to make sure that it looks
    exactly like the finished example.

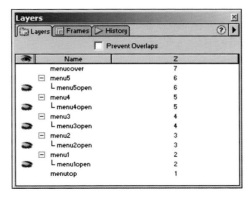

Compare the Layers palette
for your completed tree-view
menu system with this.

APPLYING THE SHOW/HIDE LAYERS BEHAVIORS

Now you will start to apply the JavaScripts that make the menu function. Let's start
with the little plus images. When the user clicks on the plus image, you want the
nested layer to become visible. That is the one that contains the minus and open folder
images. If the user clicks on the minus image, then you want the nested layer to hide
again, making only the plus image in the parent layer visible. You will apply the
Show/Hide layers behavior on each of the plus and minus links.

1   Set the Show Events selection:

    Before diving right in, make sure that the Behaviors
    panel is set up to list the correct events.

    • Open the Behaviors panel (Shift+F3).

    • Click the + button and select Show Events For.

    • Make sure that the 4.0 and Later Browsers option
      is checked.

2   Add the Show nested layer behavior on the plus
    image in menu1:

    • Click on the plus image in the first column of the
      Menu1 section.

    • Click the + button on the Behaviors panel and
      select Show-Hide Layers.

- Select the nested layer for this menu:

  layer "menu1open" in layer "menu1"

- Click the Show button

- Click OK.

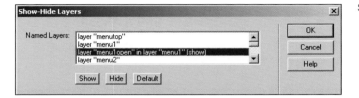

Show the nested menu1open layer.

3 Change the event handler to (onClick):

The default event for this behavior will probably be onMouseDown. Change this to (onClick).

- In the Behaviors panel, click on the down arrow in the Events column.

- From the events listing, select the (onClick) event.

- The events listed in parentheses will be applied the **<a>** tag. The Behaviors panel should look like the example in the figure.

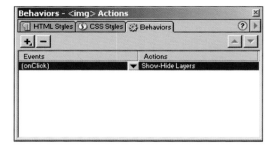

The (onClick) Show behavior applied to the menu1open layer.

4 Repeat Steps 2 and 3 to apply the Show behavior to each of the four remaining menu sections.

Be sure that in each section, you select the appropriate nested layer for that section. For example, if you are working with the plus image in menu3, you would select the layer menu3open in layer menu3 to apply the Show behavior.

5 Add the Hide nested layer behavior on the minus image for all five nested layers.

- Click on menu1open layer in the Layers panel to select the first nested layer.

- Click on the minus image in this layer.

- Click the + button on the Behaviors panel and select Show-Hide Layers.

176

- Select the nested layer for this menu:

  layer "menu1open" in layer "menu1"

- Click the Hide button and then click OK.

The onClick Hide behavior applied to the menu1open layer.

6   Change the event for the Hide nested behavior on menu1.

The default event for this behavior will probably be onMouseDown. Change this to (onClick).

- In the Behaviors panel, click on the down arrow in the Events column.

- From the events listing, select the (onClick) event.

7   Repeat for the nested layers in the remaining menu sections:

Repeat this process for each of the four remaining menu sections. Make sure that in each section you select the appropriate nested layer for that section. For example, if you are working with the minus sign in the Menu Three section, you would select the layer menu3open in layer menu3 to apply the Hide behavior.

8   Test the behaviors:

- Save and then preview (F12) this page.

- Check each plus (+) and minus (–) link to make sure that it is working correctly.

- If any of the clicks are not working correctly, go back and review the process step-by-step, and make sure that each of the events is set to (onClick). It's easy to forget to change the event or select the wrong layer when applying the behaviors.

Note: When you click on the plus image, the minus image and open folder should appear. When you click on the minus image, the plus image and the closed folder should appear. We haven't applied the behaviors to move the layers yet, but we will.

APPLYING MENU MOVEMENTS

Now that we have the proper images showing when the user clicks on the plus or minus image, it's time to apply the movements to go along with it. When a user clicks on the plus image, the detail portion of that menu section should come into view. We will "mimic" this behavior by actually sliding all the menu sections after that menu downward so that the menu detail will be exposed. Conversely, when a user clicks on the minus sign, we will slide all the menus beneath it upward so that the detail of the clicked menu is now covered by the other layers.

The whole trick to this "dance" is to know how much to move each layer. Keeping track of each layer position and whether its menu is open or closed can be complicated. Fortunately, our MultiMove Layers extension comes to the rescue! We included a Relative Movement feature in the extension that moves the layer(s) a certain number of pixels from its current position(s). That's why this method is relative targeting. You don't need to know the current position of the layer. Instead, you simply set the number of pixels to move. The MultiMove JavaScript code takes care of the necessary positioning calculations.

So, if you know the height of a menu layer, you can move all the other menu layers by that amount from their current position, no matter where they are. For example, if the user clicks on the plus sign of Menu Five (the last menu section), all you need to do is move the menu layer(s) that covers it (the menucover layer) down by just the right amount of pixels to expose the Menu Five detail. To close

the Menu Five, you just move the menucover layer back up to cover the detail of Menu Five. The whole system boils down to knowing how much to move each layer.

We have designed this menu system with images that are all the same height. This is really important. Each line is 24 pixels high. We know this because we used 18px × 24px images in each of the first cells of every table row. The first row of each table contains the title for that menu, so it is always showing. The rest of the menu section contains the detail rows, each being 24 pixels high, that you will want to reveal or hide. Menu Five has six rows, one header row, and five detail rows. When you want to reveal the detail for Menu Five, you simply move the menucover down 120 pixels. Why 120 pixels? Each row is 24 pixels high, and you have five rows to reveal. Multiply 5 × 24, and you get 120 pixels. We'll refer to this number as the *Detail Height* of each menu.

When working with this type of technique, it is always helpful to chart your movements on a table so that you can easily keep track of everything and use it as a reference when applying the movement behaviors. We've set up a table, using the layer dimensions and settings for this example. If your actual menu contains a different number of detail rows in the menu sections, remember to recalculate the values based on the layer dimensions in your actual menu. For all the movement behaviors in this project, you will use the values in the chart to enter the pixel movement amounts.

Layer	Left	Top	Width	Height	Row Height	Number of Detail Rows	Detail Height
menu1	10	112	180	144	24px	5	120
menu2	10	136	180	96	24px	3	72
menu3	10	160	180	168	24px	6	144
menu4	10	184	180	120	24px	4	96
menu5	10	208	180	144	24px	5	120

Use this table to determine the Layer Movement behaviors.

1 Apply the movements to the plus image on Menu Five:

We'll start with Menu Five because it is the easiest to apply. The menucover layer is the layer that has to be moved when the user clicks on the plus or minus signs.

• Click on the plus image in the Menu Five section.

• Click the + button on the Behaviors panel and select the Studio VII/MultiMove Layers by PVII behavior.

The first layer on the page will be displayed by default—we will have to change that.

• Select the menucover layer (the last layer listed) in the Select Layer drop-down selection list.

• Set Targeting to Relative.

We are going to use the Relative movement method for all the movements to the plus and minus images.

• In the MultiMove Layers behavior dialog, set these attributes:

    Left Pos: **0**
    Top Pos: **120**
    Method: **Relative**

• Click OK to apply the behavior.

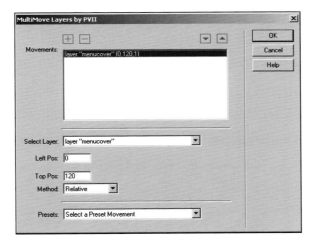

Apply the Studio VII/MultiMove Layers by PVII behavior to the menucover layer.

Note: The Left Position field controls how much the layer moves in the horizontal direction from its current position. The Top Position field controls how much the layer moves in the vertical direction from its current position. You set Left Pos to **0** because you don't want the layer to change its horizontal position. You do, however, want to slide the layer down by the number of pixels needed to completely reveal the menu5 detail rows. The table lists this value in the Detail Height column as 120, so you will set the Top Pos to **120** so that the menucover layer moves down by 120 pixels.

2 Change the event:

• In the Behaviors panel, click the down arrow on the MultiMove Layers line and select the (onClick) event. Make sure that your Behaviors panel looks like our example.

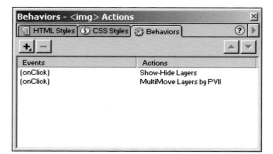

The Behaviors panel should look like this after you apply the MultiMove behavior.

3 Save and preview (F12) the page:

• In the browser preview window, click on the plus sign for Menu Five, making sure that it looks like the example.

• Make sure that the menucover layer slides down to reveal the Menu Five detail items.

The Browser preview of Menu Five.

4 Apply the movements to the minus sign on Menu Five:

What goes down must come up? In our case, yes! Next you will apply the exact opposite movement to the minus image. Because you moved the layer down 120 pixels on the plus image click event, now you will simply move the layer back up 120 pixels when the user clicks the minus image. An up movement, from the layer's current position, is expressed as a negative number: -120 pixels.

- Click on the minus sign image in the Menu Five section.
- Click the + button on the Behaviors panel and select the Studio VII/MultiMove Layers behavior.
- Select the menucover layer in the Select Layer drop-down selection list.
- In the MultiMove Layers behavior dialog, set the following attributes:

  Left Pos: **0**
  Top Pos: **–120**
  Method: **Relative**

Click OK to apply the behavior.

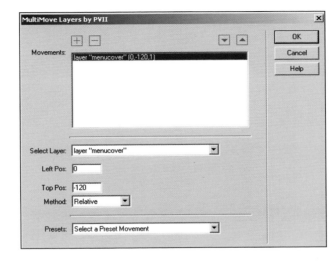

The MultiMove Layers behavior for the Menu Five minus image link.

5 Change the event:

- In the Behaviors panel, click the down arrow on the MultiMove Layers line.
- Select the (onClick) event.

6 Save the page and preview (F12) your work:

- Click the plus and minus images for Menu Five.

  The menucover layer should slide down to reveal the Menu Five detail items. When you click on the minus image, the menucover layer should slide back up into place hiding the Menu Five detail.

7 Apply the movements to Menu Four.

Menu Four has two layers on top of it—the menu5 layer and the menucover layer. When the user clicks on the plus sign for Menu Four, both menu5 and menucover move down by 96 pixels (the Detail Height for menu4; 4 rows times 24 pixels). We will apply a 96-pixel move for the menu5 and menucover layers.

- Click on the plus image in the Menu Four section.
- Click the + button on the Behaviors panel and select the Studio VII/MultiMove Layers by PVII behavior.

  The first layer on the page will be displayed by default.

- Select the menu5 layer from the Select Layer listing.
- In the MultiMove Layers behavior dialog, set these attributes for the menu5 layer:

    Left Pos: **0**
    Top Pos: **96**
    Method: **Relative**

Now add the menucover layer to the listing.

- Click the large plus sign icon at the top left of the MultiMove Layers dialog.

  An exact copy of your settings for the previous layer is made (this will save us a lot of time because we don't have to keep entering the positions).

- Select menucover from the Select Layer drop-down listing.
- Click OK to apply the behavior.
- Select the (onClick) event.

Note: Charting multiple layer movements with our MultiMove behavior is a snap. You can select as many layers as you need, set their individual move positions, and even set the Absolute or Relative targeting individually.

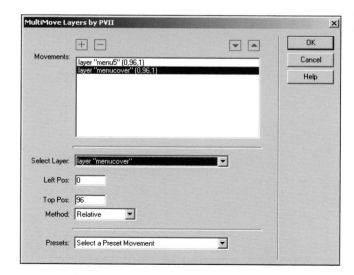

The MultiMove Layers behavior for the Menu Four plus sign.

- Repeat these steps to apply the opposite movements to the minus sign image link in Menu Four using the following settings:

  Left Pos: **0**
  Top Pos: **-96**
  Method: **Relative**

- Select the (onClick) event.

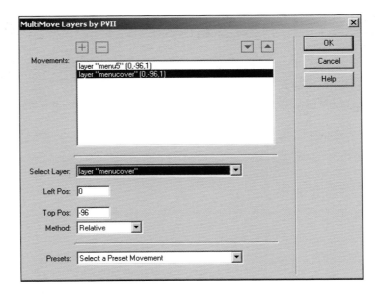

Apply these settings to the minus sign image link in Menu Four.

8 Save the page and preview (F12) it:

- In the browser preview window, click the plus sign for Menu Four.

  The menucover and menu5 layers will slide down to reveal the Menu Four detail items.

- Click on the minus sign.

  Both the menucover layer and the menu5 layer will slide back up into place hiding the Menu Four detail.

- Try opening both Menu Five and Menu Four.

- Close Menu Four.

Regardless of where the layer is vertically, it still manages to return to the exact position required to hide the menu detail above it—like Magic!

IN CASE OF DIFFICULTY...DON'T BREAK THE GLASS!

It's normal to make some errors when doing repetitive behavior applications like this. If the menu is not working perfectly, go back to each menu section and check your MultiMove Layers events. Here is a list of the most common pitfalls (errors) that can crop up:

- The movement is not set to Relative (the layer will move to extreme positions on the page).

- The event handler is not set to (onClick) (mysterious movements).

- The same layer accidentally was set to two movements.

- The wrong layer was selected.

- A positive move rather than a negative move was used on the minus sign.

As you can guess, I've fallen into each of these traps from time to time. The key to success is to take it slow, use a checklist, and preview the page after each plus or minus sign set of behaviors list is applied. It's much easier to spot the problem right after each step.

9 Apply the movements to Menu Three:

Menu Three requires that you move the three layers beneath it whenever the user clicks the plus or minus image.

- Using the techniques previously discussed, apply the MultiMove Layers behavior to the plus image of Menu Three using the table as a reference.

- Save and preview (F12) the file, checking the menu click to make sure that each layer is moving properly.

- Correct any errors now.

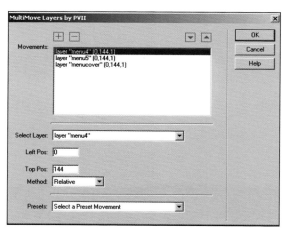

Apply these settings to the plus sign image link in Menu Three.

Layer to Move	Left Pos	Top Pos	Targeting
menu4	0	144	Relative
menu5	0	144	Relative
menucover	0	144	Relative

Use this table when setting up the movement for the plus sign image link in Menu Three.

184

- Apply the MultiMove Layers behavior to the minus image in Menu Three using the table as a reference.
- Save and preview (F12) the file, checking the menu click to make sure that each layer is moving properly.
- Correct any errors now.

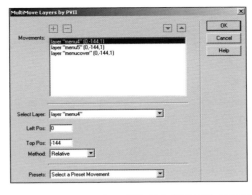

Apply these settings to the minus sign image link in Menu Three.

Layer to Move	Left Pos	Top Pos	Targeting
menu4	0	–144	Relative
menu5	0	–144	Relative
menucover	0	–144	Relative

Use this table as you set up the movement for the minus sign image link in Menu Three.

10 Apply the movements to Menu Two:

Menu Two requires that we move the four layers beneath it whenever the user clicks the plus or minus image.

- Using the techniques previously discussed, apply the MultiMove Layers behavior to the plus image in Menu Two using the table as a reference.

Note: Don't forget to set your events to (onClick).

- Save and preview (F12) the file, checking the menu click to make sure that each layer is moving properly.
- Correct any errors now.

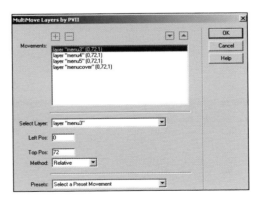

Apply these settings to the plus sign image link in Menu Two.

Layer to Move	Left Pos	Top Pos	Targeting
menu3	0	72	Relative
menu4	0	72	Relative
menu5	0	72	Relative
menucover	0	72	Relative

Use this table as you set up the movement for the plus sign image link in Menu Two.

- Apply the MultiMove Layers behavior to the minus image in Menu Two, using the table as a reference.
- Save and Preview (F12) the file, checking the menu click to make sure that each layer is moving properly.
- Correct any errors now.

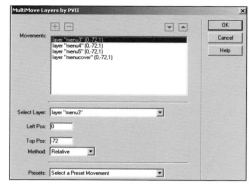

Apply these settings to the minus sign image link in Menu Two.

Layer to Move	Left Pos	Top Pos	Targeting
menu3	0	-72	Relative
menu4	0	-72	Relative
menu5	0	-72	Relative

Use this table as you set up the movement for the minus sign image link in Menu Two.

11 Apply the movements to Menu One (at last!):

Menu One requires that we move the five layers beneath it whenever the user clicks the plus or minus images.

- Using the techniques previously discussed, apply the MultiMove Layers behavior to the plus image of Menu One using the table as a reference.
- Save and preview (F12) the file, checking the menu click to make sure that each layer is moving properly.
- Correct any errors now.

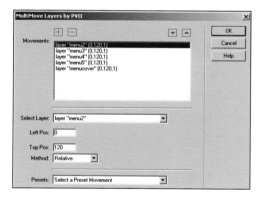

Apply these settings to the plus sign image link in Menu One.

Layer to Move	Left Pos	Top Pos	Targeting
menu2	0	120	Relative
menu3	0	120	Relative
menu4	0	120	Relative
menu5	0	120	Relative
menucover	0	120	Relative

Use this table as you set up the movement for the plus sign image link in Menu One.

- Apply the MultiMove Layers behavior to the minus image in Menu One using the table as a reference.
- Save and Preview (F12) the file, checking the menu click to make sure that each layer is moving properly.
- Correct any errors now.

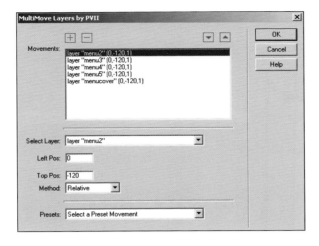

Apply these settings to the minus sign image link in Menu One.

Use this table as you set up the movement for the minus sign image link in Menu One.

Layer to Move	Left Pos	Top Pos	Targeting
menu2	0	–120	Relative
menu3	0	–120	Relative
menu4	0	–120	Relative
menu5	0	–120	Relative
menucover	0	–120	Relative

APPLYING THE EXPAND ALL AND CLOSE ALL MOVEMENTS

We're almost done! All that is left is to give the user a handy way to open all the menu choices and a quick way to close all the menu selections. To begin, we will use the Show-Hide Layers behavior to make all the nested layers (containing the minus sign and open folder images) visible.

Then we will use the Absolute targeting option of MultiMove Layers. If you think about it, opening all the menus really requires that we move each of the menu layers to a position that completely reveals the menu above it. We can calculate the where each layer should be by adding the height of each layer above it. More on that later.

1 Show the nested layers on the Expand All link:

- Click the Expand All link.

- In the Behaviors panel, click the + button and select Show–Hide Layers.

- Select each nested layer and click the Show button.

- Make sure that these five nested layers are selected:

  Layer "menu1open" in layer "menu1" (show)
  Layer "menu2open" in layer "menu2" (show)
  Layer "menu3open" in layer "menu3" (show)
  Layer "menu4open" in layer "menu4" (show)
  Layer "menu5open" in layer "menu5" (show)

- Click OK to apply the behavior.

2 Hide the nested layers on the Close All link:

- Click the Close All link.

- In the Behaviors panel, click the + button and select Show–Hide Layers.

- Select each nested layer and click the Hide button.

- Make sure that these five nested layers are selected:

  Layer "menu1open" in layer "menu1" (hide)
  Layer "menu2open" in layer "menu2" (hide)
  Layer "menu3open" in layer "menu3" (hide)
  Layer "menu4open" in layer "menu4" (hide)
  Layer "menu5open" in layer "menu5" (hide)

- Click Ok to apply the behavior.

- Save and preview (F12) the file, checking the menu click to make sure that each menu is changing the image to the minus (open) properly.

- Correct any errors now.

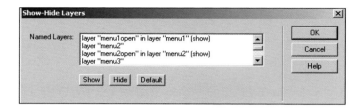

A Show-Hide layers example for the Expand All link.

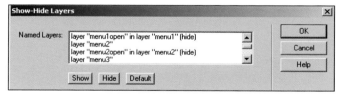

The Show-Hide layers example for the Close All link.

ABSOLUTE LAYER POSITIONING

The Absolute layer positioning option in the MultiMove extension is used when you know the exact pixel coordinate position to which you want to move the layer. When using Absolute positioning, we really don't care where the layer is currently. In fact, it could very well be out of the viewable area of the screen. The Absolute move requires that we supply the x and y pixel coordinates for the top-left corner of the layer. The x, or Left Pos, determines the distance of the left edge of the layer from the left side of the page. The y, or Top Pos, determines the distance of the top edge of the layer from the top of the page. Supplying a Left Pos of 100 and Top Pos of 20 places the layer so that its left-top corner is 100 pixels from the left side of the page and 20 pixels down from the top of the page. Setting the Left Pos to –200 places the layer 200 pixels to the left of the left side of the page (that is, not visible).

3 Apply the Expand All movements:

Now we're going to use the Absolute targeting option of MultiMove Layers. We can skip the menu1 layer. It never actually moves at all! We will start with the menu2 layer. For all the detail in menu1 to be exposed (visible) we will have to move the menu2 layer to an absolute position below menu1. Because menu1 is 144 pixels high (the Height property) and menu1 starts at 112 pixels (its Top property), then the end of the menu1 layer must be at 256 pixels (112+144). This is exactly where we want to place the beginning of the menu2 layer. Follow this through, and you can calculate the start position for the menu3 layer: menu2 now starts at 256, menu2 is 96 pixels high, so menu3 should start at 352 (256+96=352).

When applying Absolute movements, it is also necessary to supply the left position of the layer. In all cases, you will use **10**. All the layers are set to have their left edge start at 10 pixels, and you do not want to move any of them horizontally (at least not in this project!).

- Using the techniques discussed previously, apply the MultiMove Layers behavior to the Expand All link of the menu using the table as a reference and remember to select the Absolute method.
- After entering the Left Pos, Top Pos, and Absolute method for the initial layer (the menu2 layer), add the others and simply change the Top Pos for each.
- Save and preview (F12) the file checking the menu click to make sure that each layer is moving properly when clicking Expand All.
- Correct any errors now.

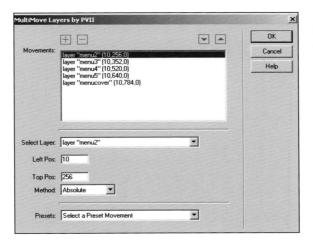

The Behaviors panel should look like this for the Expand All link.

Layer to Move	Left Pos	Top Pos	Targeting
menu2	10	256	Absolute
menu3	10	352	Absolute
menu4	10	520	Absolute
menu5	10	640	Absolute
menucover	10	784	Absolute

Use this table to apply the MultiMove Layers behavior to the Expand All link.

4 Apply the Close All movements:

The Close All series of movements is the easiest to understand. We simply move every menu layer back to its Absolute original starting point (the original Left and Top positions).

- Using the techniques discussed previously, apply the MultiMove Layers behavior to the Close All link of the menu using the table as a reference.
- Save and preview (F12) the file, checking the menu click to make sure that each layer is moving properly.
- Correct any errors now.

That's it for the movement scripts, and you're already using the menu and feeling pretty good (now that it's done!). Now you'll just finish off with some site housekeeping.

Layer to Move	Left Pos	Top Pos	Targeting
menu2	10	136	Absolute
menu3	10	160	Absolute
menu4	10	184	Absolute
menu5	10	208	Absolute
menucover	10	232	Absolute

Use this table to apply the MultiMove Layers behavior to the Close All link.

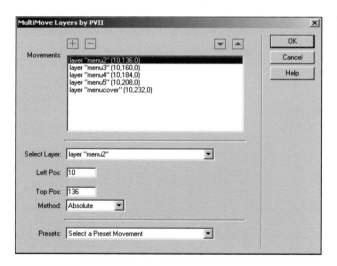

The Behaviors panel should look like this for the Close All link.

CHANGING THE MENU LAYERS BACKGROUND COLOR

Now that you're finished with all the edits in the menu layers, you can change the layer background color to match the page background. The background color for the layers is controlled by our custom class named .menulayers. If you remember, that's the style you applied to the layers when you created them. Because all the layers have this style assigned to them, all you have to do is change the .menulayers style background property.

1   Open the style sheet for editing:

- Choose Window–CSS Style (Shift+F11) to open the CSS Style Sheet panel.
- Click on the Pad and Pen icon (the second from the right) at the bottom right of the panel to open the Edit Style Sheet dialog.
- Select .menulayers and click the Edit button.

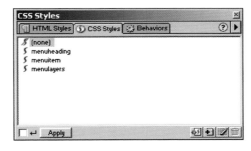

The CSS Styles panel looks like this.

Selecting the custom .menulayers style for editing.

2   Change the background color:

- Select Background in the Category listing.
- Enter the color value in the Background Color box or click on the color swatch to choose a color from the color picker. To match the page background (we are using the bg.gif image as our background) for this example, use **#333333**.
- Click the Apply button.

  Dreamweaver instantly applies the style to the page. This is an excellent way to preview your style changes.

- Click OK to save the changes.

  The menu should now look just like our example.

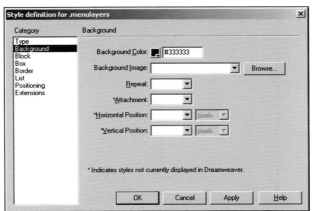

Set the .menulayers Background Color.

3 Enter the Netscape 4x Fix:

Dreamweaver writes the background property to the style sheet (or style declaration) as

background-color: #333333;

This declaration is fine for most browsers. In the case of layers, however, Netscape 4 requires that the property have a layer at the beginning of the declaration. To get around this, we have placed both declarations in our style as follows:

.menulayers { background-color: #333333; layer-background-color: #333333}

Dreamweaver will not change the layer-background-color style setting, so you must remember to do this manually whenever changing the layer background color to suit your needs. For this example, we have already set the layer-background-color to #333333 for you.

> **Note:** You may notice that the code in this book sometimes wraps to the next line. That wrapping is caused by the narrowness of the column within this book. Dreamweaver does not restrict the length of the line; the code appears on one line.

FIXING BROWSER-SPECIFIC PROBLEMS

In this section, you're going to fix three browser-specific problems. Have you noticed those pesky little dotted lines that surround your links (in Internet Explorer). You can get rid of them by applying the IE Link Scrubber. You also can prevent Netscape 4 from displaying the hourglass icon when a JavaScript link is clicked by applying the NN4 Return False Fix. Netscape will love you for it.

The third problem is that Netscape 4 has difficulty recognizing layer properties for nested layers. Currently, all the layer style properties are defined right in the HTML code on the **<div>** tag (Dreamweaver did that for you when you filled in the property inspector fields). Netscape 4 recognizes the nested layer properties only if they are defined as styles up in the head (above the HTML code) of the page. Fortunately, Jaro Von Flocken came to the rescue! His layer2style command takes all of the nested layers on the page and creates the style declarations for these layers in the head of the document.

1 Apply the Scrubber:

   • Choose Commands/Studio VII/IE Link Scrubber.

   • Click the Scrub Em! button.

   Now all your links contain an onFocus() event that kills the dotted lines.

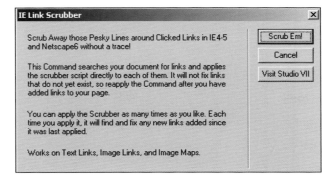

Apply the IE Link Scrubber.

2 Apply the NN4 Return False Fix:

   This fix adds a return false; JavaScript to all the **<a>** and **<area>** tags on the page.

   • Choose Commands/Studio VII/Apply NN4 Return False Fix.

   • Click the Apply button.

   Don't attempt to preview in Netscape just yet. The page will break until we apply the next fix.

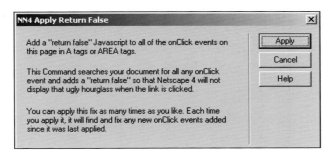

Apply the NN4 Return False Fix.

3 Apply the Layer2style fix:

   • Choose Commands/Layer2style to display a listing of all the nested layers that need to be updated.

   • Click OK to apply the fix.

   • You should apply this fix at the end of any modification process. It's easy to unknowingly nudge one of the nested layers while modifying the menu. Each time Dreamweaver detects a small change to the nested layer, it will write the properties back to the **<div>** tag, breaking Netscape.

   • Preview the menu in Netscape 4, Opera 5, Netscape 6, and all IE version 4 and higher browsers.

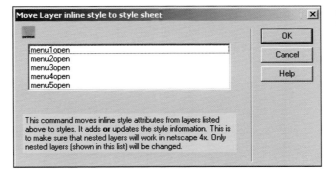

Apply the fix that makes nested layers work in Netscape.

Another issue that will surface in Netscape browsers is its unique capability to not honor (or render) the layer background color if the space in the layer is not filled. This means that fragments of a menu item may bleed through the layer on top of it if the table width is greater than the table width of the covering layer (remember, you removed the table width setting). You don't have to worry about this in this project because Link Item Three was used in all menus, bringing the width to the same for each of your menus, but you may need to address this in your projects.

The simple fix for this is to pad the longest link in the covering layer with a series of non-breaking spaces (** **) to extend the width of the table sufficiently to cover the longest link of the menu section before it. Position your cursor to the right of the link and press Ctrl+Shift+Spacebar to enter the non-breaking space. This method is preferable to other solutions that involve embedding a shim image into the table to set the width. Because that would disrupt the math used to calculate the vertical height of each menu section layer movements, it's simpler to use the non-breaking space method.

MODIFICATIONS

With this type of menu system, it is always best to incorporate all your menu link needs at the initial design time. When adding or deleting menu items, you will have to modify the layer movements contained on that menu section's plus and minus links for the movements of all the menus below it, as well as the Expand All movements.

To add a new menu section, use the same copy and paste method you used in this project to create Menu Two through Menu Five. Be sure to change the z-index for the menucover so that it is always higher than the last menu layer. Modify the layer movements for all the plus and minus images to incorporate the new layer. Then modify the Expand All and Close All links to reflect the new layer.

To delete a menu section, click the layer in the Layers panel and press the Delete key. Using the property inspector, change the Top position of each layer beneath the removed layer to move it up by 24 pixels (subtract 24 from the existing Top value). Open the MultiMove behavior on the plus and minus links for all layers above the layer you just removed. The extension will automatically adjust the layer list. Just click OK to save the revised event. Open the Show-Hide layer behavior on the Expand All and Close All links. Again, just click OK. Now modify the MultiMove behaviors on the Expand All and Close All Link to reflect the new Top Pos values for the remaining layer (just the layers beneath the layer you removed). Don't forget to reapply the layer2style command after editing your nested layers!

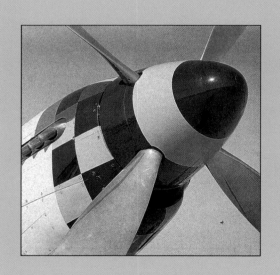

SCROLLING A LAYER WITH DREAMWEAVER, FIREWORKS, AND SOME DHTML ANIMAGIC

"You know the nearer your

destination, the more you're

slip sliding away."

—PAUL SIMON

A DHTML SIDE-SCROLLER WIDGET

The side-scroller widget is a DHTML apparatus that enables you to scroll words or images horizontally within a constrained region of the browser window. This is accomplished by using a container layer to mask the region in which the content is visible. When content moves beyond the boundaries of the mask, it is invisible. The text within the white rectangle (Link One, Link Two, and so on) scrolls horizontally, and although its length is much wider than the actual browser window, you see only the section that is within the rectangle's borders. This is accomplished with the underused (and often misunderstood) concept of nested layers (along with a sprinkling of DHTML AniMagic). Before long, you can have people slip sliding all over your site!

Project 9

Scrolling a Layer

by Al Sparber

The finished page with a side-scrolling widget.

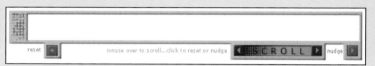

The buttons along the bottom of the widget interface control the link list's left-right movement.

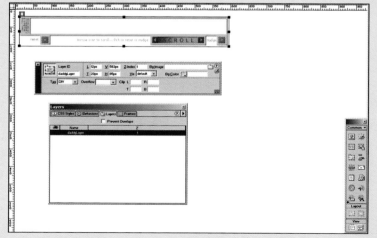

The widget interface is comprised of a single image, placed in a layer.

IT WORKS LIKE THIS

Mousing over the two scroll arrows slides the link list right or left. Taking your mouse off either of the arrows pauses all motion. Clicking the Reset button, at any time, returns the link list to its starting position. Clicking the Nudge button moves the link list 100 pixels to the left of its current position.

The range of movement takes into consideration the width of the link list. I've set the scrolling to stop after the last link comes into view. However, newer browsers (such as Netscape 6 and Internet Explorer 5–Mac) allow users to increase text size (even if a style sheet is being used), so the Nudge button permits scrolling past the initial stop point. We don't want anyone to miss a valuable link!

PREPARING TO WORK

As you've most certainly deduced by now, preparing for a Dreamweaver 4 Magic project is pretty much a routine. Install the required extensions, copy the project folder from the CD to your hard drive, and then fire up Dreamweaver and define a new site using your copied project folder as the local root folder.

1   Install the PVII Layer AniMagic behavior (if you haven't already done so):

- Browse to the Extensions folder on the CD.
- Open the Behaviors/Actions subfolder.
- Double-click LayerAnimagic.mxp to install the behavior.

2   Install the NN4 Return False Fix, layer2style, and the Scrubber commands:

- Browse to the Extensions folder on the CD.
- Open the Commands subfolder.
- Double-click the file called N4 Return False Fix.mxp to install the command.
- Repeat to install scrubber.mxp and layer2style.mxp.

3   Copy the projects folder:

- Browse to the projects folder on the CD.
- Copy the project_nine folder to a convenient location on your hard drive.

4   Define a new Dreamweaver site using the project_nine copy as your local root folder.

Note: Remember, if you want to see how the completed site looks in either Dreamweaver or your browser, you can find all the files in the finished_project folder.

BROWSER COMPATIBILITY

We have tested this interface and found that it is fully functional in the following browsers:

MSIE 4 (Windows and Mac)

MSIE 5 (Windows and Mac)

MSIE 5.5 (Windows)

NN4.08–4.76 (Windows)

NN4.5 (Mac)

Opera 5.01 (Windows)

Netscape 6 (Windows and Mac)

Note: The project also teaches you how to make the widget interface image in Fireworks 4. If you don't have Fireworks installed on your system, you can find links to Macromedia.com on the CD where you can download the 30-day trial version of Fireworks 4. However, both the editable Fireworks file and the Web-ready image are on the CD, just in case you thought you'd have to make them yourselves!

CREATING THE INTERFACE IN FIREWORKS 4

This is a Dreamweaver Magic book, but we thought it would be cool to show you how we made the widget interface in Fireworks. We think that you'll find this information useful.

1 Set up the Fireworks canvas:

  - Open Fireworks and choose File/New to create a new image.

  - When prompted, set the canvas size to **600 pixels** wide by **400 pixels** high.

  - Make sure that resolution is set to **72 pixels** per inch and that canvas color is white.

  - Save the file as **ch09iface.png**.

  Note: Fireworks uses a special PNG version as its native file format. The Fireworks PNG contains all the data necessary to recall live effects and to keep your text editable.

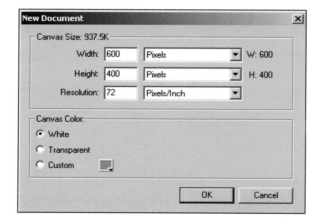

Create a new Fireworks document and set up the canvas.

2 Draw the main rectangle:

  - Select the Rectangle tool.

  - Draw a rectangle that is 580 pixels wide by 82 pixels high.

  - Position the rectangle at the top left of the canvas (x:0; y:0).

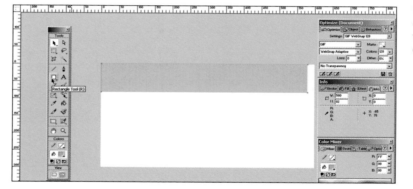

Use the Rectangle tool to draw the main rectangle, and then use the Info panel to easily size and position it.

3 Fill the rectangle:

- Select the rectangle.
- Open the Fill panel and set these properties:

  Fill color: **Solid, #FF9900**
  Edge: **Anti-Alias**
  Texture: **Line-Vert2, 32%**

Note: If you need a Fireworks panel and it's not visible, open it from the Fireworks Windows menu.

4 Divide the rectangle into fourths:

To give our widget interface its "carved from a block" look, we need to cut up the rectangle to alter its shape.

- Draw four rectangles.
- Fill each with solid black so you can see them easily.
- Use the Info panel to size and position the rectangles, referring to the settings in the table.

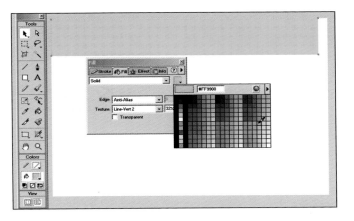

Fill the rectangle and set its texture.

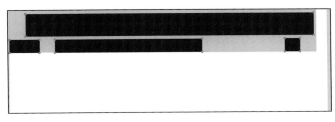

Insert the four rectangles that are used to cut up the main one.

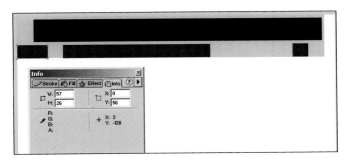

Use the Info panel to precisely set the height, width, and x-y coordinates of each rectangle.

Apply these settings to the rectangles.

Rectangle	W	H	X	Y
1	544	44	31	6
2	57	26	0	56
3	278	26	86	56
4	29	26	520	56

5 Punch through the rectangles:

- Hold down the Shift key, select the large black rectangle, and then select the main base rectangle until you see blue selection points around the perimeter of both rectangles.

- Choose Modify/Combine/Punch so that Fireworks punches out the smaller shape from the larger one, just like a cookie cutter.

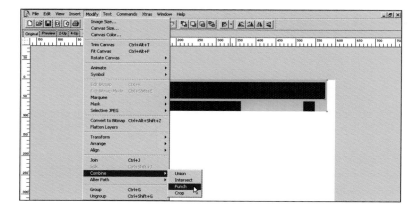

To punch out the shape of one rectangle from another, select both rectangles and then choose Modify/Combine/Punch.

Rectangle 1 is cut from the main (orange) rectangle.

- Punch out the left black rectangle from the orange one, using the preceding technique.

The remaining rectangles are cut from the main one, leaving a single orange rectangle with three outcroppings.

- Punch out the second black rectangle.

- Punch out the last black rectangle.

- Make sure that the only object remaining on your canvas at this point is the orange rectangle and that it's still positioned at the top left of the canvas (x:0; y:0).

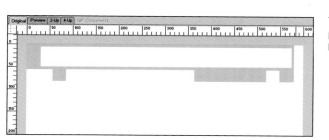

The finished shape after being punched through by the four black rectangles.

CREATING AND STYLING THE INTERACTIVE PARTS OF A FIREWORKS IMAGE

In this section, you use the Fireworks Effect panel to add a Bevel effect to the orange widget. Then you add and style the Reset control with which users will interact. You are bringing the side-scrolling widget to life.

1 Add a Bevel:

- Select the object (the orange widget) and open the Effect panel.
- Open the drop-down Effect menu and choose Bevel and Emboss/Inner Bevel.
- Enter the following settings:

  Bevel Edge Shape: **Smooth**
  Width: **4**
  Contrast: **75%**
  Softness: **2**
  Angle: **135°**
  Button Preset: **Raised**

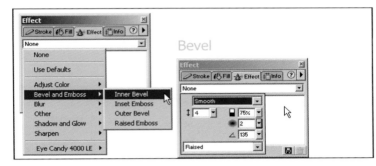

Use the Effect panel to set an Inner Bevel.

- The rectangles have an inner bevel.

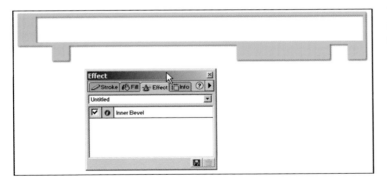

The Effect panel shows all editable effects for the selected object, which now has a bevel

2 Add and style the Reset control:

- Draw a rectangle 18×18-pixels square.
- Center the square over the first outcropping.
- Use the Fill panel to set these properties:

    Fill color: **Solid #D6D3CE**
    Texture: **Hatch 2 at 47%**

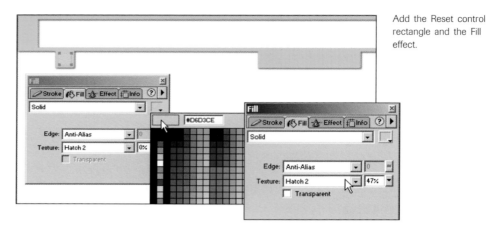

Add the Reset control rectangle and the Fill effect.

3 Add a Bevel effect to the square:

- Select the square.
- Open the Effect panel.
- Open the drop-down Effect menu and choose Bevel and Emboss/Inner Bevel.
- Enter these settings:

    Bevel Edge Shape: **Smooth**
    Width: **3**
    Contrast: **75%**
    Softness: **3**
    Angle: **140**
    Button Preset: **Inset**

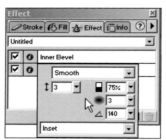

Add the Inner Bevel effect.

4 Add a Shadow effect to the square:

- Reselect the square.
- Open the drop-down Effect menu again and choose Shadow and Glow/Inner Shadow.
- Enter these settings:

    Distance: **2**
    Color: **#333333**
    Knockout: **Unchecked**
    Opacity: **65%**
    Softness: **2**
    Angle: **327°**

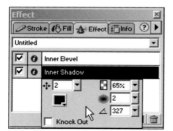

Add the Inner Shadow effect.

USING FIREWORKS COMMANDS TO COPY EFFECTS FROM OBJECT TO OBJECT

The rectangle we need to make for both the Scroll and the Nudge controls has the same properties as the Reset control square; only the dimensions are different. Fireworks has a useful feature to make our work easy: The Paste Attribute command.

1 Copy the Reset control:

- Make a copy of the Reset control square.

- Center it over the Nudge control outcropping.

- Draw a rectangle and size it 144 pixels wide by 18 pixels high.

> **Tip:** Why did you draw a new rectangle for the center outcropping? If you'd simply made a copy of the little square and stretched it, Fireworks would have distorted the bevel and shadow, so you would have needed to edit them. Copying and pasting the attributes takes far less time and requires no further edits.

- Center it over the middle outcropping (align it vertically with the Reset control). Use the table, in tandem with the Info panel, to ensure that all three rectangles are precisely positioned.

- Select the Reset control and choose Edit/Copy.

- Select the new rectangle and choose Edit/Paste Attributes, and, voilá! The attributes and effects are magically applied.

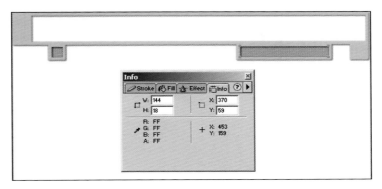

Make the Scroll control rectangle and set its properties.

Rectangle	X-Position	Y-Position
Reset	62	57
Scroll	370	57
Nudge	555	57

Using the settings in this table, carefully position the three rectangles.

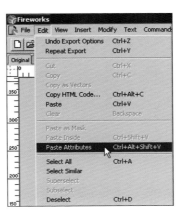

Use the Paste Attributes command to give one element all the style attributes of another.

2   Add the Scroll and Nudge controls:

- Draw a 17x17-pixel square.
- Select the square.
- Open the Fill panel.
- Set these properties:

    Fill color: **#666666**
    Edge: **Anti-Alias**
    Texture: **Lines-Horiz 1, 18%**

- Keep the square selected and open the Effect panel.
- Choose Inner Bevel and enter these settings:

    Bevel Edge Shape: **Smooth**
    Width: **3**
    Contrast: **75%**
    Softness: **2**
    Angle: **135**
    Button Preset: **Raised**

- Make three copies of the square, for a total of 4.

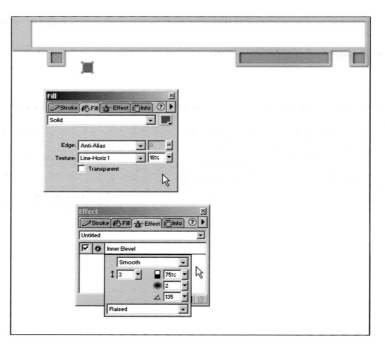

Add fill and effects to the control buttons.

- Center two of the squares atop the Reset and Nudge control insets.
- Position the remaining two squares at the outer borders of the Scroll control inset.
- Use the table as a guide to position the four button squares.

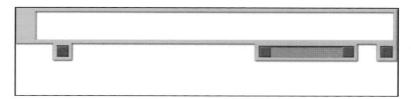

The original and three copies of the control buttons are positioned inside outcropping insets.

Rectangle	X-Position	Y-Position
Reset Button	63	58
Scroll Left	370	58
Scroll Right	497	58
Nudge	556	58

Use the settings in this table to position the four button squares.

ADDING CONTROL LABELS IN FIREWORKS

The controls are created, but they need labels that clearly indicate their functions. For arrows and such, we like to use the Marlett font that comes with all versions of Windows. It's the font that Windows uses for most of its OS controls. If you have a Mac, you can use a dingbat font or simply draw a circle and two triangles. If you open the ch9iface.png file from the CD, you will notice that we converted the Marlett text dingbats to paths.

1 Set up the right-pointing arrow:

- Select the Text tool.
- Choose Marlett font.
- Type the number **4** to render a right-pointing arrow.
- In the Text Editor, set these properties:

    Font size: **18**
    Color: **#999999**
    Anti-Aliasing: **No Anti-Alias**

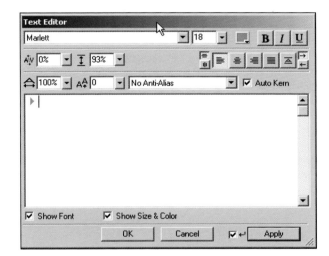

Use the Marlett Font when you create the control labels.

2 Set up the left-pointing arrow:

- Use the same technique as in task 1, except type the number **3**, Marlett's alphanumeric value for the left-pointing arrow.

3 Set up the Nudge arrow:

- Copy and paste the right-pointing arrow.
- Move it into position above the Nudge button.

4 Set up the dot for the Reset control:

- Use the same technique as in task 1, except type the letter **i**, Marlett's alphanumeric value for the dot.

5 Add helper text for each control:

reset

mouse over to scroll...click to reset or nudge

nudge

To enter text in Fireworks, select the Text tool, click a clean spot on your canvas, and the Text Editor opens. When you've finished entering your text, click OK, and it is inserted where you clicked on the canvas. You can freely move it about the canvas to position it precisely.

Tip: If you don't have the Tahoma font, good substitutes would be Verdana or Century Gothic.

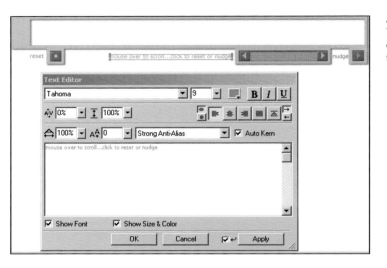

Add the helper text (like a ToolTip) that describes the control button actions to the user.

ADDING A GRADIENT FILL, ADDING A GRAPHICAL SPLASH, AND TRIMMING THE CANVAS

1 Add a gradient fill to the Scroll control:

- Select the inset rectangle in the middle outcropping.
- Open the Fill panel and choose Linear in the Fill category drop-down.
- Click the Edit button to open the Gradient Editor.
- Click the left paint bucket on the gradient ramp and set its color to **#333333**.
- Click the right paint bucket and set its color to **#D6D3CE**.
- Click in the blank space between the two paint buckets to insert a third bucket.
- Set its color to **#FFDFAE**.

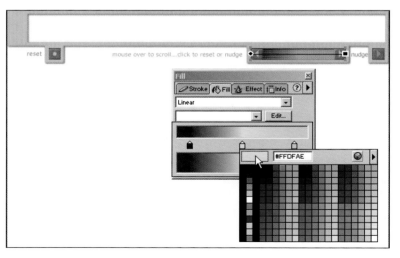

Apply a custom gradient fill to the Scroll control inset.

2 Add a graphical splash to the widget:

- Let's use Fireworks' artistic talent to create a little bit of interest in the blank space along the left side of our widget.

- Draw a rectangle 21 pixels wide by 45 pixels high.

- Set Fill to None.

- Set these Stroke properties:

  Color: **#333333**
  Category: **Oil**
  Name: **Textured Bristle**
  Tip Edge Softness: **Maximum** (slider at bottom position)
  Tip Size: **16**
  Texture: **Hatch 1**
  Texture Amount: **78%**

- Draw a second rectangle the same size.

- Set its fill to None and its stroke to 1px pencil.

- Position it, via the Info panel, at x:5 and y:6.

- Position the Oil-stroked rectangle atop the second rectangle at x:19 and y:14.

- Choose Edit/Cut.

- Select the second rectangle and then choose Edit/Paste Inside.

- Select the outside rectangle and set its stroke to None.

- Place the image on the top-left section of the widget interface.

3 Enter the Scroll label:

- Select the Text tool and click inside the scroll rectangle. Type the word **SCROLL** and use the following settings:

  Font: **Tahoma**
  Size: **14**
  Color: **#333333**
  AV: **51%**
  Smooth Anti-Alias

- Click OK to close the Text Editor.

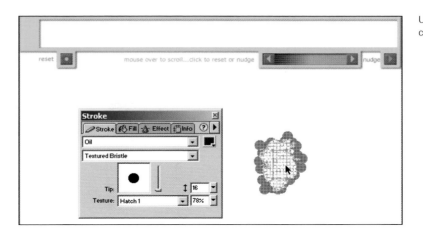

Use a textured stroke to create a graphical splash.

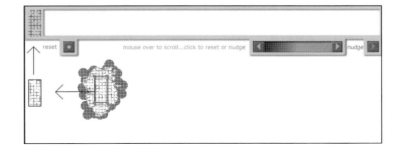

Paste the stroked rectangle inside a containing rectangle.

Tip: If you find it difficult to select the proper rectangle, use the Layer panel to select the proper one.

4   Apply a drop shadow to the Scroll label:

- Select the text SCROLL.

- Open the Effect panel and choose Drop Shadow from the Effect menu.

- Apply the following shadow settings:

  Distance: **2**
  Color: **2**
  Opacity: **65%**
  Softness: **2**
  Angle: **315**

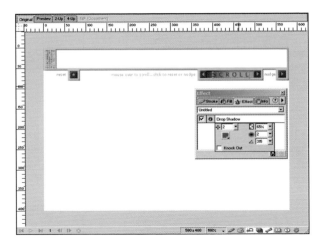

Apply a drop shadow to the Scroll label.

5   Trim the canvas:

Before slicing and optimizing our image, we need to trim the canvas to get rid of unnecessary space. Before proceeding, make sure that the widget is still positioned at the top left of the canvas.

- Select the orange widget and inspect the Info panel to ensure that the x and y coordinates are both set to 0.

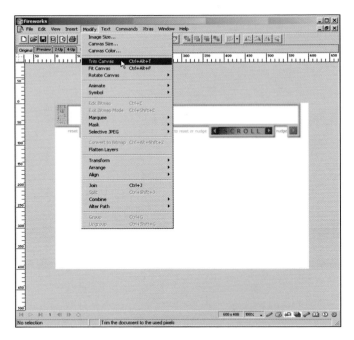

Use the Modify menu to choose the Trim Canvas command.

- Choose Modify/Trim Canvas, and Fireworks automatically reduces the canvas size to be as small as possible.

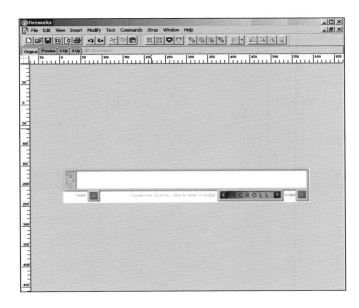

When you select the Trim Canvas command, Fireworks eliminates excess space.

OPTIMIZING AND EXPORTING THE IMAGE

Creating and styling an image are important steps in the Web site creation process. The next step is to export the interface image to the assets/images folder in the Dreamweaver site. The optimizing portion of this process is all but effortless. You use the default optimization settings in Fireworks for exporting the image.

1 Export the interface image to your Dreamweaver site:

- Choose File/Export.
- In the File Name field, type **ch09iface.gif.**
- In the Save as Type field, choose Images Only.
- Browse to the Assets folder of your project_nine Dreamweaver site.

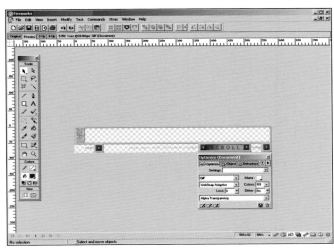

Accept the default optimization settings for this image.

- Double-click the Assets folder, double-click the Images folder, and then double-click the iface folder. You'll find the image I originally put there.

- Click the Save button.

- In the overwrite confirmation message, click OK to save your changes and overwrite my file with yours.

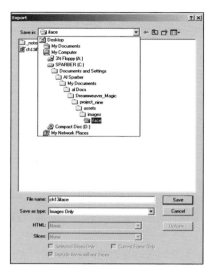

The Fireworks Export dialog showing the path to the Dreamweaver site folder where the exported image is to be saved.

2   Switch back to Dreamweaver.

SETTING UP A LAYER TO HOLD AN INTERFACE IMAGE

When you exported the image from Fireworks, you placed a Web-ready image into your Dreamweaver site. Now you'll begin the work of turning this image into the scrolling widget.

1   In Dreamweaver, Open the index.htm file in the root of your project_nine site.

2   Create a new layer to hold the interface image:

- Insert a new layer (via the Insert menu or the Object palette).

- Name the new layer **daddyLayer**.

- In the property inspector, set these properties:

    Name: **daddyLayer**
    L: **12px**
    T: **20px**
    W: **580px**
    H: **82px**
    Overflow: **Hidden**

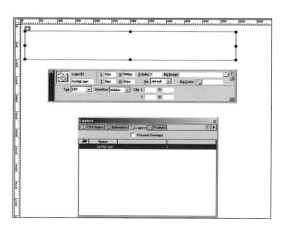

Insert daddyLayer on your page and set its properties on the property inspector.

212

3   Insert the interface image inside daddyLayer:

- Use the Assets panel to insert your interface image into daddyLayer.

- Click inside daddyLayer.

- Open the Assets panel and find the image: assets/images/iface/ch9iface.gif.

- Click the Insert button to insert it into daddyLayer.

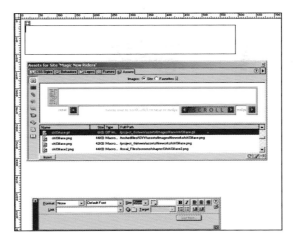

Insert the interface image into daddyLayer via the Assets panel.

NESTING LAYERS

We need to insert a layer inside daddyLayer to define a viewport through which our link list will scroll. Then we need to insert a layer containing the actual link list inside that one.

1   Insert a new layer inside daddyLayer:

The layer that contains the link list is very wide, much wider than any of the layers on our page—much wider than the page itself. We need to contain it so that the list only appears within the widget interface. We need a containing layer.

- Select the interface image inside daddyLayer.

Tip: To ensure that you have the right selection, make sure that daddyLayer is highlighted in the Layers panel, ch09iface.gif is the source image listed on the property inspector, and the **<img>** tag is highlighted on the Dreamweaver status bar.

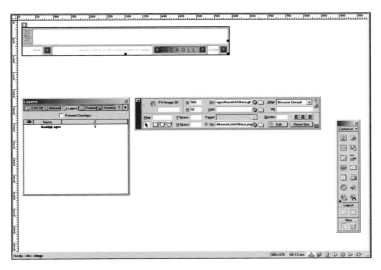

Select the interface image inside daddyLayer; and then insert a new layer, and it will nest inside.

• Choose Insert/Layer.

Dreamweaver inserts the layer inside daddyLayer, names it Layer1, and highlights it in the Layers panel.

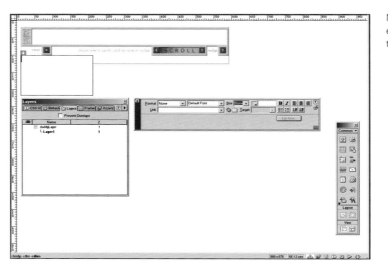

Nested layers appear in an expandable tree view below the parent layer.

• With Layer1 still selected, use the property inspector to set the following properties:

    Name: **mommyLayer**
    L: **33px**
    T: **9px**
    W: **539px**
    H: **39px**
    Overflow: **hidden**
    Clip: L: **0**   R: **539**   T: **0** B: **39**

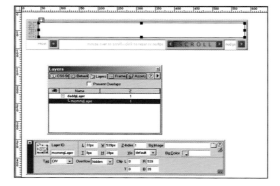

Set mommyLayer's properties with the property inspector.

Note: A nested layer's top and left positions are relative to the top-left corner of its parent layer. So mommyLayer's position is 9 pixels down from daddyLayer's top edge, and 33 pixels in from daddyLayer's left edge. The Clip properties define the viewport.

MommyLayer is clipped 539 pixels left-to-right and 39 pixels top-to-bottom, which happens to be its entire width and height. That means that the visible part of any layer nested inside mommyLayer will be the part inside its boundaries. Areas of the child layer that fall outside those boundaries will be invisible.

2 Insert the scrolling content layer:

The last layer we need to create is the one that contains the scrolling link list.

- Place your cursor in the layer named mommyLayer and make sure that Dreamweaver highlights it in the Layers panel and your cursor is flashing at its top-left corner.
- Choose Insert/Layer, and Dreamweaver inserts a new layer (named Layer1) in mommyLayer and highlights the new layer in the Layers panel.

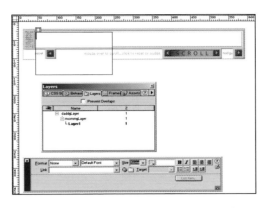

Insert the scrolling content layer inside mommyLayer.

- Use the property inspector to set the new layer's properties as follows:

    Name: **babyLayer**
    L: **0px**
    T: **11px**
    W: **2000px**
    H: **28px**

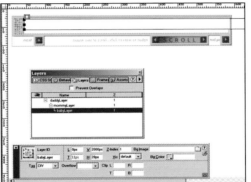

Use the property inspector to set the properties of babyLayer.

3 Insert the link list table:

The text link list should be inserted into a table. It's the easiest way to achieve structural stability in all version 4 (and higher) browsers.

- Click inside babyLayer and insert a table with the following properties:

    Rows: **1**
    Cols: **1**
    CellPad: **0**
    CellSpace: **0**
    Width: **2000 pixels**

- In the property inspector, be sure to leave all other fields blank, including height!

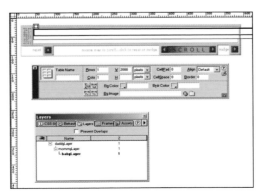

Insert the link list table inside babyLayer.

4 Type the link list:

- Type the link list all on a single line, using the pipe character as a separator:

  Link One | Link Two | Link Three | Link Four... up to Link Twenty

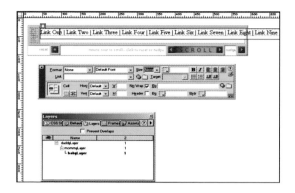

Type the link list into the table.

Note: The pipe character is usually on the same key as the backslash (\).

Tip: After typing in the text, you can optionally remove the width setting from the table. If you do, use the property inspector to set the table row to NOWRAP or Netscape 4 will break the line. Removing the width can be helpful if you anticipate that users will override your CSS and enlarge the text.

USING CSS TO STYLE THE LINK LIST

The link list looks a little bland, so let's add some style. The Dreamweaver CSS utility makes creating and applying a style a snap, but if you're an experienced CSS person, feel free to make your own.

1 Create the styles:

- Choose Window/CSS Styles to open the CSS panel.
- Click the Pencil icon on the bottom border to open the Edit Style Sheet dialog.
- Click the New button to open the New Style dialog.
- In the New Style dialog, check the Make Custom Style (Class) option.
- Type the name **.babytd** in the Name field.
- Check the This Document Only option to embed the style in the page rather than in an external CSS file.

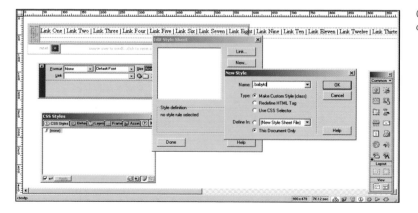

Create a new custom style called .babytd.

216

- Click OK to update the Edit Style Sheet dialog and the open Style Definition dialog with your new style name (both will happen in tandem). For this style, we are only going to set type.

- Set these properties:

    Font: **Arial, Helvetica, sans-serif**
    Size: **13 pixels**
    Color: **#FF9900**

- Click OK to close the Style Definition dialog.

- Click Done to close the Edit Style Sheet dialog.

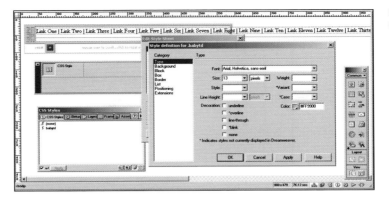

Set the type style rules for .babytd.

2 Apply your CSS style to the link list:

Now that we've created the style, we need to apply it to the link list.

- Click inside the link list table and then take a look at the status bar along the bottom border of your Dreamweaver window.

- Select the **<td>** tag and right-click (Ctrl+click) it.

- From the resultant pop-up menu, choose Set Class.

- Select the style babytd, and the link list text suddenly turns orange (hopefully, you like orange!).

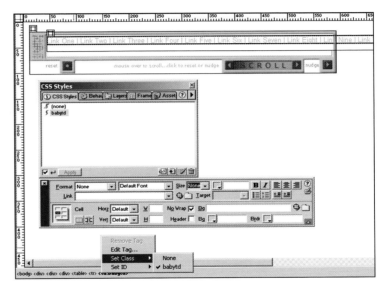

Use the tag selector on the status bar to set the class of the link list table's **<td>** tag to .babytd.

3 Set up the Anchor **<a>** style for the link list items:

All the items in the link list are hyperlinks; let's set up some styles to perk them up a bit. Because you will likely use my widget on a real page, with real content, let's go ahead and make the hyperlink styles specific to the link list. After you complete this section, you'll know how to create multiple sets of link styles that can be applied to different parts of your site.

- Open the CSS panel.

- Click the Pencil icon on the bottom border to open the Edit Style Sheet dialog.

- Click the New button to open the New Style dialog.

- In the New Style dialog, check the Use CSS Selector option.

- Type the name **.babytd a:link.**

- Set the text color to orange **#FF9900**.

- Check the None box under Decorations so that your links are not underlined.

- Click OK to close the Style Definition dialog.

- Click Done to close Edit Style Sheet dialog.

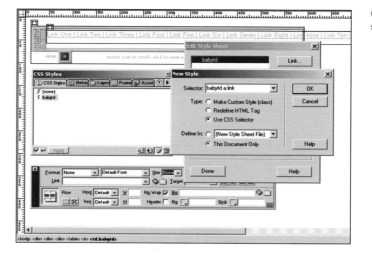

Create a new CSS selector style called babytd a:link.

Note: This style works only on links contained within elements (table cells, for example) to which is applied the babytd class. You do not have to set the font or size because this style is set by the main .babytd style and will pick up its settings.

4 Set up the remaining three Anchor **<a>** styles for the link list menu items:

- Repeat the preceding procedure to add these CSS selectors:

  For .babytd a:visited, set the text color to **#666666**.

  For .babytd a:hover, set the text color to **#333333** and select the underline decoration option.

  For .babytd a:active, set the text color to **#333333** and select the underline decoration option.

Set up the Visited, Hover, and Active selectors.

MAKING NESTED LAYERS COMPATIBLE WITH NETSCAPE 4

Because we've used nested layers, we need to do some fixing up for the sake of Netscape 4, which cannot solve for inline styles in nested layers. We need to remove all inline styles from our nested layers and place them, instead, in a style sheet. Consider the code to the right:

```
<div id="daddyLayer" style="position:absolute; left:12px;
top:20px; width:583px; height:85px; z-index:5; overflow:
hidden"></div>
```

Everything after **style="** and the closing quote are CSS rules. Instead of being in a style sheet, they are inline—inside the **<div>** tag. Netscape 4 can deal with this just fine. However, if we nest other layers inside daddyLayer (which we've certainly done!), the Netscape 4 engine gets lost. Here is the code for a nested layer:

The orange type indicates a child layer (mommyLayer) nested within daddyLayer. Notice that it, too, has an inline style. Dreamweaver writes inline styles whenever you insert, move, or resize a layer. Working around this problem is easy. We just need to remove the inline styles from all the nested layers and place those styles in a special style sheet in the **<head>** of our source code. This style sheet will consist of ID selectors. We're going to use Jaro von Flocken's Layer2Style command to automatically create the proper code.

```
<div id="daddyLayer" style="position:absolute; left:12px;
top:20px; width:580px; height:82px; z-index:1">

<div id="mommyLayer" style="position:absolute;
width:539px; height:39px; z-index:1; left: 33px; top: 9px;
overflow: hidden; clip: rect(0 539 39 0)">

</div>

</div>
```

Note: You may notice that the code in this book sometimes wraps to the next line. That wrapping is caused by the narrowness of the column within this book. Dreamweaver does not restrict the length of the line; the code appears on one line.

1   Apply the Layer2Style command:

Applying this wonderful tool is a snap.

- Open the Dreamweaver Commands menu and choose Layer2style so that the Layer2style window lists all the child layers from your document.

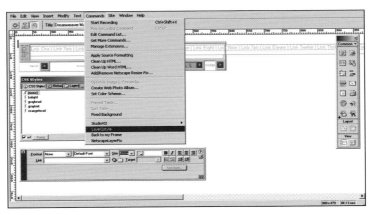

Choose Commands/Layer2Style.

• Click OK to apply the command.

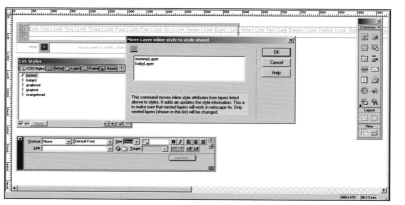

Layer2Style finds all nested layers. Click OK to apply the command.

2 Look at the changes to the code to the right:

The inline style is gone! But it's not forgotten. Jaro's command has written a style sheet in the document's **<head>** tag, as in the code.

```
<style>
#mommyLayer { position:absolute; width:539; height:39 }
#babyLayer { position:absolute; width:2000; height:28;}
</style>
```

This style sheet replaces the inline styles in the two layers nested inside daddyLayer. So instead of the type of code to the right:

```
<div id="daddyLayer" style="position:absolute; left:12px;
top:20px">
<div id="mommyLayer" style="position:absolute; width:539px;
height:39px">
<div id="babyLayer"  style="position:absolute; width:2000;
height:28">
</div>
</div>
</div>
```

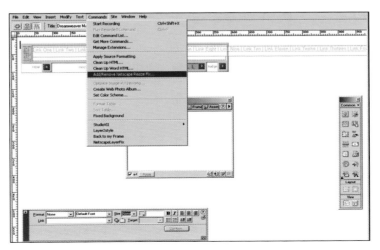

The source code at this stage reflects the new style sheet we created and the application of the Layer2style command.

We wind up with something similar to this:

Note: The code here is just a sample to convey a point and does not portray the actual project code.

Pretty cool! Netscape renders the nested layers perfectly now; that is, until you resize its browser window.

```
<div id="daddyLayer" style="position:absolute; left:12px;
top:20px">
<div id="mommyLayer">
<div id="babyLayer">
</div>
</div>
</div>
```

3 Apply the Netscape 4 Layer Fix command:

To prevent Netscape 4 from distorting your layer design when you resize its window, you need to add the Netscape Layer Fix command. This command comes pre-installed with Dreamweaver. As with the Layer2style command, the Netscape Fix is accessed from the Dreamweaver Commands menu.

Find the Netscape Resize Fix on the Commands menu.

- Open the Dreamweaver Commands menu and choose Add/Remove Netscape Resize Fix.
- Click Add.

Note: If the button reads Remove instead of Add, the layer fix has already been applied. In this case, just select Cancel. This happens if your preferences in Dreamweaver are set to automatically add the Netscape Resize Fix when inserting a layer.

Now you're fixed! And I do believe we're ready to set the widget in motion, but first refer to the tip.

Tip: If you move or resize a nested layer in Dreamweaver, even after applying the Layer2style command, Dreamweaver writes an inline style and renders the page broken in Netscape 4. But you're in luck! Layer2style can be applied over and over. Each time you apply it, it finds and fixes all nested layers that have inline styles. Moving a parent layer (like daddyLayer in this project) is totally cool and will not cause problems with the child layers. Drag daddy around all that you want. Mommy and baby will follow along happily.

The moral of the tip? Test, test, and test some more after each edit to make sure that your page continues to work as expected in all supported browsers. You never know when you may have accidentally nudged a layer that shouldn't be moved. Especially if you are using a new, ultra-sensitive optical mouse.

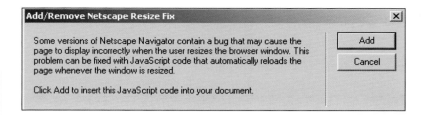

Add the Netscape Resize Fix.

MAKING AN IMAGE MAP

The Reset, Scroll, and Nudge controls are all part of a single image. Dreamweaver gives us an easy way to assign hotspots to particular areas of an image so that we can apply JavaScript behaviors. It's called image mapping.

1 Add hotspots to the control images:

• Select the widget image inside daddyLayer.

• Select the Rectangular Hotspot tool at the bottom left of the property inspector.

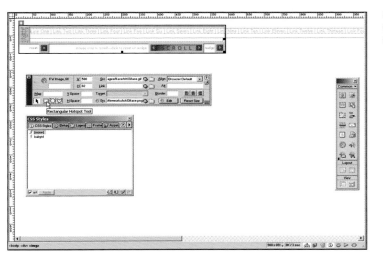

Select the widget image and then the Rectangular Hotspot tool on the property inspector.

• Draw a rectangle around the Reset control. A bright teal box marks your new hotspot.

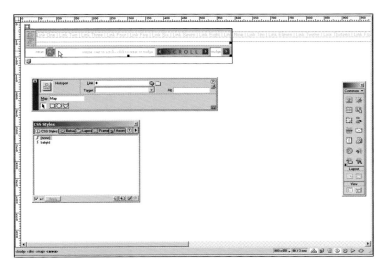

Draw a hotspot over the Reset control.

2 Add Alt text to the hotspot:

- It's a good idea to enter Alt text for this hotspot to provide mouseover feedback to visitors, as well as visual feedback to the vision impaired.

- Type **Reset the List to Start** in the Alt field.

3 Add hotspots to the remaining control images:

- Repeat the preceding procedure to add hotspots over both Scroll controls and the Nudge control.

- Add Alt text to each hotspot as follows:

  Scroll Left
  Scroll Right
  Nudge Right

Note: Dreamweaver names your map and inserts a null link (#) in the Link field.

Draw hotspots over the remaining three controls.

Tip: Hotspots have four resize points. Select one and drag to resize the hotspot. Hotspots can also be selected and nudged with your keyboard arrow keys.

APPLYING THE ANIMAGIC BEHAVIOR TO SCROLL A LINK LIST

All that's left is to attach Layer AniMagic behaviors to each of the four hotspots: Reset, Scroll Left, Scroll Right, and Nudge.

1 Apply the AniMagic behavior to the Reset control hotspot:

The Reset control launches the link list on an express scroll back to its starting position onClick.

- Select the hotspot atop the Reset control.

- Open the Behavior panel and select Studio VII/ Layer AniMagic by PVII.

- Choose babyLayer from the Layer Name list.

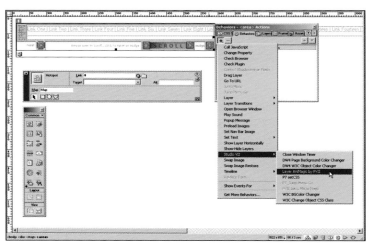

Select the first hotspot and open the Layer AniMagic behavior window.

- Set these Slide to Target Positions:

    Left Position (px): **0**

    Top Position (px): **11**

- Set these Speed Settings:

    Frame Rate (px): **24**

    Delay (in Ms): **30**

- Leave all other settings alone and click OK.

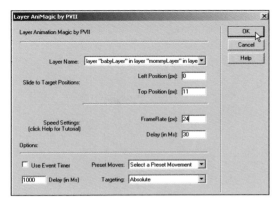

Apply Layer AniMagic to the Reset control.

- Ensure that this behavior is set to fire onClick.

Note: All AniMagic behaviors, applied to all control hotspots, must be set to the proper event: either onClick, onMouseOver, or onMouseOut. Click the arrow between the Event and the Action columns to select the required event.

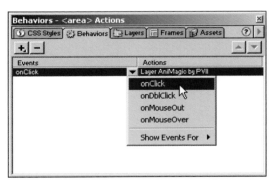

Ensure that the Reset control behavior is set to onClick.

2 Attach the Scroll Left hotspot control behavior:

The Scroll Left control scrolls the link list to the left onMouseOver and pauses scrolling onMouseOut. In this step, we apply the behavior that scrolls when the mouse is over the hotspot.

- Select the hotspot atop the Scroll Left control.
- Open the Behavior panel, select Studio VII, and then select Layer AniMagic by PVII.

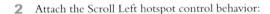

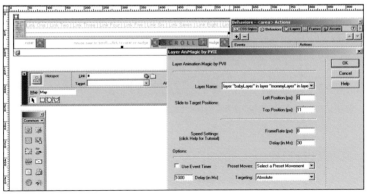

Apply Layer AniMagic to the Scroll Left control.

- Choose the babyLayer from the Layer Name list.

- Set these Slide to Target Positions:

  Left Position (px): **0**
  Top Position (px): **11**

- Set these Speed Settings:

  Frame Rate (px): **8**
  Delay (in Ms): **30**

- Leave all other settings alone and click OK.

- Set this behavior to fire onMouseOver.

3 Attach a second instance of the Scroll Left hotspot control behavior:

With the Scroll Left control still selected, select the Layer AniMagic behavior again. We're going to apply a second instance of the behavior to pause scrolling onMouseOut.

- Choose babyLayer again from the Layer Name list.

- Select Stop Moving from the Targeting list.

- Leave all other settings alone and click OK.

- Ensure that this behavior is set to fire onMouseOut.

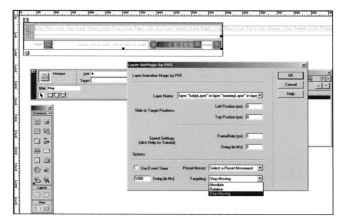

Apply the second instance of Layer AniMagic to the Scroll Left control to stop the scrolling.

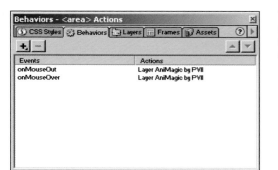

The Scroll Left control has two Layer AniMagic instances: scrolls onMouseOver, stops onMouseOut.

4 Attach the Scroll Right hotspot control behavior:

The Scroll Right control scrolls the link list to the right onMouseOver and pauses scrolling onMouseOut.

- Select the hotspot atop the Scroll Right control and select the Layer AniMagic behavior again.
- Choose babyLayer from the Layer Name list.

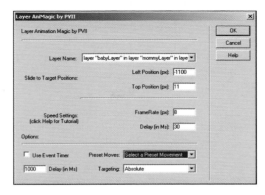

Apply Layer AniMagic to the Scroll Right control. Set its event to onMouseOver.

- Set these Slide to Target Positions:

   Left Position (px): **–1100**
   Top Position (px): **11**

- Set these Speed Settings:

   Frame Rate (px): **8**
   Delay (in Ms): **30**

- Leave all other settings alone and click OK.
- In the Behaviors panel, set the event to onMouseOver.
- Using the same technique as used on the Scroll Left control, apply a second instance of the behavior (again, by choosing the babyLayer and setting targeting to Stop Scrolling to pause scrolling onMouseOut).

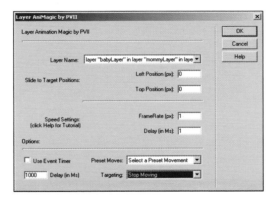

Apply an instance of Layer AniMagic to the Scroll Right control to stop the scrolling. Set its event to onMouseOut.

5 Attach the Nudge hotspot control behavior:

The Nudge control scrolls the link list to the left by 100 pixels onClick. This is a useful control because if a visitor increases the text size in his browser, part of the link list may be beyond the right edge of the view area—even after scrolling all the way right. The Nudge control can move the list past its normal stopping point to make all links accessible.

- Select the hotspot atop the Nudge control and select the Layer AniMagic behavior again.
- Choose babyLayer from the Layer Name list.

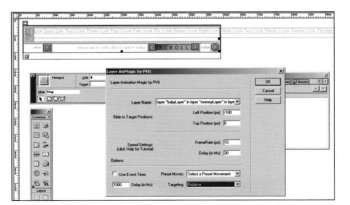

Apply Layer AniMagic to the Nudge control. Set its event to onClick.

- Set these Slide to Target Positions:

  Left Position (px): **−100**

  Top Position (px): **0**

- Set these Speed Settings:

  Frame Rate (px): **10**

  Delay (in Ms): **30**

- Select Relative from the Targeting list.

- Leave all other settings alone and click OK.

- Set the event to onClick.

Note: Relative targeting is a powerful feature of the Layer AniMagic behavior. It allows you to set a layer to move a certain number of pixels from its current position. The difference between absolute and relative targeting can thus be thought of in this way:

Absolute targeting moves a layer to a certain target position and always starts at the left position you set. Relative targeting moves a layer by the amount of pixels you enter into the left and right target positions in an additive manner. That is, the layer moves from wherever it happens to be at a given time.

CORRECTING BROWSER-SPECIFIC PROBLEMS

We need to fix a bug in Netscape 4 and a bug in Netscape 6. A real family affair! And while we're at it, we'll spruce up a little cosmetic issue with MSIE4+.

1 Apply the N4 Return False Fix:

This Project VII command adds a Return False after onClick events to alleviate a nefarious memory leak in Netscape 4 and prevents the hourglass cursor from appearing when a JavaScript link is clicked.

- Choose Commands/Studio VII/N4 Return False Fix.

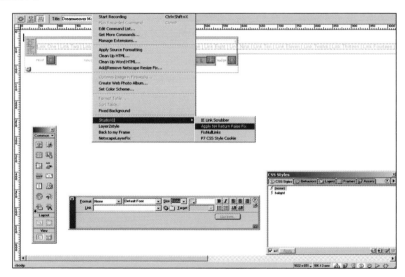

Access the N4 Netscape Return False Fix from the Studio VII/Commands menu.

- Click Apply.

Note: Layer2Style, Scrubber, and N4 Return False Fix, can be applied over and over. Each of these commands is designed to search your source code and fix situations that arise from additions or edits to your page. Run Layer2Style, for instance, if you move or otherwise edit a nested layer.

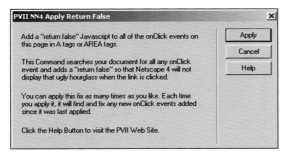

Apply the N4 Netscape Return False Fix.

2 Position the scrolling layer onLoad:

At the time of this writing, Netscape 6 has a rather annoying problem with finding some object styles when the page first loads. Without the measure we are about to take, Netscape 6 will load the scrolling layer at the wrong coordinates. After you activate the scroll controls, the layer will slide into position and work normally thereafter. Actually, it's kind of a cool effect, but because it is a bug, we thought you should know what to do.

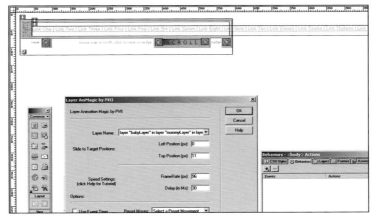

Apply Layer AniMagic to the **<body>** to position babyLayer onLoad.

- Select the **<body>** tag on the status bar.
- Open the Layer AniMagic window from the Behaviors panel.
- Choose babyLayer from the Layer Name list.
- Set these Slide to Target Positions:

   Left Position (px): **0**
   Top Position (px): **11**

- Set these Speed Settings:

   Frame Rate (px): **96**
   Delay (in Ms): **30**

- Leave all other settings alone and click OK.
- In the Behaviors panel, make sure that the event is set to onLoad.

In effect, you are moving babyLayer to where it should already be, and very quickly!

229

3 Scrub your links for MSIE:

This task is optional. The PVII Scrubber prevents focus lines from appearing around clicked links in Internet Explorer. Because the lines are an accessibility feature, we'll leave removing the lines to your discretion.

- Choose Commands/Studio VII/IE Link Scrubber.
- Click Scrub Em!.

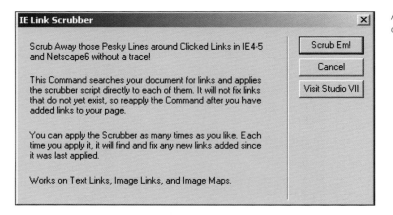

Apply the optional Scrubber command.

REPOSITIONING THE SCROLLING WIDGET AND EDITING THE LINK LIST

Now that the widget is finished, you can move it about your page to fine-tune its position, just as you move an ordinary layer in Dreamweaver. The proper way to move the widget is to select the daddyLayer, grab its handle, and then drag it to its new location. The widget behaves like a proper Victorian family. That is, wherever daddyLayer goes, mommyLayer and babyLayer follow along in harmony.

Editing the content inside the link list is done just as you would edit content in a normal table. The only caveat is that you must be careful not to move or resize any of the child layers (including the mommyLayer). If you do, Dreamweaver will rewrite the inline styles to the layer's **<div>** tag, and Netscape 4 will be totally confused. Test often by previewing the page in all target browsers. Should you accidentally cause Dreamweaver to write inline styles in a child layer, it's easy to remedy. Simply reapply the Layer2style command.

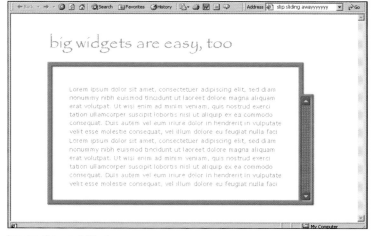

Imagine the possibilities!

Tip: Remember, you can compare your work to the author's by opening the index file in the finished_project folder.

MODIFICATIONS

With a bit of imagination, you can take what you've learned in this project and make some really cool interfaces. You can, for example, modify the images in Fireworks to make a taller widget that contains scrolling news in paragraph format. Or you can make a scrolling list of thumbnail images for a cool portfolio or gallery. The possibilities are unlimited! And remember, you can log on to our online community to discuss your *Dreamweaver 4 Magic* projects at any time and learn what other readers have done.

"Some books are to be tasted, others to

be swallowed, and some few to be

chewed and digested."

—FRANCIS BACON

PUTTING A PRESENTATION INTO MOTION

THE LETTERBOX SLIDE SHOW

The Letterbox frameset is based on the lower/wider aspect ratio of motion picture screens, HDTV, and (of course) those famous IBM commercials shown on American television. We developed a Dreamweaver Letterbox frameset object in 1999 that has been down-loaded thousands of times over. That object, along with our Layer AniMagic behavior, is the heart and soul of this project. The Letterbox provides the stage, and AniMagic acts as director and choreographer. The plot involves a Web-based presentation that emulates a PowerPoint slide show.

Project 10

Putting a Presentation into Motion

by Al Sparber

The finished page.

IT WORKS LIKE THIS

The Letterbox is designed with a central viewing frame 600 pixels wide by 320 pixels high. This central frame remains fixed but is surrounded by four border frames that expand and contract depending on the size of the browser window. All content appears in the central viewing frame. The borders are for effect.

The viewing frame is designed with CSS Layers. A layer called *logolayer* spans the top section of the frames page and contains a pretty (we think) image along with the navigation controls for the slide show.

When you click one of the three navigation buttons at the top of the viewing frame, its related content slides in, replacing what's already there (which in turn, slides out). For those times when the content is taller than 320 pixels, you choreograph scroll controls to enter from the right (or the top) on cue. The scroll controls slide out when they're not needed. It's all very cool indeed!

Tip: To inspect the source code of the frameset, select the outermost frame border in the Frames panel, and then open the source code editor.

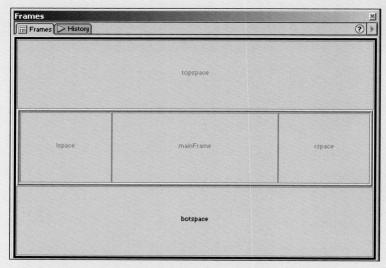

In the Frames panel (accessed via Window/Frames), four frames surround the mainFrame to create a fixed viewing area.

PREPARING TO WORK

As you've probably determined by now, preparing a *Dreamweaver 4 Magic* project is pretty much a routine. Each time, you will install the requisite extensions, copy the project folder from the CD to your hard drive, fire up Dreamweaver, and then define a new site using your copied project folder as the target. The process is outlined in more detail here:

1 Install four extensions—two behaviors, one command, and one object:

- Browse to the Extensions folder on the CD.
- Open the Behaviors subfolder and then locate and open the Actions folder.
- Double-click LayerAnimagic.mxp to install the behavior.
- Double-click DW4PageBGChanger.mxp to install that behavior.
- Browse to the Extensions folder on the CD.
- Open the Commands subfolder.
- Double-click N4 Return False Fix.mxp to install the command.
- Browse to the Extensions folder on the CD.
- Open the Objects subfolder.
- Double-click Letterbox.mxp to install the object.

2 Copy the projects folder:

- Browse to the projects folder on the CD.
- Copy the project_ten folder to a convenient location on your hard drive.

3 Define a new Dreamweaver site using the project_ten copy as your target.

Note: If you already have a copy of Letterbox installed, remove it and install the Letterbox.mxp on the CD. It has been specially adapted for use in this project. You can use the Extension Manager to perform this task.

Note: If you get confused while you're working with this project, refer to the main.htm page in the finished_project folder of the site.

BROWSER COMPATIBILITY

We have tested this interface and found that it is fully functional in the following browsers:

MSIE 4 (Windows and Mac)

MSIE 5 (Windows and Mac)

MSIE 5.5 (Windows)

NN4.08–4.76 (Windows)

NN4.5 (Mac)

Opera 5.01 (Windows)

Netscape 6 (Windows and Mac)

ASSEMBLING THE LETTERBOX AND ITS COMPONENT PAGES

In this section, you use the Object palette in a new window to insert the Letterbox frameset we created for you. The frameset automatically divides a page into five frames and sets the proper dimensions of each frame.

1 Insert the Letterbox object:

- Open Dreamweaver and your new Project_Ten site.

- Explore the contents in the root. It should contain three html files (outsides.htm, borders.htm, main.htm) and two folders (assets and finished_project).

- In the Site window, choose File/New Window.

- Select the Forms section of the Objects palette and click the Letterbox Frameset icon to insert the frameset automatically.

- Your page is now divided into five frames. The special edition Letterbox object on your *Dreamweaver 4 Magic* CD is programmed to set the proper dimensions of each frame.

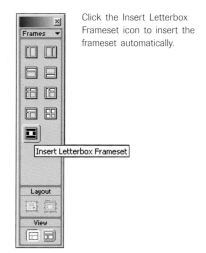

Click the Insert Letterbox Frameset icon to insert the frameset automatically.

2 Title the frameset:

- Insert your cursor in the Title field (in the toolbar along the top of your Dreamweaver window).

- Type a descriptive title for the frameset.

Note: You do not have to apply any settings to the frames; that's all taken care of by the Letterbox extension.

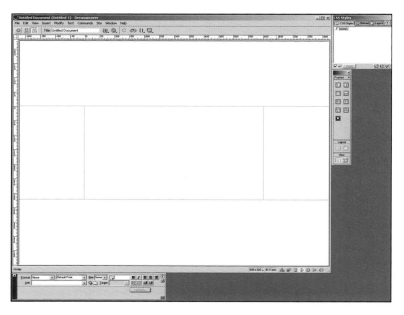

Your page now contains the Letterbox object.

3 Link the frames to their respective .htm pages:

- Choose Window/Frames to open the Frames panel.
- Select the visual representation of the top frame.
- Use the property inspector to browse to borders.htm. Then select it and click Select.
- Repeat this step for the bottom frame, which will also use borders.htm (very economical!), and for the left and right frames, both of which use the file called outsides.htm. The middle frame uses main.htm. Use the table as a handy reference.

Frame Name	Source File
topspace	borders.htm
lspace	outsides.htm
mainFrame	main.htm
rspace	outsides.htm
botspace	borders.htm

Use this table as a guide in linking the frames.

Even though your frames are populated, the frameset will still look empty. That's okay; you have not yet added any content or background to the pages that comprise it. You'll do that in a little bit!

4 Save the frameset:

- Choose File/Save Frameset.
- Browse to the root of your project_ten folder.
- Type **index.htm** as the filename and click Save.

Note: Each time you select a frame source file, you need to be careful to browse to the correct folder of your site. Dreamweaver does not always do this for you automatically. When you select the file, you might get a little warning box. This is normal because the frameset has not been saved yet. Just click OK.

When saving the frameset, you also need to make sure you have browsed to the correct folder of your site.

SETTING THE PAGE AND BACKGROUND PROPERTIES OF THE COMPONENT PAGES

To bring the letterbox metaphor to life, you need to add color to the frames pages that surround the central viewing area. You'll use a combination of image and color.

1 Set the properties for borders.htm:

   - Open borders.htm.

   - Choose Modify/Page Properties.

   - Type a page title.

   - Click the Browse button to find the background image called rosehatch.gif in the assets/images folder of your site.

   - Click the Apply button to see the background on your page.

   - Click the color square to the left of the Background field and use the eyedropper to select a color from the background image that is now on your page.

   - Delete the descriptive text from the page.

   - Leave all other settings as they are and click OK.

   - Save your changes.

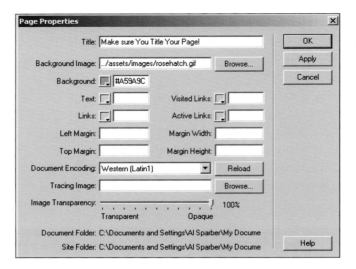

Define the properties and the background image in the Page Properties dialog.

Tip: When you use the Eyedropper tool, make sure Snap to Websafe Colors is not selected. (To find that option, click the little flyout arrow at the top right of the color picker.) The Websafe Color palette is intended for computer systems set to display 256 colors, and it won't let you pick the color you want.

2 Set the properties for outsides.htm:

   - Open outsides.htm.

   - Define the page title. (I usually like to title all pages of a frameset for the sake of search engine spiders.)

   - Define the background color by typing **#9C9A9C** into the color field.

   - Delete the descriptive text from the page.

   - Save your changes. Outsides.htm has no background image, only a color.

   - Open the index.htm page.

The project is taking on some shape! All that's left is to build the main page. Sit back and relax. This is going to take a while, but it will be well worth the effort!

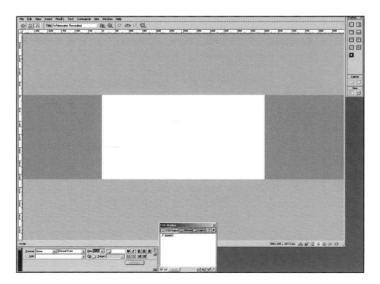

The letterbox is inserted into the page.

BUILDING AND CHOREOGRAPHING THE MAIN PAGE

Before you animate your central page, you need to build it and style it. This page is already linked to the style sheet called proj10.css, which is located in the style_sheets folder of the assets directory.

1 Open the file main.htm, which is linked to the style sheet to the right:

You can edit this Style Sheet in Dreamweaver's CSS Editor or in your favorite third-party program.

Warning: Feel free to edit any of the font families or sizes, but do not change the padding settings, or you risk the rage of Netscape 4.

Note: You may notice that the code in this book sometimes wraps to the next line. That wrapping is caused by the narrowness of the column within this book. Dreamweaver does not restrict the length of the line; the code appears on one line.

```
a:link { font-family: Verdana, Arial, Helvetica, sans-serif; font-size: 12px; color:
#333333; text-decoration: none}
a:visited { font-family: Verdana, Arial, Helvetica, sans-serif; font-size: 12px; color:
#333333; text-decoration: none}
a:hover { font-family: Verdana, Arial, Helvetica, sans-serif; font-size: 12px; color:
#FFFFFF; text-decoration: none; background-color: #A5A6AD}
a:active { font-family: Verdana, Arial, Helvetica, sans-serif; font-size: 12px; color:
#333333; text-decoration: none}
.heading { font-family: Verdana, Arial, Helvetica, sans-serif; font-size: 14px; color:
#666666; font-weight: bold}
.p3td { font-family: "Comic Sans MS", Arial, sans-serif; font-size: 13px; color: #E3E1DD;
padding-top: 16px; padding-right: 16px; padding-bottom: 16px; padding-left: 16px;
background-color: #B5AAA5}
.p3heading { font-family: Verdana, Arial, Helvetica, sans-serif; font-size: 16px; color:
#666666; font-weight: bold}
.p2td { font-family: "Comic Sans MS", Arial, sans-serif; font-size: 12px; color: #333333;
padding-top: 16px; padding-right: 16px; padding-bottom: 16px; padding-left: 16px;
background-color: #E7DBBD}
.p2heading { font-family: "Times New Roman", Times, serif; font-size: 24px; color:
#FFFFFF; font-weight: bold}
.p1td { font-family: Arial, Helvetica, sans-serif; font-size: 12px; color: #666666;
padding-top: 16px; padding-right: 16px; padding-bottom: 16px; padding-left: 16px;
background-color: #D6D3CE; vertical-align: top}
.p1td b { font-family: Arial, Helvetica, sans-serif; font-size: 12px; color: #FFFFFF;
font-weight: bold}
.p3td b { font-family: "Comic Sans MS", Arial, sans-serif; font-size: 13px; color:
#666666; font-weight: normal}
```

2 Insert the main layer:

Insert a layer on your page in whichever way you prefer (from the Insert menu or the Objects palette).

Set these properties:

Left: **0**
Top: **131**
Width: **1800 pixels**
Height: (blank)
Name: **panelayer**

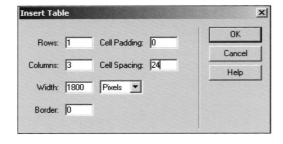

Use the Insert Table dialog to enter the correct settings for the table that goes inside panelayer.

USING A TABLE TO SHAPE CONTENT

The main layer slides in 600 pixel increments and is comprised of three distinct panels of information. The surest way to structure this is by inserting a three-column 1800 pixel-wide table within the layer and setting each column's width to 600 pixels.

1 Insert a table:

- Click inside the layer and insert a 3-column single-row table.

- Set these properties for the table:

    Width: **1800 Pixels**
    Height: (blank)
    Cell Padding: **0**
    Cell Spacing: **24**
    Border: **0**

Note: The spacing is set so that the table doesn't collapse on you. You'll set it back to 0 later.

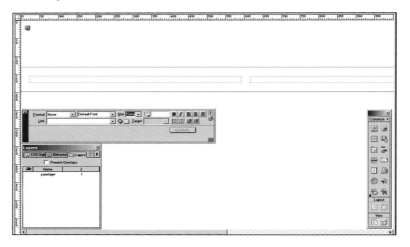

Insert a table inside panelayer.

2 Format the cells:

- Set each cell of the table to 600 pixels wide, and set its vertical alignment to Top using the property inspector.
- Do not enter any height settings.
- Select the first table cell and right-click (Ctrl+click) its **<td>** tag on the Dreamweaver status bar (on the lower left border of your window).
- Choose Set Class and then p1td.
- Repeat these actions for the other two table cells, selecting p2td and p3td as their respective classes.

3 Insert the content in the first cell:

- Click inside the first cell and type a heading.
- Press Enter (Return) to create a new paragraph.
- Type a very short marketing-oriented message (about five lines of text) to kick off the show.
- Go back and select the first paragraph and assign it a CSS class heading.

The text below the heading is automatically formatted because of the class you assigned to the **<td>** tag.

4 Insert the content in the second cell:

- Click inside the second table cell.
- Type a heading.
- Press Enter (Return) to create a new paragraph.
- Type four or five short paragraphs beneath the heading.
- Assign the heading in this cell a class of p2heading.

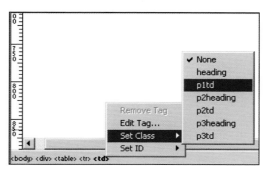

The **<td>** tag for each cell provides access to and sets its class.

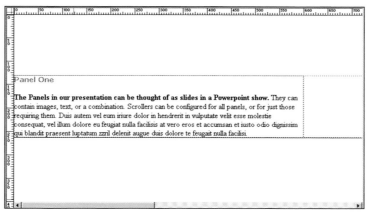

Supply the content for the first cell.

5 Insert the content in the third cell:

- Repeat the actions to add about the same amount of content to the third cell that you did to the second cell.
- Set its heading class to p3heading.

6 Change the cell spacing:

- Select the entire table.
- Change the cell spacing from 24 to 0.

SETTING UP THE LAYERS THAT CONTROL MOVEMENT, SCROLLING, AND BACKGROUND

Additional layers serve to trigger the movements of the main layer (panelayer). The navigation buttons and the scrolling controls, for instance, are all contained in layers. The background and logo are also contained in a layer.

1 Insert another layer and its image:

- Insert a new layer.
- Set these properties:

  Left: **0px**
  Top: **0px**
  Width: **600px**
  Height: **131px**
  Name: **logolayer**

- Open the Assets panel and click the Refresh Site List icon if necessary to access the images in your site.
- Insert your cursor in the new layer.
- Select the image chpparagbg.jpg.
- Click the Insert button at the bottom of the Assets panel to place the image inside the layer.

Insert the logoplayer layer and set the properties.

2 Insert the remaining layers:

Insert the layers for navigating and scrolling, using the following table as a reference for creating and placing them.

The Layers panel shows the layers you've created.

Insert the remaining layers and images at these positions.

Layer	Left	Top	Width	Height	z-index	Visibility	Notes
connectorp2	510	60	15	67	3	Default	Image to insert: p3scrollconnector.gif.
panel2ctrl	506	85	22	21	4	Default	Image to insert: panelcontrols/panel2.gif
panel1ctrl	476	85	22	21	5	Default	Image to insert: panelcontrols/panel1.gif.
connector	541	60	15	67	6	Default	Image to insert: p3scollconnector.gif. (Yes! The same image as on the other layer.)
panel3ctrl	536	85	22	21	7	Default	Image to insert: panelcontrols/panel3.gif
p2scrollers	507	-139	18	67	8	Default	Set the top to its negative setting after editing the layer. Insert a three-row by one-column table inside with the following additional attributes: Width: 18 pixels; Height (blank); Padding and Spacing: 0; Borders: 0. Insert the following images in the table rows from top to bottom: p3scrollup.gif; p3scrollmid.gif; p3scrolldown.gif.
p3scrollers	800	58	18	67	9	Default	Insert a three-row by one-column table inside. Insert the following images in the table rows from top to bottom: p3scrollup.gif; p3scrollmid.gif; p3scroll-down.gif. (Yes, the same images as in p2scrollers.)

CHOREOGRAPHING THE MOVES

Before you apply the AniMagic behaviors, you should chart the position of each moving layer so that you have easy access to its beginning and ending locations. This is a good habit to get into if you will be using this project as a basis for your own presentations. Charting the positions of each layer throughout the course of the presentation will be a tremendous timesaver when you begin to apply the AniMagic behaviors. Refer to this table for the beginning and ending positions of the moving layers:

Layer	Start Left	Start Top	End Left	End Top
connector	541	60	557	60
connectorp2	510	60	541	60
panel1ctrl	476	85	448	85
panel2ctrl	506	85	476	85
panel3ctrl	Does not move			
panelayer	0	131	Moves only left or right, depending on the panel control button clicked.	
p2scrollers	507	-139	507	58
p3scrollers	800	58	572	58

Chart the beginning and ending positions of the layers.

All that's left now is to make everything dance! Here's the plot in a nutshell:

User clicks panel button 2, buttons one and two move left, connectorp2 moves right, p2scrollers move down next to button 2, and the panelayer moves left to expose the middle table column.

User clicks panel button 3, buttons one and two move back to their starting positions, connector moves right, p3scrollers move in from the right, and panelayer moves left to expose the third table column.

User clicks panel button 1 and everything returns to the state it was in when the page first loaded.

APPLYING THE BEHAVIORS

To make things move and scroll, you must apply JavaScript behaviors to trigger the changes. For example, you'll apply an instance of Layer AniMagic to each panel button that causes the main layer to move the appropriate table cell into view. When scrolling is necessary, you also need for your scroll controls to come into the scene as the panel buttons shift position to make room. Finally, each time you move a panel into view, you'll dynamically change the background color of the page itself so that everything appears to comprise a nice, cohesive whole.

You apply the behaviors to the panel images and to the scroller images. Let's start with the panel buttons.

1   Apply the first behavior to panel1.gif:

- Select panel1.gif in Layer panel1ctrl.
- Click the + sign on the Behaviors panel to apply a new behavior.
- Choose DW4 Page Background Color Changer from the Studio VII flyout menu.
- Click the color cube to open the color picker.
- Use the Eyedropper tool to pick up the color from the first table cell.
- Click OK and make sure to set the event to onClick before leaving the Behavior panel.
- With panel1.gif still selected, click the + sign to add another behavior.

Select the image and then use the Behaviors panel to apply a new behavior.

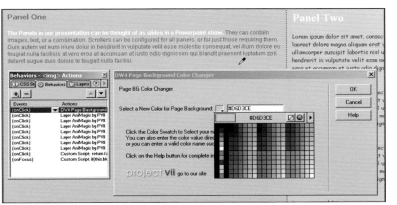

Apply the DW4 Page Background Color Changer behavior.

2 Apply the second behavior to panel1.gif:

- Choose Layer AniMagic by PVII from the Studio VII flyout menu.
- In the Layer Name list, choose layer p2scrollers.
- Set these properties:

  Left: **507**
  Top: **−139**
  Frame Rate: **24**
  Delay: **30**
  Leave all the other settings as they are.

- Click OK and make sure the event set is onClick.

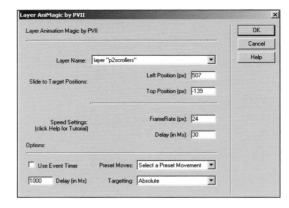

Use the Layer AniMagic Behavior's dialog to chart the movement of each layer.

3 Apply the DW4 Page Background Color Changer behavior to the remaining panel button images.

- Now that you know how to apply the behaviors, use the table as a guide for applying the remaining DW4 Page Background Color Changer actions.

4 Finish applying the Layer AniMagic by PVII behavior to the scroller and panel button objects. Use the table as a guide for applying the behaviors. Notice that the objects have multiple instances of the behavior applied. For example, panel1.gif has seven separate instances of Layer AniMagic (applied onClick) that move seven different layers.

Apply to Image	In Layer	Color (or use Eyedropper)	Event
panel1.gif	panel1ctrl	#D6D3CE	onClick
panel2.gif	panel2ctrl	#E7DBBD	onClick
panel3.gif	panel3ctrl	#B5AAA5	onClick

Apply the DW4 Page Background Color Changer behavior to the remaining panel button images.

In Layer	Apply to Image	Moves Layer	Left Position1	Top Positon	FrameRate	Delay	Event
panel1ctrl	panel1.gif	p2scrollers	507	–139	24	30	onClick
		connector	541	60	24	30	onClick
		p3scrollers	800	58	8	30	onClick
		panelayer	0	131	24	30	onClick
		panel2ctrl	506	85	3	30	onClick
		panel1ctrl	476	85	3	30	onClick
		connectorp2	510	60	12	30	onClick
panel2ctrl	panel2.gif	connector	541	60	12	30	onClick
		p3scrollers	800	58	8	30	onClick
		panelayer	–600	131	24	30	onClick
		panel2ctrl	476	85	12	30	onClick
		panel1ctrl	448	85	12	30	onClick
		p2scrollers	507	58	6	30	onClick
		connectorp2	496	60	12	30	onClick
panel3ctrl	panel3.gif	panelayer	–1200	131	48	30	onClick
		connector	557	60	12	30	onClick
		p3scrollers	572	58	6	30	onClick
		panel2ctrl	506	85	3	30	onClick
		panel1ctrl	476	85	3	30	onClick
		p2scrollers	507	–139	12	30	onClick
		connectorp2	510	60	24	30	onClick

Apply the Layer AniMagic by PVII behavior to the scroller and panel button objects.

5 Apply the AniMagic behaviors to the remaining scroll controls.

Apply the behaviors to the remaining scroll controls.

In Layer	Apply to Image	Moves Layer	Left Position	Top Position	Frame Rate	Delay	Event
p3scrollers	p3scrollup.gif	panelayer	-1200	131	10	30	onMouseOver
		panelayer	Select Stop Moving from the Targeting drop-down. No othersettings are needed.				onMouseOut
p3scrollers	p3scrolldown.gif	panelayer	-1200	-360	10	30	onMouseOver
		panelayer	Select Stop Moving from the Targeting drop-down. No other settings are needed.				onMouseOut
p2scrollers*	p3scrollup.gif	panelayer	-600	131	10	30	onMouseOver
		panelayer	Select Stop Moving from the Targeting drop-down. No other settings are needed.				onMouseOut
p2scrollers*	p3scrolldown.gif	panelayer	-600	-360	10	30	onMouseOver
		panelayer	Select Stop Moving from the Targeting drop-down. No other settings are needed.				onMouseOut

AFTERTHOUGHTS

I wrote this project during the Christmas season. As I played with my son's
Legos, all the little pieces reminded me of this interface. So I thought it would be
a good idea to provide you with a parts manifest of the layers on the main page—
just so you can make sure you have all the pieces you need to build this baby. If
you're missing anything, please contact us immediately and we will send you a
replacement part post haste.

The Panelayer contains the information that viewers see. This layer moves left or right when one of the panel buttons is clicked. Panelayer also moves up and down as necessary when the user mouses over the scroll controls.

Logolayer contains the image that tops the main page. The image needs to be placed precisely—to the pixel. Placing it inside a layer allows that precision.

The two scroller layers both use the same images: mouse over and mouse out to scroll or pause the panelayer as it scrolls up and down.

The two scroller layers.

The two connector layers also use the same image. These are the little lines that visually connect the scroll controls with their respective panel buttons.

The two connector layers.

The three panel buttons are what you click on to make things go!

The three panel buttons.

FIXES AND WORKAROUNDS FOR NETSCAPE 4

To keep the interface from coming apart when a Netscape 4 user resizes the browser, you need to apply the Netscape Layer Fix.

1 Apply the Netscape Layer Fix to the main.htm page.

- Choose Commands/Add/Remove Netscape Resize Fix.
- Click Apply.

Note: If you try to apply the fix and it is already present, a dialog appears, telling you so. In that case, just click Cancel.

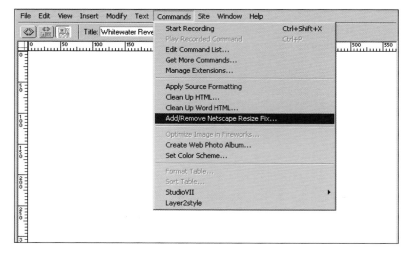

Use the Add/Remove Netscape Resize Fix command to fix problems that might occur when resizing the Netscape 4 browser.

2 Apply the PVII NN4 Apply Return False Fix.

The next fix will make for a smoother operating page. Netscape 4 has some problems with onClick events, and it needs a little kick in the rear to straighten it out. The symptoms are described here.

You click on a null link that exists only to house a JavaScript event, and Netscape 4 displays an hourglass cursor until you move completely off and away from the link. To eliminate this unsightly problem, you can append the onClick event with an instruction to "return false." Where the Resize Fix is imperative because your layers will come unglued without it, this is more of a cosmetic fix.

- Choose Command Studio VII/PVII NN4 Apply Return False.
- Click Apply.

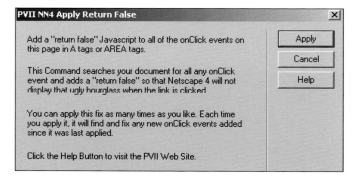

Use the N4 Return False Fix command to avoid the hour-glass cursor nightmare.

MODIFICATIONS

I really like this interface so don't touch it (just kidding). There are a lot of possibilities here. A project like this can be a special part of an existing site, or it can be made to stand on its own. Instead of having text in the panels, you can easily place images. Perhaps you could make this project a container for your graphic or Web design portfolio. Imagination rules. Think and be cool!

Both Madison Avenue and Park Avenue can be test driven at our Web site:

www.projectseven.com/dreamweaver.

Project VII's Madison Avenue site was the inspiration for the Letterbox Frameset object. Released in May, 2000, it's been one of the most successful and enduring design packs. The About page contains a north-south DHTML scrolling layer, and the Portfolio page uses an east-west DHTML scroller to present a series of clickable thumbnail images.

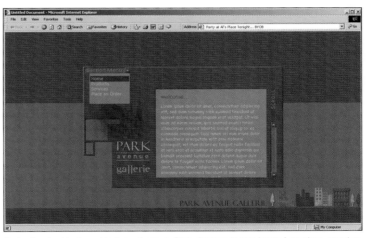

A short cab ride from Madison Avenue, Park Avenue is our latest Letterbox creation and is a virtual showcase for our Layer AniMagic behavior. This site contains a sliding drop-down menu that links viewers to pages that slide, scroll, and scoot while always maintaining the poise and dignity that comes naturally to those having prestigious midtown Manhattan addresses.

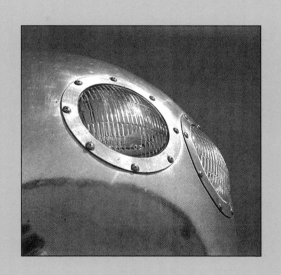

CREATING SIMPLE AND DISJOINT ROLLOVERS

"The unexpected always happens!"

—ANONYMOUS

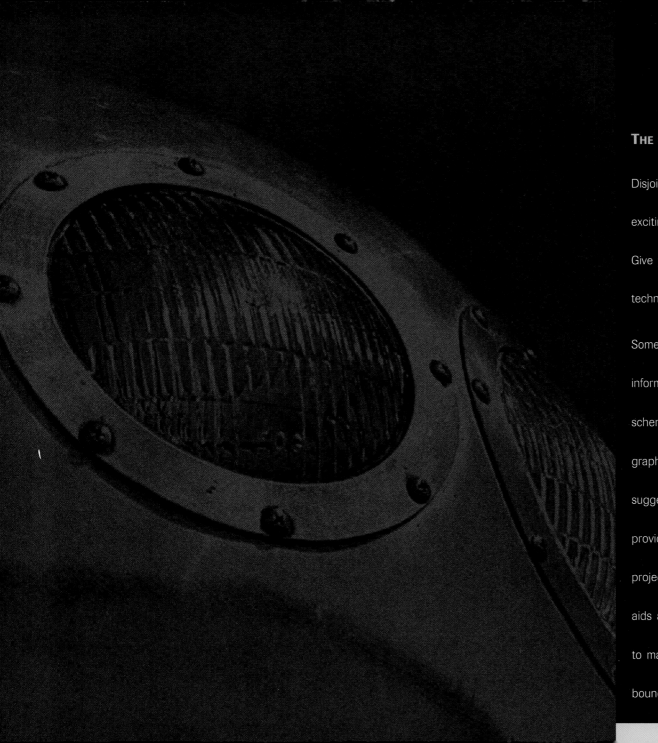

THE ELSEWHERE ROLLOVER

Disjoint rollovers provide an easy way to add exciting interactivity to your Web pages. Give your site life with one of these simple techniques.

Sometimes a word or two is just not enough information to make your page's navigation scheme clear. Arrows, pointers, and other graphical elements can guide the user by suggesting what his next action might be, while providing visual clues in the bargain. In this project, you will see how to make these user aids appear anywhere on your page and how to manage them, even across frame boundaries.

Creating Simple and Disjoint Rollovers

by Murray R. Summers

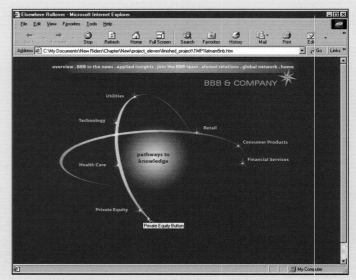

The finished site.

It Works Like This

The Web changed radically with the introduction of Netscape 3. This was the first browser to bring a functional set of JavaScript routines to the Internet and, as a result, Web pages have visible motion. Perhaps the most commonly used motion effect since has been the image rollover. This project will show you, in detail, how to have a single trigger produce visible changes in several places on your page, using this JavaScript technique first devised by Netscape.

The phrase *disjoint rollover* is used to describe any rollover or mouseover event that causes a visible (or invisible) change at some other location. At the extremes, the two locations could be physically adjacent or at locations that are not even in the same browser window! But the procedure is basically the same for all these variations.

Although mouseover events can trigger a variety of Dreamweaver behaviors, our simple examples will be confined to image swaps. The procedure for this is simplicity itself when you're using a tool like Dreamweaver. Each disjoint rollover involves at least one image and one trigger. Select the trigger, apply the Swap Image behavior, select the images to swap out and the images to swap in, make two decisions about how to manage these images, click OK, and you're done!

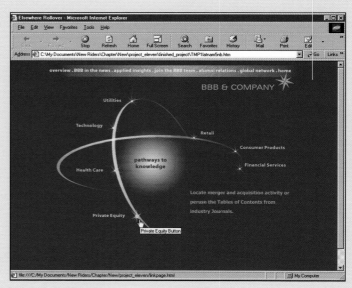

A mouseover event triggers a change in the site.

PREPARING TO WORK

This project depicts a page for the fictitious BBB Company. Because some businesses still use low-resolution displays, we are building the page so that it will fit in a 640×480-pixel window. The page will contain centered tables so that it will look good in larger windows.

Dreamweaver comes with a Swap Image JavaScript behavior, so your setup for this project will not require using any extensions. Let's get right to it by defining your site.

1 Copy the projects folder.

   • Browse to the projects folder on the CD.

   • Copy the project_eleven folder to a convenient location on your hard drive.

2 Define a new Dreamweaver site, using the project_eleven copy as your local root folder.

Note: Each of the images that will be used in this project is already included in the images folder of your project_eleven site. They are named with a convention that begins each image filename with the characters "i_" followed by two optional characters that describe which side of the table (built later) they will be used on (that is, "l_" or "r_" for left and right, respectively). All filenames are lowercase.

It's always a good idea to keep filenames simple and to avoid (at all costs!) the use of any special characters, such as spaces, ampersands, tildes, percent signs, and so on.

Note: Remember, if you want to see how the completed site looks in either Dreamweaver or your browser, you can find all the files in the finished_project folder.

BROWSER COMPATIBILITY

We have tested this interface and found that it is fully functional in the following browsers:

MSIE 4 (Windows and Mac)

MSIE 5 (Windows and Mac)

MSIE 5.5 (Windows)

NN4.08–4.76 (Windows)

NN4.5 (Mac)

Opera 5.01 (Windows)

Netscape 6 (Windows and Mac)

CREATING THE INFRASTRUCTURE OF A PAGE

This project uses nested tables to hold both the trigger element (what you mouseover) and the disjoint elements (those that change in response to the mouseover). We will center align the outer tables so that they are always shown in the middle of the page, regardless of the size of the browser's viewport.

Dreamweaver offers two methods for handling changes to tables—that is, the Deferred Update setting can be either turned on or off in your preferences. When this setting is turned off, all changes to tables are immediately reflected on the layout page. With it turned on, you must click outside the table or click the Refresh button on the property inspector to see your changes take effect. So that we can work on these tables most conveniently, I prefer to leave this option selected. (The following directions were prepared assuming that you have your preferences set similarly.)

Note: A browser's viewing window is often referred to as its *viewport*. This is that portion of the browser not occupied by "chrome"—toolbars, icons, and so on. The browser's viewport is that portion of the total browser screen's window that is exclusively devoted to displaying HTML content. Using this term is just another, and perhaps less ambiguous, way of saying "window."

1 Open the file called index.html in the root of your project_eleven defined site.

This file has the page's title already defined and its background color set. Particularly note that the page's margins are set by redefining the **<body>** tag in a linked external CSS file. In this case, the top margin is set to 5 pixels.

Note: Although you can easily set page margins by selecting Modify/Page Properties in Dreamweaver and filling in a margin value for all four margin fields on the resulting panel, this method will produce code that does not validate because margin settings for both Netscape and Internet Explorer's requirements are added. In addition, minor screen anomalies can be caused when this method is used. A much less problematic and more standards-compliant method is to use CSS to set these margins, as I have done here.

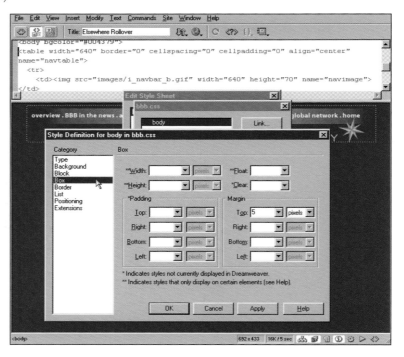

This figure shows how the page's top margin has been set in Dreamweaver's CSS Editor. Notice the top margin setting of 5 pixels.

This page already contains a table (navtable) and an image (navimage). The table has the following properties:

Rows: **1**
Columns: **1**
Width: **640px**
Align: **Center**
CellPad: **0**
CellSpace: **0**
Border: **0**

2   Insert a table beneath navimage:

- Select navimage by either clicking on the image or by clicking on **<img>** in the Quick Tag Selector (QTS).

- Press the Tab key to insert a new table row beneath navimage that will contain the rest of the "cosmos."

- The cursor should appear in this new row after you insert it, but if it does not, click in this new row so that the cursor appears beneath navimage.

- Insert a new table nested inside this row.

3   In the Insert Table dialog, enter the following parameters:

Rows: **1**
Columns: **2**
Width: **640px**
CellPad: **0**
CellSpace: **0**
Border: **0**

- Use the property inspector to set Align to Default and to name the table **bodytable**.

Each cell of this two-column, one-row table will hold another table for the images.

Note: Notice that the names referred to throughout the narrative are those entered into the Name field of the property inspector (PI).

Note: This Quick Tag Selector is one of the more useful navigational tools in Dreamweaver! I cannot build pages without it.

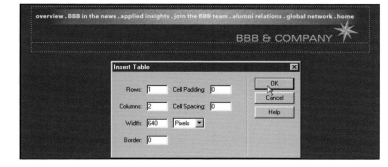

Insert the nested table beneath navimage.

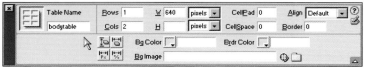

Use the property inspector to name the table.

- Click inside the left cell of bodytable (make sure that you can see **\<table>\<tr>\<td>\<table>\<tr>\<td>** in the QTS area to verify that you are actually in the cell of the inner table) and set its vertical alignment to Top using the Vert field in the property inspector.

- Set the same alignment for the right cell of bodytable.

Now we will add another nested table in each of these two cells to hold the page's images.

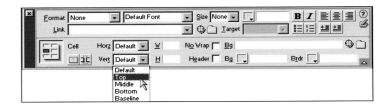

Use the property inspector to change the vertical alignment to Top.

Note: You must have the property inspector fully expanded to see the Vert align field. To fully expand the property inspector, click on the small white triangle in the lower-right corner.

4   Insert a nested table inside the left cell of bodytable:

- Click inside the left cell of bodytable.

- Insert another table with the following properties:

    Rows: **1**
    Columns: **1**
    Width: **350px**
    CellPad: **0**
    CellSpace: **0**
    Border: **0**

- Use the property inspector to name the table **leftsidetable** and to verify that the Align field is set to Default.

5   Insert the right nested table inside bodytable.

- Click inside the right cell of bodytable.

- Insert a table with the following properties using the insert table dialog and the PI:

    Rows: **1**
    Columns: **1**
    Width: **290px**
    CellPad: **0**
    CellSpace: **0**
    Border: **0**

- Use the property inspector to name the table **rightsidetable** and to verify that the Align field is set to Default.

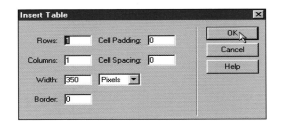

Insert a table inside the left cell of bodytable.

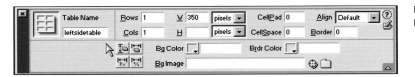

Enter the properties of leftsidetable.

PLACING IMAGES THAT SERVE AS TRIGGERS

Each of the inner tables will hold a column of images that will not only provide content and meaning to the page, but also will serve as the triggers for simple and disjoint rollovers. One of the images will serve as the placeholder for the disjoint rollover target. Use the Assets panel to put these images in place.

1   Place the images in leftsidetable:

> **Note:** You are inserting only the Up image states of the images for both leftsidetable and rightsidetable.

- Click in the only cell in leftsidetable (the innermost **<td>** tag will be bold in the QTS area).
- Locate the image i_l_utilities_up.gif in the Assets panel and select it.
- Click the Insert button.
- Press the Tab key to insert a new row in the table.
- Repeat the preceding actions with the i_l_technology_up.gif and i_l_healthcare_up.gif images in each newly inserted row in leftsidetable.
- Repeat the actions with i_l_privateequity_up.gif image, but don't insert a new row beneath it.

> **Note:** To hold the top cell of rightsidetable open, we need to add a *shim*—a transparent GIF image set to the intended size of the cell—to it.

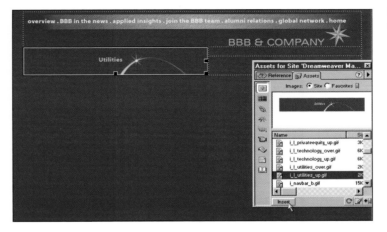

Use the Assets panel to place the first image in leftsidetable.

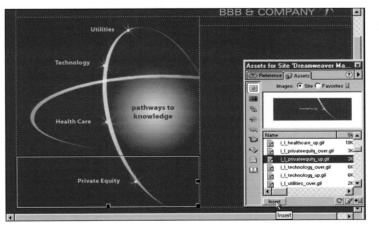

With leftsidetable filled, your page should now look like this.

2 Add a shim to the only cell of rightsidetable:

- Click in the single cell of rightsidetable (verify your position with the QTS).

- Select the image shim.gif in the Assets panel.

- Click the Insert button.

- Use the property inspector to set the following properties for this image to force this cell to the correct height and width so that you can properly position the images below it:

    Width: **290**
    Height: **80**

- Click on the shim in the design window to select it, if it is not already selected.

- Press the Tab key to insert another row beneath this shim in rightsidetable.

3 Place the images in this new row and below in rightsidetable:

- Repeat in rightsidetable the actions used to load leftsidetable with the following four images, in the order listed:

    i_r_retail_up.gif
    i_r_consprods_up.gif
    i_r_financialserv_up.gif
    i_blankswap.gif

Now you have ignited the heavens for this site. Let's take care of some details before proceeding with the rest of the work.

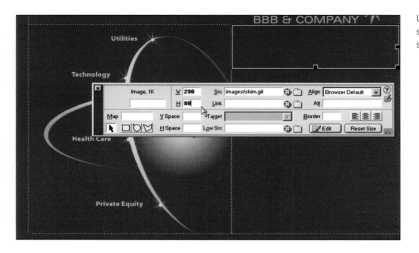

Use the property inspector to set the dimensions for the shim.gif file.

Note: When you place an image on the page, you are actually creating an image object on the page and setting its default source file. The source file for this image object can be changed with JavaScript. That's how the Swap Image behavior works. The source file is always an image file (GIF or JPG). The object is named separately, and this object name is referenced in the JavaScript.

4 Assign the image's object name:

- Using the property inspector, name each of these image objects so that you can easily locate and refer to them later (from top to bottom):

 utilitiesimage
 technologyimage
 healthcareimage
 privateequityimage

5 Name the image objects in rightsidetable:

- From top to bottom in rightsidetable, name the images:

 blankimage
 retailimage
 consumerimage
 financialimage
 swapimage

6 Add the **<alt>** tags for each image in leftsidetable (from top to bottom):

- Select utilitiesimage.
- Type **Utilities Button** into the Alt field of the PI.
- Repeat this process with each image in leftsidetable, using these as entries in the Alt field of each:

 Technology Button
 Health Care Button
 Private Equity Button

Note: Alt text appears in a browser when the user has images turned off. It's also read by search engine spiders crawling through a Web site, and it's vocalized in accessibility utilities for the blind.

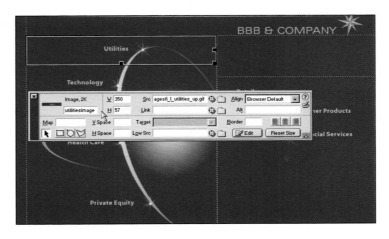

Set the image's object name in leftsidetable, beginning with utilitiesimage.

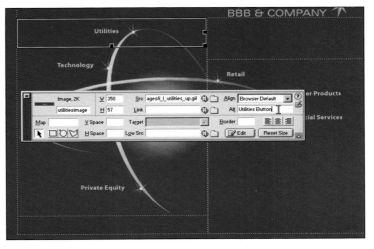

Use the Alt field of the property inspector to enter Alt text for the utilities button image.

7 Add the **<alt>** tags for the images in rightsidetable (from top to bottom) by selecting each image in turn:

- For blankimage, enter a null **<alt>** tag manually in the code—a pair of double quotation marks—to prevent page readers from saying "unidentified image!."

Note: An easy way to do this is to split the Dreamweaver window into code and layout rows, as shown in many of the figures in this project. Select the image and add a character in the Alt field, and you will see the code for this image selected in the Code View Split window. Find the **<alt>** tag there and delete the character you just inserted, leaving a null tag.

- Continue entering **<alt>** tags for each of the other images in rightsidetable, using these as entries in the Alt field of each:

  Retail Button
  Consumer Products Button
  Financial Services Button

- Enter another null **<alt>** tag for swapimage.

Note: Notice that because some of these images would probably be links to other pages, they will have borders applied to them by the browser. To prevent this from happening, in the property inspector, enter a zero in the Border field for each image, if there is not one already there.

At this point, the page is built and is ready for the rollover behaviors to be applied. Your page should look like the one shown in the figure.

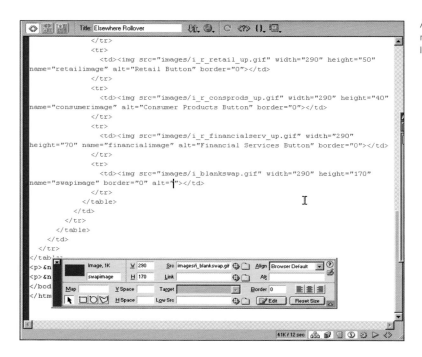

Add the images and Alt tags, making the code window look like the one in this figure.

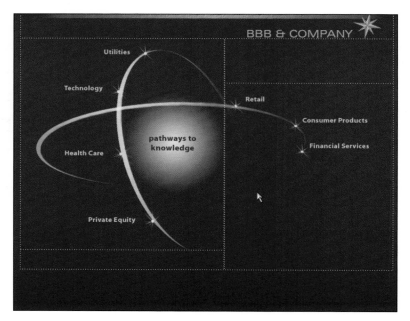

When the images are placed in leftsidetable and rightsidetable, your page should look like this.

Using the Dreamweaver Swap Image Behavior to Create Disjoint Rollovers

Now that we have built the page in Design mode and inserted the images, it is a simple matter to select each image and apply the rollover behaviors. But there is more that we need to do with the images in the leftsidetable. Each of these images will not only swap an image with itself, but also will swap an image with the rightsidetable image called swapimage. This is the disjoint rollover—on mouseover, the trigger's Up image is replaced with its Over image, and the swapimage is replaced with the image appropriate for the trigger's context. On mouseout, each of these images will be swapped back to the default image source files.

1 Insert the swap:

- Click on utilitiesimage to select it.
- Access the Behaviors panel.
- Click the + button in the Behaviors panel to open the dropdown list of behaviors.
- Select the Swap Image action.
- In the Swap Image dialog, scroll down the Images list and make sure that utilitiesimage is selected.
- Click the Browse button (and browse to the images folder if necessary).
- In the Select Image Source dialog, select the i_l_utilities_over.gif image.
- Make sure that the Relative To dropdown of this dialog panel is set to Document.
- Click Select to set the rollover behavior.
- Keep the Swap Image dialog open.

Note: The asterisk after the object name utilitiesimage in the Swap Image dialog indicates that a swap behavior has been applied to that object. You may see many asterisks in a single behavior panel, showing that the single behavior has been applied to multiple objects.

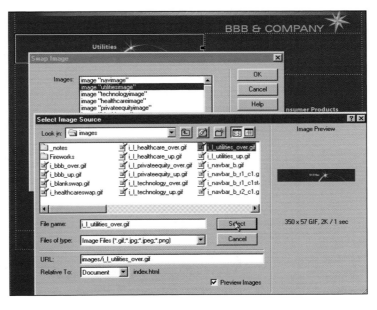

Apply the Swap Image behaviors to each image in turn, using the Select Image Source dialog.

2 Before clicking OK on the Swap Image dialog, piggyback the disjoint rollover:

Because this trigger also initiates a disjoint rollover, we need to add a second image swap while the Swap Image dialog is open.

- Scroll down the list of images to see and then select the image swapimage.

- With swapimage selected in the Images list, use the Browse button once again to choose the second part of the disjoint rollover, image i_utilityswap.gif.

- Make sure that the Relative To dropdown on this browse panel is set to Document.

Note: This setting is "sticky," so after it is set it will retain that setting from one session to the next!

- Click Select.

- Leave both check boxes at the bottom of the Swap Image dialog checked so that the rollover images are preloaded and the onMouseOver event is automatically added.

- Click OK to conclude rollover definition for this trigger.

- Check your work by using the F12 key to preview it in a browser.

Note: I always leave my Events For setting at 4.0 and Later Browsers except for the cases when I may need to apply a special W3C DOM behavior, such as the PVII Change Object Background Color, for instance.

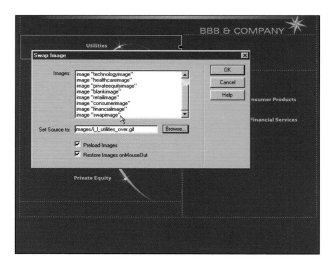

Select the second image to swap to complete the Disjoint Rollover.

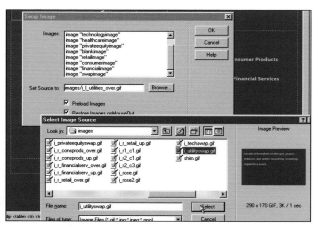

This figure shows the selection of the second part of the disjoint rollover, swapping swapimage with i_utilityswap.gif.

Check that your Swap Image dialog for this rollover matches this figure before you click OK to close it.

Note: Notice that onMouseOut is placed higher than onMouseOver in the Behaviors list. This is of no concern. Obviously you cannot trigger an onMouseOut event without also triggering an onMouseOver event first!

You may change the order of behaviors within the same event by using the up and down placement arrows on the upper-right corner of the tab. Several onMouseOut events can be rearranged in this way to ensure that one particular event occurs first, if necessary.

3 Insert two other image rollovers for leftsidetable:

- Repeat this rollover definition process for technologyimage and healthcareimage, selecting the appropriate onMouseOver file and the appropriate swapimage file for the swap.

- Leave privateequityimage at the bottom unlinked for later use.

4 Save the file and check your work:

- Choose File/Save As and enter a name of your choice. Because all the original files are on the CD, you can always restore this lesson's files to their initial state, but it will be less confusing if you use your own name here and in subsequent saves.

- Check your work in the browser of your choice.

- Verify that the mouseover events trigger the proper image both on itself and in the disjoint swap area on rollover.

Tip: You could also apply a link to all these images by using the Link field of the PI and browsing to, or pointing at, the file to be linked (see the section "Entering the Links for a Page" later in this project).

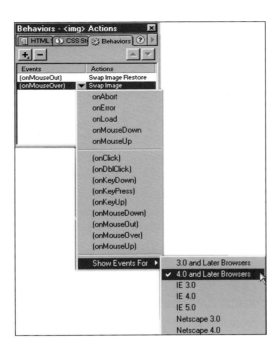

The Behaviors panel shows the choices available for events and the location of the Show Events For choices.

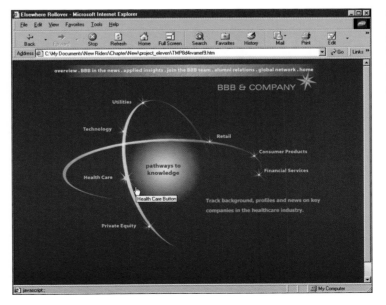

At this point, your page should look like this in your browser. Check the behaviors, too. For example, Health Care and its star are lit when you move your mouse over the button.

USING A HOTSPOT AS THE TRIGGER FOR AN EVENT

You may notice that these images are much larger than the actual area of the text/star graphic portion. Because the mouseover event is applied to the whole image, this could lead to some confusion as the user moves the mouse over the image and sees a link cursor (finger) in an unused part of the screen. A good way to avoid this confusion is to use a hotspot as the trigger for the event rather than the entire image, and we will do that to the last image in leftsidetable.

1 Create the hotspot:

- Select privateequityimage.
- Locate the Hotspot tool in the lower-left corner of the image's property inspector.
- Click on the Rectangular Hotspot tool.
- Trace a rectangle on the screen that includes the Private Equity text and the bulk of its associated star by clicking in one corner of the intended location of the hotspot and dragging the mouse to the opposite corner diagonally.
- Accept the name of privateequityimageMap shown in the Map field of the PI, and the placement of the hotspot itself.

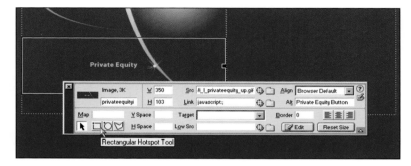

Use the property inspector to access the Rectangular Hotspot tool.

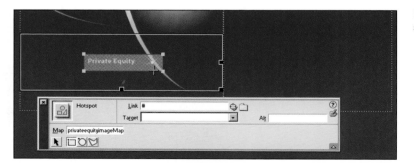

Draw a hotspot that is much smaller than the entire image.

266

2 Apply the Swap Image behavior to the hotspot:

• Select the hotspot you just created in the previous step.

• Apply a Swap Image behavior to it just as you did to all the other images in this table, swapping both the privateequity swap image and the button states for privateequity image.

Note: You might have noticed that the events presented in the list are different when an image map is selected than they are when an image is selected. This selection is context sensitive and works like this for all other page elements.

Choose Behavior/Swap Image.

These events are available for hotspots.

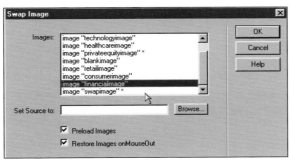

The Swap Image dialog shows both swaps for privateequityimage and blankimage as asterisks.

3 Save the page (using your preferred name) and check your work.

• Preview it in the browser.

• Evaluate the benefit of the hotspot rollover compared to the full image rollover. You may want to convert your page to use only hotspots, based on being able to confine the rollover trigger with the hotspot. If so, I will leave that as an exercise for the reader (I have waited most of my professional life to use that often frustrating and never informative phrase!)

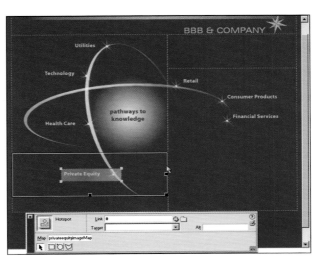

After you insert the hotspot and its behaviors, your page should look like this.

CREATING SIMPLE ROLLOVERS

Let's complete the page by assigning rollover behaviors to the middle three images in rightsidetable.

1 Apply the Swap Image behavior to retailimage (just as you did earlier when applying the behaviors to the images in leftsidetable), selecting its matching Over state image.

- Select retailimage.
- Apply a simple image swap to bring in i_r_retail_over.gif (onMouseOver).

2 Select i_r_consprods_over.gif and i_r_financialserv_over.gif for swaps with consumerimage and financialimage, respectively.

- Leave blankimage and swapimage alone, for obvious reasons!

ENTERING THE LINKS FOR A PAGE

There's just one more step that you would need to do if you were building this page for a real site, and that's entering the links for each of the rollover images.

1 Link each of the trigger images in leftsidetable:

- Select utilitiesimage.

> **Note:** After applying a behavior to an image, you may notice that DW4 has automatically added javascript:; in the Link field of the property inspector, if you chose 4.0 and Later Browsers under Events For.
>
> This null link is automatically added to any image when a bracketed event, such as <onMouseOver> and <onMouseOut>, is used with a behavior.

- Drag the bull's-eye to linkpage.html in the Site Manager and drop it to create the link. This step results in linkpage.html being loaded when utilitiesimage is clicked.

2 If you were actually building a page, you would repeat this linking with each of the remaining trigger images in rightsidetable.

Project 11 is now complete.

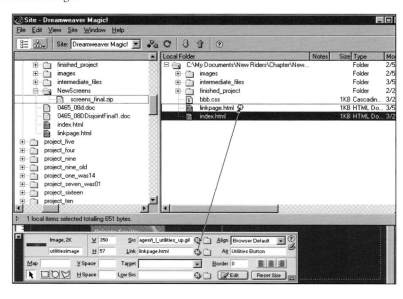

Drag and drop the bull's-eye to create a link in Dreamweaver. The Site Manager pops to the top when the bull's-eye is hovered over any part of it.

MODIFICATIONS

Now that you know how to swap images (here, there, and anywhere!), you are free to let your imagination soar. Project 11 showed you how to create a special-purpose interface intended for a home page. We've included a special bonus page, along with a fully editable Fireworks PNG file, that will serve to illustrate how simple and disjoint image rollovers can be used in a more conventional navigation schema.

The bonus interface is comprised of a horizontal button row. Mouse over the buttons and they become highlighted, and a descriptive phrase pops up above the main textual content.

The finished files can be found in the project_11\modifications folder. Enjoy!

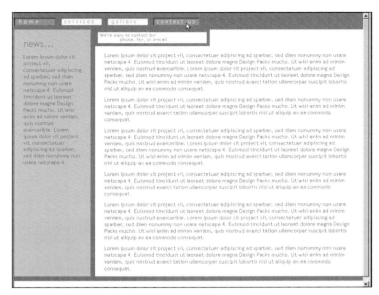

Mouse over the buttons to highlight them and see a descriptive message pop up at the top of the main content table cell.

TAKING CONTROL WITH TEMPLATES AND LIBRARY ITEMS

"Always design a thing by considering

it in its next larger context—a chair

in a room, a room in a house, a house

in an environment, an environment

in a city plan."

—ELIEL SAARINEN, TIME, JULY 2, 1956

Templates and Library Items

Dreamweaver templates and library items are

enormously important productivity tools.

Templates make designing a large site fast and

easy, and library items provide the extra control

you need.

Taking Control with Templates and Library Items

by Craig Foster

An example of a site that uses templates and library items.

IT WORKS LIKE THIS

Templates are comprised of editable and locked regions. Editable regions, which can be modified outside the template, should be labeled for the type of content they are designed to hold. This will help content editors determine where specific content should be placed. Typically, all that is required is an editable region for the main content and editable regions for other content unique to different pages or departments of a company. You can create library items for a departmental submenu, for instance, and place them in a designated editable region of the template to speed production, maintain appearance throughout the site, and decrease the

chances of broken links. We're going to create a simple company Web page that contains a main menu and submenus that change based on the main menu item selected. The base page and its main menu are managed in a template. The submenus are managed with library items.

The main menu is locked so that changes made in the template update all pages to which the template is applied. The submenu library items are contained in an editable region so that the appropriate submenus can be placed on the actual pages.

PREPARING TO WORK

Preparing for a *Dreamweaver 4 Magic* project is pretty much a routine. Copy the project folder from the CD to your hard drive, fire up Dreamweaver, and define a new site using your copied project folder as the local root folder.

1 Copy the projects folder:

   • Browse to the projects folder on the CD.

   • Copy the project_twelve folder to a convenient location on your hard drive.

2 Define a new Dreamweaver site by copying the project_twelve folder onto your hard drive and using it as your local root folder.

Note: Remember, any time you want to see how the completed site looks in either Dreamweaver or your browser, you can find all the files in the finished_project folder.

3 Open the file called index.htm in the root of your p12root defined site.

4 Save the file as the site's template:

   • Choose File/Save as Template.

   • Type **main** for the template name.

   • Click Save.

Note: Moving templates from the template folder or moving the template folder from the local site root will break Dreamweaver's connection with the template.

BROWSER COMPATIBILITY

We have tested this interface and found that it is fully functional in the following browsers:

MSIE 4 (Windows and Mac)

MSIE 5 (Windows and Mac)

MSIE 5.5 (Windows)

NN4.08–4.76 (Windows)

NN4.5 (Mac)

Opera 5.01 (Windows)

Netscape 6 (Windows and Mac)

DEFINING EDITABLE REGIONS AND CREATING TEMPLATE-BASED DOCUMENTS

You will define the entire second table of the template as an editable region. This table holds both the sidebar in the left cell where submenus will be placed and the main content area.

The mock company in this project has four departments: Customer Service, Finance, Marketing, and Personnel. You will create a document for each of these departments and an index file as a starting point for the site.

1   Select the area to define as an editable region:

   • Click in the cell with the header text.

   • Click the **<Table>** tag at the bottom of the window.

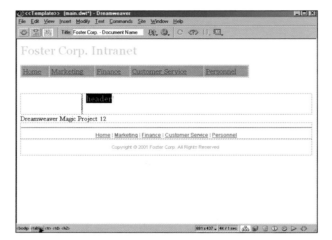

Select the area to define as an editable region.

2   Define the area as editable and give it a unique name:

   • Choose Modify/Templates/New Editable Region.

   • Type **maincontent** for the name of the editable region.

   • Click OK.

3   Save the template:

   • Choose File/Save.

   • Choose File/Close.

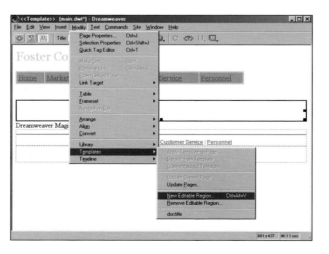

Choose Modify/Templates/New Editable Region.

4 Apply a template to previously created documents:

- Choose File/Open.
- Select the file named index.htm in the root of your project_twelve folder.
- Click Open.
- Choose Modify/Templates/Apply Template to Page.
- Select the template named main.
- Click Select.
- Click (none).

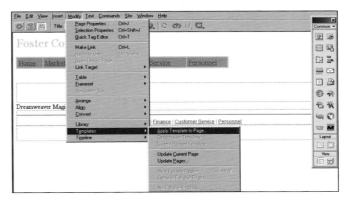

In an open file, choose Modify/Templates/Apply Template to Page to apply a template to a previously created document.

In this dialog, you select the template and then click Select.

If you are unsure whether to preserve content in previously created documents or throw it away, select the largest editable region for Dreamweaver to place it in (in this case the maincontent editable region). After Dreamweaver is finished applying the template to the page, the original content of the document will be available in the selected editable region. From there, you can decide the fate of the content.

- Click OK.
- Choose File/Save.
- Choose File/Close.

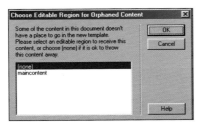

In the Choose Editable Region for Orphaned Content dialog, you choose whether to preserve content in previously created documents or throw it away.

5 Create template-based documents:

- Choose File/New from Template.
- Select the template named main.
- Click Select.
- Choose File/Save As.
- Select the root of your local site.
- Type **marketing.htm** for the filename.
- Click Save.
- Repeat the previous steps in Step 5 to save the three other files, using the names **finance.htm**, **customerservice.htm**, and **personnel.htm**.

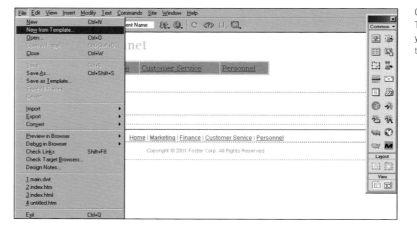

Choose File/New from Template. Select the template you want to use, and click the Select button.

Select the template to apply to the page.

6 Set the site links in the template.

- Choose Window/Templates.
- Right-click (Ctrl+click) the template named main.
- Select Edit.
- Click the text Home.

Choose Window/Templates to access the template you want to edit.

Select the template, right-click (Ctrl+click), and then choose Edit.

- Choose Modify/Change Link.
- Browse to and select the index.htm file.
- Click Select.

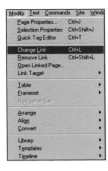

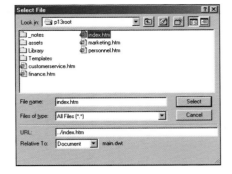

Choose Modify/Change Link to access the Select File dialog.

In the Select File dialog, browse to and select the index.htm file.

- Repeat the previous four steps until all menus at the top and bottom of the page are linked to the appropriate files—for example, the Marketing menus link to the marketing.htm file.
- Choose File/Save.
- Click Update.
- Click Close.
- Choose File/Close.

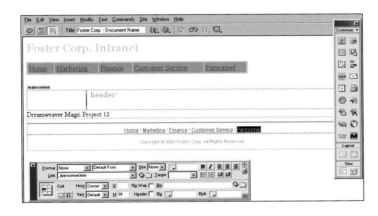

When you have set all the site links in the template, you're ready to save, update, and close it.

INSERTING AND EDITING LIBRARY ITEMS

Library items can be created from any content you would find between the body tags of HTML pages. You can edit library items in Dreamweaver just as you would any other HTML content.

Five library items are available in the Assets folder. One library item is for the index page of the mock company in this project, and one is for each of the company's departments. The library items are submenus to be placed in the sidebar of the editable region.

We'll insert each department's submenu library item into the appropriate HMTL file and then modify the text on the email link to the Personnel department.

1 Insert a library item into the Personnel department's page:

- Choose File/Open.
- Select the personnel.htm file.
- Click Open.
- Choose Window/Library.
- Highlight the contents of the leftmost cell of the table you just defined as an editable region to indicate the area of document to insert library item.
- Click the personnel library item in the Library Asset window.
- Click Insert.

2 Repeating the previous steps, insert the remaining library items into their corresponding file—for example, the marketing library item into the marketing.htm file.

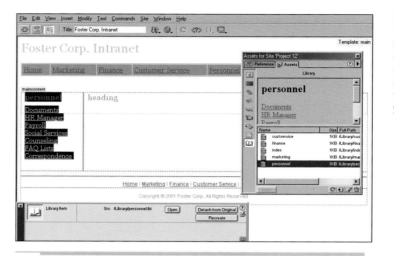

Use the Assets panel to insert the library item. When you click Insert, the item appears n the page and is highlighted in black. When you then move your mouse away from the item, the highlight turns yellow.

Tip: When links or images with applied behaviors are made into library items, only the behavior call to the JavaScript function is contained in the library item; the function from the head of the document is not. When library items are placed into pages without the JavaScript function in the head of the document, Dreamweaver places the function in the head of the document automatically.

3 Edit and Save the library item:

Note: You can access your library item at any time from the Assets panel or from any document containing it by selecting the item and clicking the Open button on the Properties palette.

- Open the personnel.htm file.
- Right-click (Crtl+click) the library item in the document window.
- Choose Open Library Item.

Note: To prevent broken links, always save newly created documents, library items, and templates in the local defined site prior to inserting images or creating links.

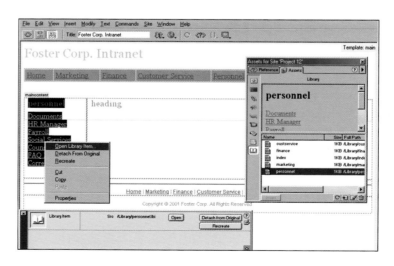

Open the library item from the document window.

- Change the text Personnel Dept. Head to **Correspondence**.
- Choose File/Save.
- Click Update.
- Click Close.
- Choose File/Close.
- When prompted to Save, choose Yes.
- Click Update.

Note: If you want to test changes without updating all documents in your site with the library item or template, click Don't Update after saving. Open a document containing the library item and choose Modify/Library/Update Current Page.

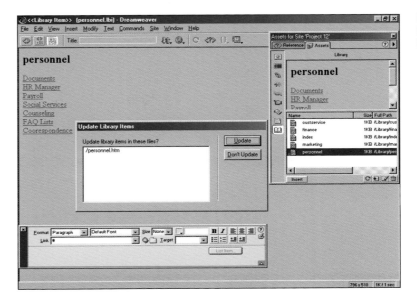

Edit the text in the library item, save the file, and click Update.

MODIFICATIONS

Although you cannot place one template inside another (this is referred to as nesting), you can use more than one template for your site. In this intranet example, a template can be created for each department's site using any design desired. You can preserve the overall site navigation by making the main menu into a library item and inserting it into each department's template.

Nesting library items is another level of control library items provide. For example, displaying the date and time of a Personnel and Finance department monthly meeting may be required. A library item of the information inserted into the Personnel and Finance department submenu library item would be a quick way of maintaining this information without displaying it throughout the company or burdening the server with a Server-Side Include.

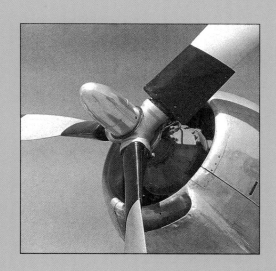

"Experience is something you don't get

until just after you need it."

—ANONYMOUS

APPENDIX A

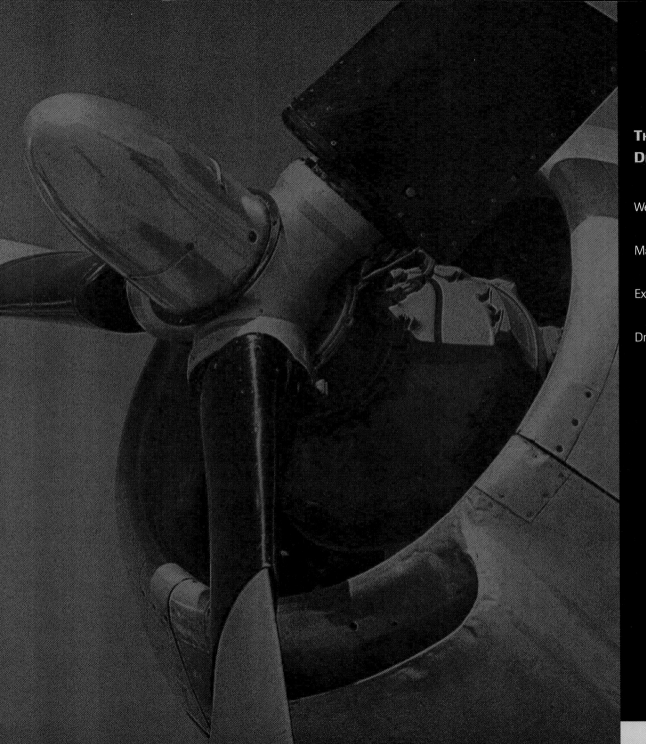

THE TRUE POWER OF
DREAMWEAVER: EXTENSIBILITY

We asked Francoise Bollerot, Product Line

Manager of the Macromedia Extension

Exchange, to give us overviews of the

Dreamweaver platform and Extension Exchange.

DREAMWEAVER PLATFORM

Since its introduction in December 1997, the Macromedia Dreamweaver platform has become the platform of choice for over 1.3 million professional Web developers, garnering 72% market share—more popular than every other professional Web authoring product combined, on both the Windows and Macintosh platforms (Source: *PC Data*).

Right from the beginning with Version 1, Dreamweaver has had an open, extensible architecture based on HTML and JavaScript, languages familiar to Web developers. Today, nearly everything about the application can be customized, including the menu system, objects, behaviors, commands, and translators. Developers can create custom Floaters that let them inspect the properties of any part of a document in a modeless palette.

In June 2000, Macromedia debuted a powerful new product built on the Dreamweaver platform, Dreamweaver UltraDev. Dreamweaver UltraDev is the solution for ensuring the presentation quality of professional Web sites with dynamic content, letting developers see live server side data from within the application development environment and allowing them to create and edit their design accordingly. Dreamweaver UltraDev includes all of the powerful HTML rendering features of Dreamweaver 4 plus an optimal design environment for ASP, JSP, and CFML sites.

The Power of Extensibility

Dreamweaver JavaScript-based API (Application Programming Interface) lies at the core of the Dreamweaver platform. The Dreamweaver API consists of more than 300 custom JavaScript functions that can be used to automate any task that can be accomplished through the menus in Dreamweaver. This makes it easy for partners to create a set of extensions that will turn Dreamweaver into a custom authoring environment for any back-end server.

More importantly, the JavaScript-based API puts the power of extensibility in the hands of the typical Dreamweaver customer. Traditionally, product APIs require extension developers to know C++, which puts them out of reach for most Web developers. With Dreamweaver, anybody proficient in JavaScript, HTML, and

XML can create custom commands, behaviors, property inspectors, objects, floating palettes, and data translators.

While Dreamweaver has been recognized as a leader in Web authoring, it is even more powerful as a platform. Dreamweaver allows customers, partners, and corporate Web teams to customize, enhance, and extend it to suit their needs. They have already realized benefits including

- **Productivity Gains.** Extensions allow Web developers to automate repetitive tasks and create custom versions of the product tuned to their own needs. This speeds up Web development.
- **Rapid Iteration.** Web developers no longer depend on Macromedia to add new features to Dreamweaver. They can extend the product to suit their needs on a daily basis.
- **Technology Integration.** Web technology vendors such as Allaire, Pervasive, Calico Commerce, and BEA Systems have customized Dreamweaver to help Web developers implement their products. As new Web technologies emerge, Dreamweaver can quickly grow to handle them as well.
- **Vertical Market Solutions.** Custom Dreamweaver-based solutions can be developed to serve individual vertical markets.

Using Extensibility to Create Custom Solutions

Dreamweaver's extensibility architecture has allowed Macromedia's partners to create entirely new solutions based on Dreamweaver's core authoring feature set. For example, BroadVision created a suite of extensions for their 1-to-1 personalization architecture called the BroadVision Design Center, based on the Dreamweaver UltraDev application building tool. These extensions allow users to interact directly with the BroadVision server while authoring in Dreamweaver UltraDev.

Similarly, Nokia used the Dreamweaver platform as the foundation for their WML Studio, a set of extensions that allows Dreamweaver users to create WML pages and preview them on a built-in phone simulator before uploading them to a Wireless Application Protocol (WAP) server. Users can select the type of phone they are designing for and can also monitor how large their WAP pages will be. Using the Studio, Dreamweaver authors can create pages for wireless devices as seamlessly as they do traditional Web pages.

THE MACROMEDIA EXCHANGE FOR DREAMWEAVER

The Macromedia Exchange for Dreamweaver provides a central location where partners and individual extension developers can share their work with the Dreamweaver community at-large. Any Dreamweaver user can easily search through hundreds of extensions that add helpful new features to Dreamweaver.

The Exchange also works to foster a sense of community among Dreamweaver users. In the Exchange, each extension is accompanied by reviews written by other Web developers. Members can also review extensions and interact with other Dreamweaver customers and extension developers in threaded discussion groups.

Extensions You Can Trust

Every extension on the Macromedia Exchange site has been individually tested by a trained Macromedia QA engineer to make sure it installs correctly and will not cause harm. Select extensions will be awarded the "Macromedia Approved" Rating. These extensions have undergone a series of additional tests to ensure they will function as described and behave in a manner familiar to the Dreamweaver user. Macromedia-approved extensions provide an ideal starting point for people just learning to use extensions.

All the Benefits of a Community

Because this is a community site, each visitor can benefit from the work of others. For instance, each extension will have a numeric rating and a set of written reviews from other professional Web developers who have used the extension in a real-life setting. Also, each extension has its own threaded discussion where users can post questions about the extension, and get support from the extension's creator and others who have used it.

A Thriving Community

In less than a year of existence the Macromedia Exchange for Dreamweaver already offers over 350 extensions that automate or simplify nearly every aspect of Web development. This is truly a case of users helping each other by sharing their productivity tool with the community and constantly augmenting the functionality of Dreamweaver.

The Dreamweaver community is thriving. With over 2.5 million extension downloads the Dreamweaver Exchange is one of the top destinations for Web professionals. In response to the success of the Exchange for Dreamweaver, Macromedia has launched additional Exchanges for Dreamweaver UltraDev and Flash.

by Francoise Bollerot
Product Line Manager
Macromedia Exchange

POWER TO THE MASSES

The power of Dreamweaver is in its extensibility. Macromedia had the wonderful foresight to include this capability. The result is that you or I can log onto the Dreamweaver Exchange or a third party developer site and acquire commands, objects, and behaviors that extend the ability of Dreamweaver. What is an extension? Well, you may very well have already used one without knowing it. When you use the Swap Image behavior or the Insert Table object, you are using an extension written by Dreamweaver engineers that is included in the shipping program.

When Macromedia released Dreamweaver 3 it also released the first edition of the Macromedia Exchange and the Extension Manager program. In the old days of Dreamweaver Versions 1 and 2, extensions had to be manually installed by the user. This involved copying one or more files to various directories within the Dreamweaver program folders. The Extension Manager takes the guesswork out. Simply double-click a Macromedia Extension Package file (.MXP) and the Extension Manager comes to life and installs the extension for you. The Extension Manager can be invoked in several ways, including the following:

- From the Commands Menu in Dreamweaver (Commands/Manage Extensions).
- By double-clicking a file with the .MXP extension.

- Through the Program menu of your operating system. In Windows, for example, the path would be Start/Programs/Macromedia Extension Manager/ Macromedia Extension Manager.

- You can drag a shortcut onto your desktop or taskbar (as I have on mine).

Dreamweaver 4's new Extension Manager program adds some very useful functionality. It allows us to turn extensions on or off by checking or unchecking a box next to the installed extension's name.

You should familiarize yourself with this powerful addition to your Dreamweaver software. And, of course, you should take full advantage of the wealth of powerful extensions available.

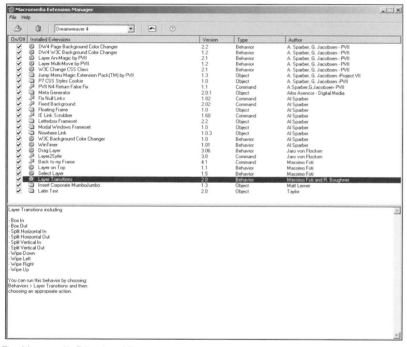

The Macromedia Extensions Manager.

THE IMPORTANCE OF USING THE LATEST VERSION OF THE EXTENSION MANAGER

The current version of the Extension Manager, and the one that ships with Dreamweaver 4, is Version 1.2. Please check the Dreaweaver Exchange Web site for any updates. The Web address of the Exchange is:

http://dynamic.macromedia.com/bin/MM/exchange/dreamweaver/main.jsp

Before we go any further, there is, at the time of this book's publishing, a rare anomaly involving extension installation. Many extensions write to a special .xml file in Dreamweaver's configuration folder called menus.xml. This is a rather complex file, and under certain conditions installing an extension can corrupt that file and make your Dreamweaver menus disappear. This is neither the fault of the extension's author or Macromedia. The anomaly seems more likely to occur if you have made changes to the menus yourself or if you have ever used a Beta version of Dreamweaver.

If you encounter the anomaly, here's how to fix it:

1. Launch the Extension Manager.

2. Quit Dreamweaver.

3. Make a copy of your Menus.xbk file. Be sure to save this file somewhere safe and easy to find, as you might need to access it later.

4. Using the Extension Manager, uninstall the extension causing the problem.

Note: If it is not apparent which extension triggered the problem, you will have to troubleshoot by starting with the most recent extension you've added, follow Steps 5 through 7, and, if that does not work, try the next most recent extension. We want to emphasize that the extensions included with this book are fully tested and error-free; and the Extension Manager issue, although quite rare, is due to a bug in Dreamweaver, not the extensions. If you have problems, please feel free to log onto our News Server for updates and assistance at

news://forums.projectseven.com/pviiwebdev

5. Delete the Menus.xml file associated with Dreamweaver 4.

6. Change the name of the Menus.xbk file to Menus.xml.

7. Launch Dreamweaver and test. If the error message no longer occurs, try reinstalling the extension.

8. If the problem persists, your Menus.xbk file was corrupted during the process of uninstalling the corrupted extension. Fortunately, you made a back-up copy of the Menus.xbk file prior to uninstalling the extension!

9. Delete the new Menus.xml you just created.

10. Drag the back-up copy of the Menus.xbk file into the Menus folder located inside your Dreamweaver 4 Configuration folder. Change the name of this Menus.xbk file to Menus.xml. Finally, reinstall the extension.

OUR FAVORITE EXTENSIONS

There are more than 300 free extensions available at the Exchange. Out of those, I've made a small list of my favorites. Essentially, they are the ones that I can't live without. Some of them were used in the development of this book, in which case it is on the CD. We've chosen not to include the others for a very good reason. Extensions go through version cycles just like full programs do. To ensure you are getting the latest version of an extension, it's best to be a frequent visitor to the Dreamweaver Exchange and to the Web sites of the top extension developers.

Massimo Foti

www.massimocorner.com

Massimo is one of the masters of DHTML extensions. Heck, he's a master of all kinds of extensions! One visit to his Web site will tell you why. He's got a treasure trove of commands, objects, and behaviors.

Our favorite Massimo extension is Select Layer. This is an awesome behavior that simplifies the task of showing and hiding multiple layers with a minimum of work. For animation addicts, Massimo recently released a Netscape 6 compatible suite of Layer Transition behaviors aptly named Layer Transitions.

We asked Massimo to discuss his own personal favorites with us and following is his response:

"My all time favorite extension is, without a doubt, Meta Manager, a command that inserts up to six different **<meta>** tags that you enter into fields contained in a dialog window. This is one of my 'Sitewide' commands that can insert the **<meta>** tags in a single document or in a whole Web site with just one click. Another plus is that you can also save your presets for later use. It was the first extension I made with Sitewide capabilities, and its tabbed interface inspired many other developers and started a major trend in extension GUIs.

Another powerful tool is RegExp Validator, a behavior to validate a form's data entries. It is completely built around a set of regular expressions that allow sophisticated validations while keeping the code very compact. Power users especially appreciate the ability to use custom regular expressions.

Probably, my most underrated extension is Base Target—a small, simple object, but a huge time saver. When working with frames, especially if used for navigation menus, you soon find yourself entering the same value for the target attribute of your link. Use this object and forget about it. It will create a default target for all the links inside the page."

—Massimo Foti; February 14, 2001

Jaro Von Flocken

www.yaromat.com

If DHTML were rocket science, Jaro would be its Werner von Braun. Our favorite Jaro extension is called Layer2style and is absolutely necessary for any Web developer wanting to take advantage of nested layers while maintaining compatibility with Netscape Navigator 4.

Timeline Extensions

These extensions are a suite of behaviors that allow you to play and reverse timelines. It even allows the playing of random timelines.

Hal Pawluk

www.pawluk.com

Our favorite Pawluk extension is called FrameJammer. Framed pages that are opened "naked" outside of their frameset will find the parent frameset and position themselves in the correct frame. This is great when pages that should be framed are indexed by search engines. JavaScript fans can tweak it to simplify framed site navigation.

Eddie Traversa

www.dhtmlnirvana.com

Eddie Traversa is synonymous with bleeding edge. If you want to see what the Web will look like two years from now, head on over to his site with the latest W3C-compliant browser. You'll be glad you did. Looking at Eddie's work is kind of like looking at a Renoir that moves. He also has some very special extensions that do some very remarkable things. My favorite is the Linear Animation Looping Synthesizer command. It is quite amazing.

We asked Eddie to discuss his own personal favorite with us and following is his response:

> "My favourite extension is an extension suite called Ultimate Windows Behaviours. These allow for more functionality than the standard Open Browser Window behaviour that comes with Dreamweaver. This particular extension suite adds features such as these three: centering of new windows, positioning windows at any x, y position, and also opening a new window in fullscreen mode for Internet Explorer.
>
> The standard Dreamweaver Open Browser Window behaviour features are also included, thus giving users options like adding or removing status, menu, scroll bars, and so on. In essence, this extension suite is a highly enhanced version of the standard Dreamweaver behaviour."
>
> —Eddie Traversa; February 14, 2001

Gerry Jacobsen and Al Sparber

www.projectseven.com

Gerry is a programming genius and although the jury is still out on Al, he is reputed to have his moments. Our favorite PVII extension is Layer AniMagic, the Swiss Army knife of layer animation extensions. Some of the projects in this book would not have been possible without it, or certainly would have required hundreds of lines of additional code.

Gerry has also rewritten the Dreamweaver Jump Menu and we have named it Jump Menu Magic (we like the word *magic*). It includes a much more flexible and intuitive interface, allows for targeting links individually within the menu, and has a much more powerful go button logic.

Gerry is also the mastermind behind the PVII CSS Cookie Monster extension, which is also featured in this book.

Actually, if you frequent the Dreamweaver Newsgroup or the PVII Design Pack Newsgroup, you'll regularly get links to places deep within the PVII skunkworks that provide sneak peeks at magic in process. We've got some awesome stuff in the works!

Following is a list of some of PVII's other available extensions:

DW4 W3C Object Color Changer

This behavior allows you to access the W3C Style properties of table cells, paragraphs, **<divs>**, and more to make cool rollover effects without images. These effects are compatible with IE5 and NN6, and fails gracefully in older browsers.

DW4 Page BG Color Changer

This behavior allows you to change your page's background color on the fly.

W3C Change Object Class Behavior

Dynamically change the CSS Style of an object in W3C browsers (IE5 and NN6). You will have access to all Styles from your page and from Linked External CSS Files in the Behaviors Window!

DW4-DW3 WinTimer Behavior

Apply to any link or image to close a window after a time delay that you set!

DW4-DW3 Floating Frame Object

This command allows you to place a floating frame (i-frame) on your page, fully configured to show alternate content for Netscape 3 and 4. i-frames are supported by IE3, IE4, IE5, and NN6.

DW4-DW3 Nowhere Link Object

Insert a preformatted text link ready to accept behaviors and actions.

DW4-DW3 Letterbox Frameset Object

Download an object that automatically inserts a framset that looks like a letterbox movie or those trendy new television commercials by IBM.

Ultimate IE Link Line Scrubber Command

This command works at the **<a>** tag level and will take care of existing links on your page. It makes the lines disappear completely; you won't even see them on mouseover! The Scrubber also coexists flawlessly with forms and popup windows. You can reapply the command each time you add links to your page and it will detect only the new ones.

Instant CSS 101 Command

Automatically adds a preformatted Style Sheet to your page.

Fix Null Links Command

This command turns all # links into **javascript:;** so your page doesn't jump to top onClick.

Andrew Wooldridge

www.andrewwooldridge.com/dreamweaver

Wooldridge has not written any Dreamweaver 4 extensions yet, but he bears mentioning as one of the Dreamweaver extension pioneers. Keep an eye on his site because when he does begin writing extensions again, they will probably be very cool. If you want to take a first crack at writing a Dreamweaver behavior, you must get his Action Builder command. It will help you take a simple JavaScript and make it into a Dreamweaver behavior.

public domain

www.publicdomain.to

Paul Boon and company are recent additions to the Dreamweaver extension community, and they have been quite prolific, indeed! We enjoy using their Splash Window behavior, which opens up a "chromeless" window that can be timed to close by itself. Netscape 4 viewers see a normal popup window.

"I went to the museum where they had all

the heads and arms from the statues that

are in all the other museums."

—STEVEN WRIGHT

APPENDIX B

TOP TEN DREAMWEAVER WEB SITES

Throughout the years that we've been using

Dreamweaver, we've seen how the software

has increasingly enabled really imaginative

people to create some pretty incredible Web

sites. We thought you might like to see a list

of some of our favorites.

We chose not to include photographs because

these sites are evolutionary and tend to be

updated on a regular basis. But rest assured,

these are some great designs!

New Image

http://www.n-image.com/2k/frame.html

by Jaro von Flocken

This site is from one of the masters of DW DHTML. The site is in German, but well worth the visit even if you can't speak the language. This is a constantly evolving site that gets better with each update.

n-image definitely pushes the DHTML envelope.

Massimo's Corner

http://massimocorner.com

Everyone talks about Massimo's extensions, but they forget about the simply wonderful site he keeps.

Massimo's Corner is a marvelously easy site to navigate. His DHTML mastery is under the hood and not quite as obvious as Jaro's. But do spend some time marveling at the simplicity of Massimo's menu system.

Project VII

http://www.projectseven.com

by Al Sparber and Gerry Jacobsen

If you are a Dreamweaver user and you do not have projectseven.com bookmarked, you must not be serious about Dreamweaver. The free tutorials and extensions alone make checking in with this site regularly a must for Dreamweaver users on just about any level.

Reviewed by J. Scott Hamlin
Director, Eyeland Studio (www.eyeland.com)
Co-author: *Flash 5 Magic* (New Riders Publishing)

Eveline Frings

http://www.eveline-frings.com/intro.html

by Marion Kaltenschnee

Marion is a regular contributor on the Dreamweaver Newsgroup, and I can remember when she was putting this site together. It is a hauntingly beautiful design that showcases the medieval-style work of a German artist.

Close the lights and view this site at night. You may hear King Arthur holding court down the hall.

DS Design

http://www.divsoft.com/dsdesign/

This is one of those sites that just makes me feel good all over. It's a very clean and refreshing design done in a PVII Letterbox frameset.

Full Upright Position, Inc.

http://www.fup.com

Minimalism at its best! This design shows how to use Dreamweaver and CSS Layers to make pages exude style and class.

Playing with Fire

http://www.playingwithfire.com

Linda Rathgeber is a Macromedia Evangelist who operates a marvelous resource site for Fireworks users all over the world. Linda has come up with a design that I never tire of looking at. Her use of color, type, and imagery are impeccable. Of course, her Fireworks tutorials are awesome!

Escogitando

http://www.escogitando.it

Japi Honoo's site is one of my favorites. Talk about color and images. Wow! Japi is the Italian queen of Fireworks, and her site is a wonder to behold. You've never seen such gorgeous rollovers.

Tin Crow

http://www.tincrow.co.za

This site shows a really good use of timelines. The site takes a long time to load, and the navigation is not always the most intuitive, but there's a lot to like here and some good tricks to learn.

Orchimedia

http://www.orchimedia.com/eng

Orchimedia.com was made with Dreamweaver and Flash. It has a very hip and modern design. The look is metaphorically *Star Trek*. The layout is clean, uncluttered, and quite logical. Perhaps it was created by Mr. Spock?

Evil Films

http://www.evilfilms.com

This site has a nice frameset implementation and excellent color work. This site is amazing with its use of composites and textures. As complex and inspiring as the images are, the site is very economical in terms of bandwidth.

Code Design

http://code-design.com

by Joseph Ternes

I normally don't like sites that are done in popup windows, but this one is different. The clean design and appropriate use of DHTML animations are right on.

Furturcom

http://www.futurcom.co.uk

This site never ceases to amaze me with its perfect use of pastel colors. If you never thought you could achieve a professional look and still use more than the most basic of colors, give this site a once over.

APPENDIX C

"Sponges grow in the ocean. That just kills me.

I wonder how much deeper the ocean would be if

that didn't happen."

—STEVEN WRIGHT